PORTABLE

Nantucket & Martha's Vineyard

2nd Edition

by Laura M. Reckford

Here's what critics say about Frommer's:

"Amazingly easy to use. Very portable, very complete."
—*Booklist*

"Detailed, accurate, and easy-to-read information for all price ranges."
—*Glamour Magazine*

Wiley Publishing, Inc.

Published by:

WILEY PUBLISHING, INC.
111 River St.
Hoboken, NJ 07030-5774

ISBN 13: 978-0-7645-7629-4
ISBN 10: 0-7645-7629-1

Editor: Michael Kelly
Production Editor: Donna Wright
Photo Editor: Richard Fox
Cartographer: Tim Lohnes
Production by Wiley Indianapolis Composition Services

For information on our other products and services or to obtain technical support, please contact our Customer Care Department within the U.S. at 800/762-2974, outside the U.S. at 317/572-3993 or fax 317/572-4002.

Wiley also publishes its books in a variety of electronic formats. Some content that appears in print may not be available in electronic formats.

Manufactured in the United States of America

5 4 3 2 1

Contents

List of Maps

ABOUT THE AUTHOR

Laura M. Reckford is a writer and editor who lives on Cape Cod. Formerly the managing editor of *Cape Cod Life Magazine,* she has also been on the editorial staffs of *Good Housekeeping* magazine and *Entertainment Weekly.* She is currently the news editor of the *Falmouth Enterprise* newspaper. She is also the author of *Frommer's Cape Cod, Nantucket & Martha's Vineyard.*

AN INVITATION TO THE READER

In researching this book, we discovered many wonderful places—hotels, restaurants, shops, and more. We're sure you'll find others. Please tell us about them, so we can share the information with your fellow travelers in upcoming editions. If you were disappointed with a recommendation, we'd love to know that, too. Please write to:

Frommer's Portable Nantucket & Martha's Vineyard, 2nd Edition
Wiley Publishing, Inc. • 111 River St. • Hoboken, NJ 07030-5774

AN ADDITIONAL NOTE

Please be advised that travel information is subject to change at any time—and this is especially true of prices. We therefore suggest that you write or call ahead for confirmation when making your travel plans. The authors, editors, and publisher cannot be held responsible for the experiences of readers while traveling. Your safety is important to us, however, so we encourage you to stay alert and be aware of your surroundings. Keep a close eye on cameras, purses, and wallets, all favorite targets of thieves and pickpockets.

FROMMER'S STAR RATINGS, ICONS & ABBREVIATIONS

Every hotel, restaurant, and attraction listing in this guide has been ranked for quality, value, service, amenities, and special features using a **star-rating system.** In country, state, and regional guides, we also rate towns and regions to help you narrow down your choices and budget your time accordingly. Hotels and restaurants are rated on a scale of zero (recommended) to three stars (exceptional). Attractions, shopping, nightlife, towns, and regions are rated according to the following scale: zero stars (recommended), one star (highly recommended), two stars (very highly recommended), and three stars (must-see).

In addition to the star-rating system, we also use **seven feature icons** that point you to the great deals, in-the-know advice, and unique experiences that separate travelers from tourists. Throughout the book, look for:

Finds	Special finds—those places only insiders know about
Fun Fact	Fun facts—details that make travelers more informed and their trips more fun
Kids	Best bets for kids and advice for the whole family
Moments	Special moments—those experiences that memories are made of
Overrated	Places or experiences not worth your time or money
Tips	Insider tips—great ways to save time and money
Value	Great values—where to get the best deals

The following **abbreviations** are used for credit cards:

AE	American Express	DISC	Discover	V	Visa
DC	Diners Club	MC	MasterCard		

FROMMERS.COM

Now that you have the guidebook to a great trip, visit our website at **www.frommers.com** for travel information on more than 3,000 destinations. With features updated regularly, we give you instant access to the most current trip-planning information available. At Frommers.com, you'll also find the best prices on airfares, accommodations, and car rentals—and you can even book travel online through our travel booking partners. At Frommers.com, you'll also find the following:

- Online updates to our most popular guidebooks
- Vacation sweepstakes and contest giveaways
- Newsletter highlighting the hottest travel trends
- Online travel message boards with featured travel discussions

The Best of Nantucket & Martha's Vineyard

Megastars and CEOs, vacationing families, honeymooning couples, and carefree students are among those who seek refuge on Nantucket and Martha's Vineyard, two picturesque islands off the coast of Cape Cod in Massachusetts. Both islands have much to offer families with children and couples seeking a romantic getaway. But there's something for everyone on both islands, and an island vacation is bound to be one that's cherished for years to come. Their fame as summer resorts doesn't begin to take into account their rich history, diverse communities, and artistic traditions.

While only about 25 nautical miles apart, each island has its own distinct personality. Nantucket, flash-frozen in the mid–19th century through zealous zoning, has long been considered a rich and traditional Republican haven. Social scene aside, Nantucket has more pristine public shores than the Vineyard, as well as the best upscale shopping in the region.

Martha's Vineyard, large enough to support a year-round population spanning a broad socioeconomic spectrum, is not quite as rarefied as Nantucket. Vineyarders pride themselves on their liberal stances. True, a prime oceanside estate may fetch millions here, but residents still dicker over the price of zucchini at the local farmers' market.

The popularity of these islands means that if you go in the middle of summer, expect crowds. Consider visiting in the quiet "shoulder" seasons in May, June, September, and October, when the Islands are far less crowded, reservations are easier to come by, and prices are lower.

1 Best of Nantucket

THE BEST BEACHES

Jetties Beach: Nantucket's beaches as a rule have the best amenities of any beaches in the region; most have restrooms, showers, lifeguards, and food concessions. For families and active types, Jetties Beach (just a half-mile from the center of town) can't be beat. There are boat and windsurfing rentals, tennis courts, volleyball nets, a playground, and great fishing (off the jetties). It's also scenic (those jetties again), with calm, warm water. See p. 76.

Surfside Beach: Three miles south of town via a popular bike/skate path, Surfside—equipped with lifeguards, restrooms, free parking, and a snack bar—is quite popular. The parking lots fill up early, so consider biking or taking the shuttle bus. Also, be aware that the surf can be heavy here, so keep an eye on children. See p. 76.

THE BEST BIKE ROUTES

Nantucket Town to Madaket: Only 3 miles wide and 14 miles long, Nantucket is a snap to cover by bike. The 6-mile Madaket bike path crosses undulating moors to reach a beach with boisterous surf. See chapter 3.

Nantucket Town to Surfside: An easy, flat 3 miles from town, Surfside Beach is a perfect mini-excursion for the whole family. The bike path has benches along the route if you'd like to stop and admire the scrub pine and beach plums. When you return to town, pause at Brant Point to watch the yachts maneuver in and out of Nantucket Harbor. See chapter 3.

THE BEST LUXURY HOTELS & INNS

Cliffside Beach Club (© 800/932-9645 or 508/228-0618): On the beach and within easy walking distance from town, this establishment may not be as fancy as others, but it remains the premier lodging in town. The place has a sublime beachy-ness to it, from simply decorated rooms and cheerful staff to antique wicker in the clubhouse and colorful umbrellas on the beach. See p. 45.

The Wauwinet (© 800/426-8718 or 508/228-0145): Far from the bustle of Nantucket Town, and nestled between a bay beach and an ocean beach, this opulently restored landmark offers the ultimate retreat. Everything a summering hedonist could want is close at hand, including tennis courts, a launch to drop you off on your own secluded beach (part of a 1,100-acre wildlife refuge), and an outstanding New American restaurant, **Topper's at The Wauwinet** (see below). See p. 48.

THE BEST LODGING DEALS

The Woodbox Inn (© 508/228-0587): Located on a quiet street a short walk from the center of town, this small inn's prices are very reasonable. Built in 1709, Nantucket's oldest inn is an atmospheric place, with cozy and spacious rooms decorated with period antiques and reproductions. The Woodbox Inn restaurant on-site is one of the island's best. See p. 56.

The Nesbitt Inn (© **508/228-0156**): This old-fashioned Victorian inn in the center of town has been run by the same family for 95 years. You'll feel like you stepped back in time, and you'll be sure to enjoy the extra spending money. All rooms share bathrooms. See p. 56.

THE BEST FINE-DINING RESTAURANTS

Òran Mór (© **508/228-8655**): Chef/owner Peter Wallace has worked his magic on this humble space, transforming it into an elegant and romantic setting for his unusual and creative cuisine. His eclectic style ranges from very hot and spicy fusion to international dishes, with many grilled items on the menu. An excellent sommelier is on hand to assist wine lovers. See p. 64.

The Summer House (© **508/257-9976**): The classic Nantucket atmosphere, 'Sconset-style, distinguishes this fine-dining experience from others on the island: wicker and wrought-iron, roses and honeysuckle. The pounding Atlantic is just over the bluff. Service is wonderful and the food is excellent, though expensive. See p. 60.

Topper's at The Wauwinet (© **508/228-8768**): This 1850 restaurant—part of a secluded resort—is a tastefully subdued knockout that turns fine dining into an event. To get there in the summer, you may want to arrive by sea on the complimentary launch from Nantucket Harbor. The menu features the finest regional cuisine and unusual delicacies. See p. 61.

THE BEST FAMILY RESTAURANTS

The Even Keel Café (© **508/228-1979**): This low-key cafe in the heart of town serves breakfast, lunch, and dinner both indoors and outside on the patio in the back. Unlike much of Nantucket's dining scene, you'll find reasonable prices and non-exotic fare such as burgers and sandwiches here. There's a kid's menu, as well as high-speed Internet access. See p. 70.

Nantucket Lobster Trap (© **508/228-4200**): When only a bowl of chowder and a giant lobster roll will do, bring the family to this over-sized clam shack where the big game is usually on the TV behind the bar. Seating is on large picnic tables, and lobsters and other shellfish come straight from local waters. See p. 68.

THE BEST BARS & CLUBS

The Chicken Box (© 508/228-9717): This raucous bar has been jumping since the mid-1970s, and if you want to work up a sweat on the dance floor, the Box is a good bet most any night. Ska bands, a staple of what might be called New England Beach Music, are a favorite, along with reggae, funk, and rock. See p. 90.

The Club Car (© 508/228-1101): While one side of The Club Car is a fine dining establishment, the bar located in an actual old club car is a fun piano bar where you'll make lots of new friends and have a great time singing along to your old favorites. See p. 58.

2 Best of Martha's Vineyard

THE BEST BEACHES

Aquinnah Beach (Moshup Beach): These landmark bluffs on the western extremity of Martha's Vineyard offer a picturesque backdrop to a wide beach unencumbered by development. The bluffs are suffering from erosion, so it's no longer politically correct to engage in multi-colored mud baths as the hippies once did. Still, it's an incredibly scenic place to swim. Come early to beat the crowds. See p. 128.

Joseph A. Sylvia State Beach: Midway between Oak Bluffs and Edgartown, State Beach stretches a mile and is flanked by a paved bike path. This placid beach has views of Cape Cod and Nantucket Sound, and is prized for its gentle and (relatively) warm waves, which make it perfect for swimming. This is a popular place midsummer, so you may want to take a shuttle bus or a bike rather than try to find a parking space. See p. 129.

THE BEST BIKE ROUTES

Chilmark to Aquinnah (Gay Head): The Vineyard's awe-inspiring vistas of ponds, inlets, and ocean greet you at every turn as you bike along State Road and then turn onto the Moshup Trail, a road that takes you along the coast up to Aquinnah (formerly known as Gay Head). It's a strenuous ride with perhaps the best scenic views in the region. On the way back, treat yourself to a bike-ferry ride to the fishing village of Menemsha. See chapter 6.

Oak Bluffs to Edgartown: All of Martha's Vineyard is easily accessible for two-wheel recreationalists. This 6-mile path hugs the water almost the whole way, so you're never far from a refreshing dip. See chapter 6.

THE BEST LUXURY HOTELS & INNS

The Beach Plum Inn & Restaurant (Menemsha; ✆ 877/ 645-7398 or 508/645-9454): Recently refurbished top to bottom, this family-run inn just up the road from the fishing village of Menemsha is set on 8 lush acres overlooking Vineyard Sound. The decor is appropriately cottage-y, and amenities are top-notch. As a bonus, on-site is one of the island's finest restaurants (see below). See p. 112.

Charlotte Inn (Edgartown; ✆ 508/627-4751): Edgartown tends to be the most formal enclave on Martha's Vineyard, and this Anglicized compound of exquisite buildings is by far the fanciest address in town. The rooms are distinctly decorated: One boasts a baby grand piano, another its own thematic dressing room. The conservatory restaurant, **L'étoile** (see below), is among the finest you'll find on this side of the Atlantic. See p. 100.

The Winnetu Inn & Resort (Edgartown; ✆ 978/443-1733): Martha's Vineyard's newest resort, which is just a short walk from the beach, is trying hard to be the top lodging venue on the island. Though only a couple of years old, it succeeds on a number of fronts. Noteworthy elements are the fine-dining restaurant **Lure** (Katama; ✆ 508/627-3663), with its second-floor deck overlooking South Beach; the comfortable suites fully furnished for beach living; and the slate of activities for children and families. See p. 104.

THE BEST LODGING DEALS

Edgartown Inn (Edgartown; ✆ 508/627-4794): This is a quirky, old-fashioned inn, centrally located in the heart of Edgartown. Aromas of fresh-baked goodies swirl around, and the staff is friendly and helpful. Most important, prices have stayed reasonable, a rarity on the Vineyard. See p. 107.

Wesley Hotel (Oak Bluffs; ✆ 800/638-9027 or 508/693-6611): The Wesley is one of the great bargains on the Vineyard. The hotel is ultra-convenient. It is across the street from Oak Bluffs Harbor, around the corner from the center of the rollicking town of Oak Bluffs, and a short walk from two ferry terminals. Rooms are no-frills, but some are spacious with harbor views. See p. 110.

THE BEST FINE-DINING RESTAURANTS

Atria (Edgartown; ✆ 508/627-5850): This fine-dining restaurant earns raves for its consistent excellence in food and service. Set in an old captain's house on Upper Main Street in Edgartown, Atria has a comfortable yet elegant atmosphere. The food is beautifully presented, creatively prepared, and in ample portions. See p. 116.

The Beach Plum Inn & Restaurant (Menemsha; ✆ **508/645-9454**): This jewel of a restaurant is located on a bluff overlooking the fishing village of Menemsha. The decor is spare and purposefully understated, the better to appreciate the wonderful sunset views of the harbor. Prime seating on a clear night is outside on the new tiled patio. Service is particularly gracious. Chef James McDonough's elegant cuisine includes the bounty of the Vineyard, from freshly caught fish to home-grown vegetables. See p. 124.

L'étoile (Edgartown; ✆ **508/627-5187**): This exquisite conservatory at the elegant Charlotte Inn has long been the best restaurant on the Vineyard, if not the entire region. The fixed-price dinner, a triumph of French cuisine, may be a tad extravagant; for a special occasion, you can't do any better than this. See p. 115.

THE BEST FAMILY RESTAURANTS

Home Port (Menemsha; ✆ **508/645-2679**): When the basics—a lobster and a sunset—are what you crave, bring the family to one of the Vineyard's most cherished restaurants, set with perfect views of Menemsha Harbor. You can save money by ordering your lobster dinners to go, and then head down to the beach for a private picnic supper. See p. 125.

The Newes from America (Edgartown; ✆ **508/627-4397**): Kids love the atmosphere of this subterranean tavern, built in 1742, which also had two dining rooms. The food is better than average, and the kid's menu has all the standards. While the tots nosh on chicken fingers, parents can enjoy the unusual beer selection. See p. 119.

THE BEST BARS & CLUBS

Atlantic Connection (Oak Bluffs; ✆ **508/693-7129**): There's entertainment nightly in season at this island institution on Oak Bluff's main drag, Circuit Avenue. You may find live bands, disco, or karaoke, but you'll be sure to find a crowd enjoying themselves. See p. 151.

Offshore Ale Company (Oak Bluffs; ✆ **508/693-2626**): The Vineyard's first and only brewpub is an attractively rustic place featuring eight locally made beers on tap. There's also good grub, including a raw bar. Local acoustic performers entertain 6 nights a week in season. See p. 152.

2

Planning Your Trip to
Nantucket & Martha's Vineyard

In this chapter, you'll find everything you need to know to handle the practical details of planning a trip to Nantucket and Martha's Vineyard: airlines, airports, ferries, parking, a calendar of events, resources for those of you with special needs, and much more.

1 Visitor Information

For the free *Getaway Guide,* which covers the whole state, contact the **Massachusetts Office of Travel & Tourism,** 10 Park Plaza, Suite 4510, Boston, MA 02116 (© **800/227-MASS** or 617/973-8500; fax 617/973-8525; www.massvacation.com).

The **Cape Cod Chamber of Commerce,** Routes 6 and 132, Hyannis, MA 02601 (© **888/332-2732** or 508/362-3225; fax 508/362-2156; www.capecodchamber.org); **Martha's Vineyard Chamber of Commerce,** Beach Road, Vineyard Haven, MA 02568 (© **800/505-4815** or 508/693-0085; fax 508/693-7589; www.mvy.com); and **Nantucket Island Chamber of Commerce,** 48 Main St., Nantucket, MA 02554 (© **508/228-1700;** fax 508/325-4925; www.nantucketchamber.org), can provide location-specific information and answer any questions that may arise.

Members of the **American Automobile Association (AAA)** (© **800/222-8252;** www.aaa.com) can request a complimentary map and guide covering the area.

HOSTEL INFORMATION

Hostelling International (© **202/783-6161;** www.hihostels.com) offers low-cost dorm accommodations in five sites on the Cape and the Islands. Rates are $24 per person per night for non-members; members pay somewhat less (membership $28 a year for adults, $18 for adults over 54, free for youths under 18). Note that there's a "lockout" period (typically 10am–5pm daily) and, likely, a limit on the length of stay. Hostels on the Islands are located next to the Manuel F. Correllus State Forest in West Tisbury on Martha's

Nantucket

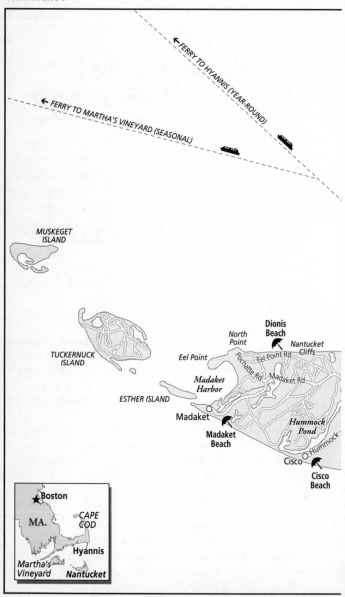

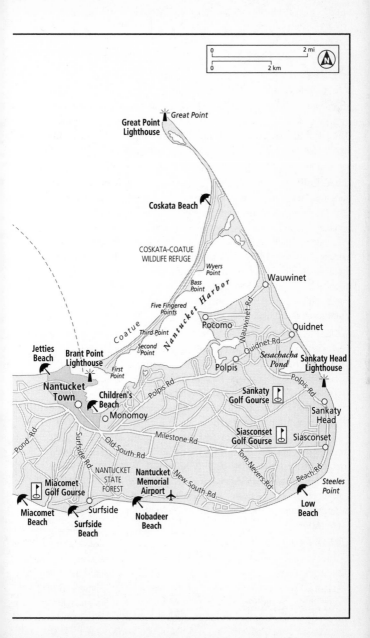

Vineyard, and in an 1874 lifesaving station on Surfside Beach on Nantucket. For details, see "Where to Stay" in chapters 3 and 5.

MONEY

The Islands are pricey destinations with costs comparable to those in large U.S. cities. If you're looking for an inexpensive vacation, you should look elsewhere. Most of the nicer rooms cost between $250 and $350 a night in season, and fine-dining restaurants with exorbitant prices are the norm. Nonetheless, many island beaches are free and open to the public, as are numerous walking trails.

TRAVELER'S CHECKS   Traveler's checks are accepted at hotels, motels, restaurants, and most stores, as are credit cards. They are something of an anachronism these days, but since many banks now impose a fee every time you use your card to withdraw money from an ATM in a different city or bank, you may be better off with traveler's checks. You can get traveler's checks at almost any bank; American Express cardholders can charge them over the phone and avoid the 1% fee by calling © **800/221-7282.** If you opt to carry traveler's checks, make sure to record their serial numbers and keep them separate from the checks themselves.

ATMs   ATMs are available on both islands, at banks and supermarkets, so you can get cash as you travel. Call one of the major networks, such as **Cirrus** (© **800/424-7787;** www.mastercard.com) or **PLUS** (© **800/843-7587;** www.visa.com), to find the nearest location. Make sure you know your bank's daily withdrawal limit. Foreign travelers should check with their banks beforehand to make sure their PINs work abroad.

Should you require personal service, the banks with the greatest number of branches on Cape Cod include **Bank of America,** which merged with Fleet in 2004 (© **800/900-9000;** www.bankofamerica.com), and **Banknorth Massachusetts** (© **800/747-7000;** www.banknorthma.com). Both banks exchange all foreign currencies, although you may want to stop at the exchange booth at Logan Airport in Boston.

CREDIT CARDS   Credit cards are a safe way to carry money and provide a convenient record of your expenses. You can also withdraw cash advances from your credit cards at any bank (though you'll start paying hefty interest on the advance the moment you receive the cash, and you won't receive frequent-flier miles on an airline credit card). At most banks you don't even need to go to a teller; you can get a cash advance at an ATM if you know your PIN. If you've forgotten your PIN or didn't even know you had one, call the phone number on the back of your credit card and ask the bank to send it to you. It usually takes 5 to 7 business days, though some banks provide the number over the phone if you pass some security clearance such as telling them your mother's maiden name.

THEFT Almost every credit card company has an emergency 800 number that you can call if your wallet or purse is stolen. They may be able to wire you a cash advance off your credit card immediately, and in many places, they can deliver an emergency credit card in a day or two. The issuing bank's toll-free number is usually on the back of the credit card—though, of course, that won't help you very much if the card has been stolen. The **toll-free information directory** will provide the number if you dial ℂ **800/555-1212. Citicorp Visa**'s U.S. emergency number is ℂ **800/336-8472. American Express** cardholders and traveler's check holders should call ℂ **800/221-7282** for all money emergencies. **MasterCard** holders should call ℂ **800/307-7309.**

Odds are that if your wallet is gone, it won't be recovered. However, after you realize that it's gone and you cancel your credit cards, it is still worth informing the police. Your credit card company or insurer may require a police report number.

2 When to Go

Once strictly a seasonal destination, opening with a splash on Memorial Day weekend and shuttering up come Labor Day, the Islands now welcome more and more tourists to witness the tender blossoms of spring and the fiery foliage of autumn. During these "shoulder seasons," lodging tends to cost less, and a fair number of restaurants and attractions remain open. Most important, traffic is non-existent. In addition, the natives tend to be far more accommodating in the off season, and shopping bargains abound.

August is the most popular month, followed by July (especially the July 4th weekend). You are virtually guaranteed good beach weather in July and August. September and October, though, are splendid, too; the ocean retains enough heat to make for bearable swimming in lakes and ponds during the sunny days of Indian summer, though the Atlantic is bone-chillingly cold. In autumn, the subtly varied hues of the trees and moors are always changing, always lovely. May and June are also enticing as gardening goes way beyond hobby in this gentle climate, and blooms are profuse from May through the summer. Unless your idea of the perfect vacation

Martha's Vineyard

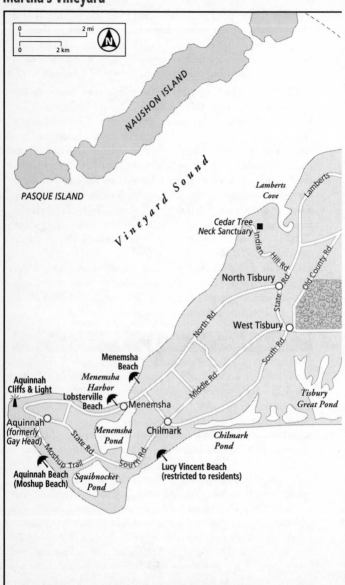

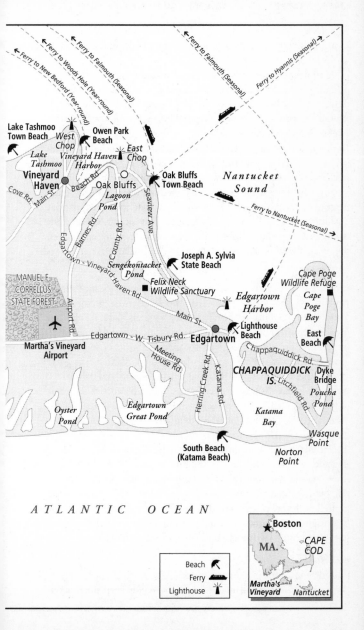

Lake Tashmoo
Town Beach

West
Chop

Owen Park
Beach

East
Chop

*Lake
Tashmoo*

*Vineyard Haven
Harbor*

Vineyard Haven

Oak Bluffs

Oak Bluffs
Town Beach

*Nantucket
Sound*

← Ferry to New Bedford (Year-round)
← Ferry to Woods Hole (Year-round)
← Ferry to Falmouth (Seasonal)
← Ferry to Falmouth (Seasonal)
Ferry to Hyannis (Seasonal) →
Ferry to Nantucket (Seasonal) →

Cove Rd.

Main St.

Beach Rd.

*Lagoon
Pond*

Barnes Rd.

County Rd.

Seaview Ave.

Edgartown - Vineyard Haven Rd.

*Sengekontacket
Pond*

Joseph A. Sylvia
State Beach

Felix Neck
Wildlife Sanctuary

MANUEL F.
CORRELLUS
STATE FOREST

Airport Rd.

Martha's Vineyard
Airport

Edgartown - Vineyard Haven Rd.

Main St.

*Edgartown
Harbor*

Cape Poge
Wildlife Refuge

*Cape
Poge
Bay*

Edgartown - W. Tisbury Rd.

Edgartown

Lighthouse
Beach

East
Beach

Chappaquiddick Rd.

**CHAPPAQUIDDICK
IS.**

Dyke
Bridge

Meeting
House Rd.

Herring Creek Rd.

Katama Rd.

Litchfield Rd.

*Poucha
Pond*

*Oyster
Pond*

*Edgartown
Great Pond*

*Katama
Bay*

Wasque
Point

South Beach
(Katama Beach)

Norton
Point

ATLANTIC   OCEAN

★ Boston

MA.

*CAPE
COD*

*Martha's
Vineyard*   Nantucket

Beach 🏖
Ferry ⛴
Lighthouse 🗼

13

requires a swim in the ocean, you're better off (fewer people and better deals) visiting the Islands slightly off-season: May, June, September, or October.

A number of entertaining town festivals and events attract crowds in the spring and fall. Some say the most crowded time on Nantucket is during the **Christmas Stroll** in early December; the entire month before Christmas is known as **Nantucket Noel,** with lots of holiday events. Martha's Vineyard also rolls out the red carpet in December with events in Edgartown and Vineyard Haven, including Santa arriving on the ferry. Spring brings the **Daffodil Festival** on Nantucket (book your ferry reservations way in advance for this one).

Some establishments stay open straight through the truly quiet season—January through March—and it's a rare treat to enjoy these historic towns and pristine landscapes with almost no one but natives stirring about. To avoid disappointment in the off season, however, always be sure to call ahead to check schedules.

WILDLIFE

The Islands' wetlands are part of one of the country's greatest annual wildlife spectacles: the passage of thousands of migratory sea-, shore-, and songbirds in spring and fall. Warblers, herons, terns and oystercatchers, shorebirds such as avocets and the endangered piping plover, dozens of species of ducks, huge flocks of snow geese, owls, and hawks—these are just a few of the birds that take a rest stop on the Islands as they pass along the Atlantic Flyway, which for some birds extends from winter homes in South America to breeding grounds in the vast, marshy tundra within the Arctic Circle. March, April, October, and November are all good months to see migrating waterfowl. August is the month to observe migrating shorebirds. Fewer shorebirds stop on the Islands in spring, but those that do will be decked out in the bird equivalent of a tux—their breeding plumage. Songbirds pass through in May, in their brightest plumage and in full-throated song (both color and voice are muted in the fall migration). If you're birding on the Islands during the height of the summer season, you'll find plenty of herons, egrets, terns, and osprey wherever you find sand and wetlands.

CLIMATE

During winter, the Gulf Stream renders the Islands about 10 degrees warmer than the mainland, and offshore winds keep them about

10 degrees cooler in summer (you'll probably need a sweater most evenings). The only downside of being surrounded by water is the tendency for fog, particularly on Nantucket, which is known as Fog Island; it's sunny about 2 days out of 3—not bad odds. And the foggy days can be rather romantic.

SUMMER   The official beginning of summer in the region is heralded by the **Figawi sailboat race** from Hyannis to Nantucket on Memorial Day weekend. Traffic all over the Cape is horrendous, and ferries are booked solid. It's a rowdy party weekend, but then, strangely, things slow down for a few weeks until late June. The first few weeks of June can be a perfect time to visit the Islands, but be forewarned: You may need to request a room with a fireplace. Weather this time of year can be unpredictable at best. At worst, it's cold and rainy (pack some good books for when it pours). Don't count on swimming in the ocean unless you're a member of the Polar Bear Club. Late June weather is usually lovely. July 4th is another major mob scene weekend to be avoided. July and August can be perfect—sunny and breezy—or damp, foggy, and humid. Usually it's a combination of the two. Heavily trafficked Labor Day is another weekend you'll probably want to avoid.

AUTUMN   It usually starts feeling like fall around mid-September on the Islands. Leaves start to change color, roads start to unclog, and everyone seems happier. Day temperatures are perfect for long hikes along the seashore. By October, you'll need a sweater during the day, and evenings can be downright chilly. But this is a lovely time of year on the Islands.

WINTER   It rarely snows on the Islands, but when it does, it's beautiful. One recent winter, the region received virtually no snow until a surprise blizzard on April 1. The holidays are quite popular for family gatherings on the Islands. January through March are on the bleak side. This is when a lot of locals head south to sunnier climes.

SPRING   April is a cheerful time on the Islands, particularly Nantucket, where the Daffodil Festival is a major event. Folks in the tourism business are gearing up for the summer season. It's a time for last-minute fix-up jobs: painting and repairing. In May and June, the Islands blossoms but the weather can be quite rainy this time of year.

Nantucket's Average Monthly Temperatures

	Jan	Feb	Mar	Apr	May	June	July	Aug	Sept	Oct	Nov	Dec
High (°F)	40	41	42	53	62	71	78	76	70	59	48	40
High (°C)	4	5	6	12	17	22	26	24	21	14	9	4
Low. (°F)	26	26	32	40	48	58	63	61	66	47	37	26
Low (°C)	–3	–3	0	4	9	14	17	16	18	8	3	–3

Martha's Vineyard's Average Monthly Temperatures

	Jan	Feb	Mar	Apr	May	June	July	Aug	Sept	Oct	Nov	Dec
High (°F)	37	38	45	54	63	72	78	78	71	62	53	43
High (°C)	3	3	7	12	17	22	26	26	22	17	12	6
Low (°F)	21	21	29	37	46	56	62	62	55	45	37	27
Low (°C)	–6	–6	–2	3	8	13	17	17	13	7	3	–3

CALENDAR OF EVENTS

April

Daffodil Festival, Nantucket. Spring's arrival is heralded with masses of yellow blooms adorning everything in sight, including a cavalcade of antique cars that parade down Main Street. Call ✆ **508/228-1700.** Late April.

May

Nantucket Wine Festival, Nantucket. Vintners converge on Nantucket for wine tastings and cuisine provided by some of the Island's top chefs. The Grand Cru is the main event. Call ✆ **508/228-1128;** www.nantucketwinefestival.com. Mid-May.

Figawi Sailboat Race, Hyannis to Nantucket. The largest—and wildest—race on the East Coast. Intense partying in Hyannis and on Nantucket surrounds this popular event. Call ✆ **508/771-3333;** www.figawi.com. Late May.

June

A Taste of the Vineyard, Martha's Vineyard. Island restaurateurs offer samplings of their specialties at Edgartown's Whaling Church to benefit the Martha's Vineyard Preservation Trust. Call ✆ **508/627-8017.** Mid-June.

Harborfest Celebration, Nantucket. You can sample competing chowders and board tall ships. Call ✆ **508/228-1700.** Mid-June.

Nantucket Film Festival, Nantucket. Annual event focuses on storytelling through film and includes showings of short- and feature-length films, documentaries, staged readings, panel discussions, and screenplay competition. Call © **212/708-1278;** www.nantucketfilmfestival.org. Late June.

July

Nantucket's Fourth of July, Nantucket. Main Street festivities are followed by community games, races, and a band concert on Jetties Beach. Fireworks are set off at dusk on Jetties Beach. Call © **508/228-1700.** Early July.

Edgartown Regatta, Martha's Vineyard. A highly social sailing event. Call © **508/627-4364.** Early July.

August

Possible Dreams Auction, Martha's Vineyard. Resident celebrities give—and bid—their all to support the endeavors of Martha's Vineyard Community Services. Call © **508/693-7900;** www.possibledreamsauction.org. Early August.

In the Spirit Arts Festival, Martha's Vineyard. Oak Bluffs celebrates its cultural diversity with food, music, and children's fun. Call © **508/693-0085.** Early August.

Agricultural Society Livestock Show and Fair, Martha's Vineyard. In West Tisbury, a classic country carnival, and a great leveler. Call © **508/693-9549.** Mid-August.

Sandcastle and Sculpture Day, Nantucket. A fairly serious contest, but fun; categorization by age group ups the odds of winning. Call © **508/228-1700.** Mid-August.

Opera House Cup Regatta, Nantucket. A classic wooden sailboat regatta that benefits the Nantucket Community Sailing program. Call © **508/325-7755.** Mid-August.

Illumination Night, Martha's Vineyard. The Oak Bluffs campground is lit with hundreds of Japanese lanterns. Campground officials keep this event a secret until the last minute, so it's hard to plan ahead. Call © **508/693-0085.** Late August.

Oak Bluffs Fireworks and Band Concert, Martha's Vineyard. The summer's last blast. Call © **508/693-5380.** Late August.

September

Martha's Vineyard Striped Bass and Bluefish Derby, Martha's Vineyard. The region's premier fishing derby and one of the country's oldest is a month-long classic contest. Call © **508/627-3471;** www.mvderby.com. Mid-September to mid-October.

October

Nantucket Arts Festival, Nantucket. This weeklong event includes a wet-paint sale, mini–film festival, writers and their works, gallery exhibitions, artist demonstrations, theater, concerts, photography, and more. Call ✆ **508/325-8588.** Mid-October.

Happy Haunting Weekend, Martha's Vineyard. Edgartown hosts Halloween festivities, including a pumpkin-carving contest and trick or treating. Call ✆ **508/627-4711.** Late October.

November

Fall Festival, Edgartown, Martha's Vineyard. Family activities at the Felix Neck Wildlife Sanctuary, including a treasure hunt, wildlife walks, and wreath making. Call ✆ **508/627-4850.** Late November.

December

Christmas Stroll, Nantucket. The island stirs from its winter slumber for one last shopping/feasting spree, with costumed carolers, Santa in a horse-drawn carriage, and a "talking" Christmas tree. This event is the pinnacle of **Nantucket Noel,** a month of festivities starting in late November. Ferries and lodging establishments book up months before this event, so you'll need to plan ahead. Call ✆ **508/228-1700.** Early December.

First Night, Vineyard Haven and Edgartown, Martha's Vineyard. Boston-inspired jamborees featuring local artists and performers. Call ✆ **508/693-0085.** New Year's Eve.

3 Tips for Travelers with Special Needs

FOR TRAVELERS WITH DISABILITIES

A disability shouldn't stop anyone from traveling. The free *Getaway Guide* offered by the **Massachusetts Office of Travel & Tourism** (✆ **800/227-MASS** or 617/973-8500; www.massvacation.com) is keyed for handicapped accessibility. Though the larger, more popular establishments, as well as newer (1990s) construction, are generally up to code, a great many of the Islands' older, historic buildings are difficult to retrofit, and the task is prohibitively expensive for many small-business owners, much as they may like to upgrade. Your best bet is to check accessibility when calling ahead to confirm hours or make reservations. You'll find most places eager to do whatever they can to ease the way; if you run into problems, you may want to contact the **Cape Organization for Rights of the Disabled** (✆ **800/541-0282** or 508/775-8300; www.cordonline.org). For information on services available in the state, call the **Massachusetts Network of Information Providers** (© 800/642-0249 or 800/764-0200; www.mnip-net.org) during business hours.

The **Steamship Authority** (© 508/477-8600; www.islandferry.com), which runs ferries year-round to Martha's Vineyard and Nantucket, has made great strides in ensuring that their boats are handicapped accessible and that travelers with special needs are given appropriate attention and care, though some ferries remain difficult to access. Call ahead to ensure the accessibility of the vessel you're boarding.

For travelers to Nantucket, *Guide for Visitors with Special Needs,* published by the Nantucket Commission on Disability (NCD) is available through the **Nantucket Island Chamber of Commerce** (© 508/228-1700), **Nantucket Visitor Services** (© 508/228-0925), or by calling **NCD** (© 508/228-8085).

The U.S. National Park Service offers a **Golden Access Passport** that gives free lifetime entrance to all properties administered by the National Park Service—national parks, monuments, historic sites, recreation areas, and national wildlife refuges—for persons who are visually impaired or permanently disabled, regardless of age. You may pick up a Golden Access Passport at any NPS entrance fee area by showing proof of medically determined disability and eligibility for receiving benefits under federal law. Besides free entry, the Golden Access Passport also offers a 50% discount on federal-use fees charged for such facilities as camping, swimming, parking, boat launching, and tours. For more information, go to www.nps.gov/fees_passes.htm or call © 888/467-2757.

Many travel agencies offer customized tours and itineraries for travelers with disabilities. **Flying Wheels Travel** (© 507/451-5005; www.flyingwheelstravel.com) offers escorted tours and cruises that emphasize sports and private tours in minivans with lifts. **Access-Able Travel Source** (© 303/232-2979; www.access-able.com) has extensive access information and advice for traveling around the world with disabilities. **Accessible Journeys** (© 800/846-4537 or 610/521-0339; www.disabilitytravel.com) caters to slow walkers and wheelchair travelers and their families and friends.

Avis Rent a Car has an "Avis Access" program that offers such services as a dedicated 24-hour toll-free number (© 888/879-4273; www.avis.com) for customers with special travel needs; special car features such as swivel seats, spinner knobs, and hand controls; and accessible bus service.

Organizations that offer assistance to travelers with disabilities include **MossRehab** (www.mossresourcenet.org), with a library of accessible-travel resources online; **SATH** (Society for Accessible Travel & Hospitality) (© **212/447-7284;** www.sath.org; annual membership fees: $45 adults, $30 seniors and students), which offers a wealth of travel resources for all types of disabilities and informed recommendations on destinations, access guides, travel agents, tour operators, vehicle rentals, and companion services; and the **American Foundation for the Blind (AFB)** (© **800/232-5463;** www.afb.org), a referral resource for the blind or visually impaired that includes information on traveling with Seeing Eye dogs.

For more information specifically targeted to travelers with disabilities, **iCan** (www.icanonline.net/channels/travel/index.cfm) has destination guides and regular columns on accessible travel. Also check out the quarterly magazine *Emerging Horizons* ($14.95 per year, $19.95 outside the U.S.; www.emerginghorizons.com), and *Open World* magazine, published by SATH (see above; subscription: $13 per year, $21 outside the U.S.).

FOR SENIORS

With relatively mild winters and splendid summers, the Islands attract their share of seniors. Businesses from museums to B&Bs cater to this clientele with attractive discounts. Mention that you're a senior when you make your travel reservations, and be sure to carry some form of identification that establishes your birth date, such as a driver's license or passport. Both **Amtrak** (© **800/USA-RAIL**) and **Greyhound** (© **800/752-4841**), which serves Boston, offer discounted fares to persons over 62.

You should also inquire about the resources of **Elder Services of Cape Cod and the Islands** (© **800/244-4630** or 508/394-4630).

Members of **AARP** (formerly known as the American Association of Retired Persons), 601 E St. NW, Washington, DC 20049 (© **888/687-2277;** www.aarp.org), get discounts on hotels, airfares, and car rentals. AARP offers members a wide range of benefits, including *AARP The Magazine* and a monthly newsletter. Anyone over 50 can join.

The **U.S. National Park Service** offers a **Golden Age Passport** that gives seniors 62 years or older lifetime entrance to all properties administered by the National Park Service—national parks, monuments, historic sites, recreation areas, and national wildlife refuges—for a one-time processing fee of $10, which must be purchased in person at any NPS facility that charges an entrance fee.

Besides free entry, a Golden Age Passport also offers a 50% discount on federal-use fees charged for such facilities as camping, swimming, parking, boat launching, and tours. For more information, go to www.nps.gov/fees_passes.htm or call ℂ **888/467-2757.**

Many reliable agencies and organizations target the 50-plus market. **Elderhostel** (ℂ **877/426-8056;** www.elderhostel.org) arranges study programs for those 55 and over (and a spouse or companion of any age) in the U.S. and in more than 80 countries around the world. Most courses last 5 to 7 days in the U.S. (2–4 weeks abroad), and many include airfare, accommodations in university dormitories or modest inns, meals, and tuition.

Recommended publications offering travel resources and discounts for seniors include: the quarterly magazine *Travel 50 & Beyond* (www.travel50andbeyond.com); *Travel Unlimited: Uncommon Adventures for the Mature Traveler* (Avalon); *101 Tips for Mature Travelers,* available from Grand Circle Travel (ℂ **800/221-2610** or 617/350-7500; www.gct.com); and *Unbelievably Good Deals and Great Adventures That You Absolutely Can't Get Unless You're Over 50* (McGraw-Hill), by Joann Rattner Heilman.

FOR GAY & LESBIAN TRAVELERS

Gay and lesbian travelers, singly or in pairs, should feel quite comfortable on the Islands. These are sophisticated destinations, and you'll rarely encounter a bigoted innkeeper, shopkeeper, or restaurateur—if you do, report them to the **Massachusetts Commission Against Discrimination,** 1 Ashburton Place, Room 601, Boston, MA 02108 (ℂ **617/994-6000;** www.mass.gov/mcad). To avoid unpleasant situations, read between the lines of promotional literature ("fun for the whole family" may mean rampant bedlam and not much fun for you), or be blunt in stating your expectations (for example, "It will be for myself and my partner, and we'd like a queen bed, if possible"). The descriptions of each establishment listed in this book should give some idea of their suitability and compatibility.

The **International Gay and Lesbian Travel Association (IGLTA)** (ℂ **800/448-8550** or 954/776-2626; www.iglta.org) is the trade association for the gay and lesbian travel industry, and has an online directory of gay- and lesbian-friendly travel businesses.

Many agencies offer tours and travel itineraries specifically for gay and lesbian travelers. **Above and Beyond Tours** (ℂ **800/397-2681;** www.abovebeyondtours.com) is the exclusive gay and lesbian tour operator for United Airlines. **Now, Voyager** (ℂ **800/255-6951;** www.nowvoyager.com) is a well-known San Francisco–based gay-owned and operated travel service. **Olivia Cruises & Resorts** (© **800/631-6277;** www.olivia.com) charters entire resorts and ships for exclusive lesbian vacations and offers smaller group experiences for both gay and lesbian travelers.

The following travel guides are available at most travel bookstores and gay and lesbian bookstores, or you can order them from **Giovanni's Room** bookstore, 1145 Pine St., Philadelphia, PA 19107 (© **215/923-2960;** www.giovannisroom.com): *Frommer's Gay & Lesbian Europe* (Wiley Publishing, Inc.), an excellent travel resource; *Out and About* (© **800/929-2268;** www.outandabout. com), which offers guidebooks and a newsletter ($20/year; 10 issues) packed with solid information on the global gay and lesbian scene; *Spartacus International Gay Guide* (Bruno Gmünder Verlag; www.spartacusworld.com/gayguide) and *Odysseus: The International Gay Travel Planner* (Odysseus Enterprises Ltd.), both good, annual English-language guidebooks focused on gay men; the *Damron* guides (www.damron.com), with separate, annual books for gay men and lesbians; and *Gay Travel A to Z: The World of Gay & Lesbian Travel Options at Your Fingertips* by Marianne Ferrari (Ferrari International; Box 35575, Phoenix, AZ 85069), a very good gay and lesbian guidebook series.

FOR FAMILIES

Basically a giant sandbox with a fringe of waves, the Islands are an ideal family vacation spot. A number of the larger hotels and motels offer deals whereby kids can share their parent's room for free. But beware of the fancier B&Bs: Although it's quite illegal for them to do so, some actively discriminate against children. The kind that do are apt to be the kind that children dislike, so it's no great loss. For the most part, the local tourism industry is big on serving family needs, so you'll need to do little by way of advance preparation.

To locate accommodations, restaurants, and attractions that are particularly kid-friendly, look for the "Kids" icon in this guide.

Recommended family travel Internet sites include **Family Travel Forum** (www.familytravelforum.com), which offers customized trip planning; **Family Travel Network** (www.familytravelnetwork.com), an award-winning site with travel features, deals, and tips; **Traveling Internationally with Your Kids** (www.travelwithyourkids.com), which offers sound advice for long-distance and international travel with children; and **Family Travel Files** (www.thefamilytravelfiles. com), with an online magazine and a directory of off-the-beaten-path tours and tour operators for families.

4 Getting There

GETTING TO NANTUCKET

BY FERRY From Hyannis (South St. Dock), the **Steamship Authority** (© 508/477-8600; www.islandferry.com; on Nantucket, © 508/228-0262) operates year-round ferry service (including cars, passengers, and bicycles) to Steamship Wharf in Nantucket by fast ferry (1 hr.) and regular ferry (2 hr. 15 min.).

The Steamship Authority's fast ferry to Nantucket, *The Flying Cloud* (© 508/495-3278), is for passengers only (no cars), takes 1 hour and runs five to six times a day in season. It is cheaper than the Hy-Line ferry (see below), at $27.50 one-way ($55 round-trip) for adults, $20.75 one-way ($41.50 round-trip) for children 5 to 12. Parking costs $8 to $10 per day. Passenger reservations are highly recommended. No pets are allowed on *The Flying Cloud.*

If you plan to travel to Nantucket with your car in summer, you must reserve *months in advance* to secure a spot on the regular ferry because only six boats make the trip daily in season (three boats daily off season). Before you call, have several alternatives for departure dates. Remember to arrive at least 1 hour before departure to avoid your space being released to standbys. If you arrive without a reservation and plan to wait in the standby line, there is no guarantee you will get to the island that day. There is a $10 processing fee for canceling reservations. No advance reservations are required for passengers traveling without cars on the regular ferry.

Total trip time on the regular ferry is 2 hours and 15 minutes. A round-trip fare for a car costs a whopping $350 to $380 from May to October; $230 to $250 from November to April. (Do you get the impression your car may not be welcome?) Fare does not include drivers or passengers; you must get tickets for each person going to the island. For passengers, a one-way ticket is $14 ($28 round-trip) for adults, $7.25 one-way ($14.50 round-trip) for children 5 to 12, and $12 round-trip for bikes. Remember that parking costs $8 to $10 per day; you do not need to make parking reservations.

Also from Hyannis, passenger ferries to Nantucket's Straight Wharf are operated by **Hy-Line Cruises,** Ocean Street Dock (© **888/778-1132** or 508/778-2602; for high-speed ferry reservations, call © **800/492-8082** or 508/778-0404; www.hy-linecruises.com). Hy-Line offers year-round service with its high-speed passenger catamaran, *The Grey Lady II,* which makes five to six hourly trips per day. The cost of a one-way fare is $35 for adults ($61 round-trip), $26 for children 5 to 12 ($43 round-trip), and $5 extra for bicycles ($10 round-trip). It's best to make a reservation in advance.

From early May to October, Hy-Line's standard, 1-hour-and-50-minute ferry service is also offered. Round-trip tickets are $30 for adults, $16 for children ages 5 to 12, and $10 extra for bikes. On busy holiday weekends, try to order tickets in advance; otherwise, be sure to buy your tickets at least a half-hour before your boat leaves.

The standard ferry has a first-class section with a private lounge, bathrooms, bar, and snack bar; a continental breakfast or afternoon cheese and crackers is also served onboard. One-way fare is $24 for adults and children ($48 round-trip).

Hy-Line's "Around the Sound" cruise is a 1-day, round-trip excursion from Hyannis with stops in Nantucket and Martha's Vineyard that runs from early June to late September. The price is $45 for adults, $24 for children 4 to 12, and $15 extra for bikes.

Hy-Line runs three passenger-only ferries from Oak Bluffs, Martha's Vineyard, to Nantucket from early June to mid-September (there is no car-ferry service between the Islands). The trip time from Oak Bluffs is 2 hours and 15 minutes. The one-way fare is $15 for adults, $8 for children 5 to 12, and $5 extra for bikes.

From Harwich Port, you can avoid the summer crowds in Hyannis and board one of **Freedom Cruise Line**'s (702 Rte. 28 in Harwich Port, across from Brax Landing, © **508/432-8999;** www.nantucket islandferry.com) passenger-only ferries to Nantucket. From mid-May to early October, boats leave from Saquatucket Harbor in Harwich Port; the trip takes 1 hour and 30 minutes. A round-trip ticket is $48 for adults, $38 for children ages 2 to 11, $6 for children under 2, and $10 extra for bikes. Parking is free for day-trippers, $12 for overnight; advance reservations are recommended.

BY BUS **Plymouth & Brockton Bus Line** (© 508/746-0378; www.p-b.com) offers direct service from Boston to Hyannis. **Bonanza Buslines** (© 888/751-8800; www.bonanzabus.com) carries passengers from Providence, Rhode Island, to Hyannis.

BY AIR You can also fly into **Nantucket Memorial Airport** (© 508/325-5300; www.nantucketairport.com), which is about 3 miles south of Nantucket Road on Old South Road. The flight to Nantucket takes 30 to 40 minutes from Boston, 15 minutes from Hyannis, and a little more than an hour from New York City airports.

Tips Parking

You do not need a car on Nantucket, so plan to park your car in Hyannis before boarding the ferry to the island. For **Hy-Line** ferry service from Ocean Street Dock in Hyannis in July and August, it's a good idea not only to reserve tickets in advance, but also reserve a parking spot ahead of time. The all-day parking fee is $15 per calendar day in season. If the Hy-Line lot is full, there are two competing lots next to the Hyannis Harbor Motel across the street. Choose the one where the attendants are wearing yellow shirts (not yellow jackets!); they have the more reliable rates. Travelers on **Steamship Authority** vessels do not need a parking reservation, but when the lots near the ferry terminal are full, satellite lots are used and passengers take shuttle buses to the terminal. When the nearby lot across from Cape Cod Hospital is full, parking is at a lot several blocks away on Yarmouth Road. From the Yarmouth Road lot, you access the ferry terminal via a free shuttle bus. Overflow ferry parking is at the Cape Cod Community College parking lots just north of Route 6 on Route 132 (exit 6 off Rte. 6). Be sure to arrive at least 1 hour before sailing time to allow for parking. Parking at the Steamship Authority lots is $8 to $10 per day. Free shuttle buses take passengers to the Hy-Line and Steamship Authority terminals, which are on opposite ends of Hyannis Harbor. In season, watch signs on Route 6 as you drive to Hyannis for up-to-the-minute ferry parking information.

Airlines providing service to Nantucket include **Cape Air/ Nantucket Air** (© 800/352-0714 or 508/771-6944; www. flycapeair.com) year-round from Hyannis, Boston, Martha's Vineyard, Providence, and New Bedford; **Continental Express** (© 800/ 525-0280; www.continental.com) from Newark, seasonally; **Island Airlines** (© 800/248-7779 or 508/228-7575; www.nantucket.net/ trans/islandair) year-round from Hyannis; and **US Airways Express** (© 800/428-4322; www.usairways.com) year-round from Boston and New York.

Island Airlines and Nantucket Airlines both offer year-round charter service to the island. Another recommended charter company is **Ocean Wings** (© 800/253-5039).

GETTING TO MARTHA'S VINEYARD

BY FERRY   Most visitors get to Martha's Vineyard by ferry. If you're traveling via car or bus, you'll most likely catch the ferry from Woods Hole on Cape Cod; however, boats do run from Falmouth, Hyannis, New Bedford, Rhode Island, and Nantucket. On weekends in season, the Steamship Authority ferries make about 26 trips a day to Martha's Vineyard from Woods Hole (two other companies provide an additional 12 passenger ferries a day from Falmouth Harbor). Schedules are available from the **Martha's Vineyard Chamber of Commerce** (*©* 508/693-0085; fax 508/693-7589; www.mvy.com) or the Steamship Authority (see below).

The state-run **Steamship Authority** (www.islandferry.com) runs the show in Woods Hole (*©* **508/477-8600** early Apr to early Sept daily 7am–9pm, and reduced hours the rest of the year; or 508/693-9130 daily 8am–5pm) and operates every day, year-round (weather permitting). It maintains the only ferries to Martha's Vineyard that accommodate cars in addition to passengers. These large ferries make the 45-minute trip to Vineyard Haven throughout the year; some boats go to Oak Bluffs from late May to late October (call or check the website for seasonal schedules). During the summer, you'll need a reservation to bring your car to the island, and you must reserve *months in advance* to secure a spot. If you are planning to bring your car over to the island, you need to arrive at the Woods Hole terminal at least 30 minutes before your scheduled departure.

Many people prefer to leave their cars on the mainland, take the ferry (often with their bikes), and then rent a car, Jeep, or bicycle on the island. You can park your car at the Woods Hole lot (always full in the summer) or at one of the many lots in Falmouth that absorb the overflow of cars during the summer months; parking is $8 to $10 per day. Plan to arrive at the parking lots in Falmouth at least 45 minutes before sailing time to allow for parking, taking the free shuttle bus to the ferry terminal, and buying your ferry ticket. Free shuttle buses (some equipped for bikes) run regularly from the outlying lots to the Woods Hole ferry terminal.

The cost of a round-trip passenger ticket on the ferry to Martha's Vineyard is $12 for adults and $6.50 for children 5 to 12 (kids under 5 ride free). If you're bringing your bike along, it's an extra $6 round-trip. You do not need a reservation on the ferry if you're traveling without a car, and there are no reservations needed for parking. The cost of a round-trip car passage from May to October is $114 (vehicles over 16 ft. long, typically large SUVs, pay slightly more); in the

> *Tips* **Reservations-Only Policy for Car Passage to Martha's Vineyard**
>
> You must make reservations to bring your car to Martha's Vineyard on Friday through Monday from mid-June to mid-September. During these times, standby is in effect only on Tuesday through Thursday. Vehicle reservations are also required to bring your car to Martha's Vineyard during Memorial Day weekend. There will be no standby service available during these dates. Although technically, reservations can be made up to 1 hour in advance of ferry departure, ferries in season are almost always full, and you cannot depend on a cancellation during the summer months. Also be aware that your space may be forfeited if you have not checked into the ferry terminal 30 minutes prior to departure. Reservations may be changed to another date and time only with at least 24 hours' notice; otherwise, you will have to pay for an additional ticket for your vehicle.
>
> If you arrive without a reservation on a day that allows standby, come early and be prepared to wait in the standby line for hours. The Steamship Authority guarantees your passage if you're in line by 2pm on designated standby days only. For up-to-date **Steamship Authority** information, check out their website (www.islandferry.com).

off season it drops to $70. Car rates do not include drivers or passengers; you must buy tickets for each person going to the island.

Once you are aboard the ferry, you have won the right to feel relieved and relaxed. Now your vacation can begin. Ferries are equipped with bathrooms and snack bars. Your fellow passengers will be a gaggle of kids, dogs, and happy-looking travelers.

From Falmouth, you can also board the *Island Queen* at Falmouth Inner Harbor (© **508/548-4800;** www.islandqueen.com) for a 35-minute cruise to Oak Bluffs (passengers only). The boat runs from late May to mid-October; round-trip fare is $12 for adults, $6 for children under 13, and an extra $6 for bikes. There are seven crossings a day in season (eight on Fri and Sun), and no reservations are needed. Parking costs $15 a day. Credit cards are not accepted.

The **Falmouth-Edgartown Ferry Service,** 278 Scranton Ave. (© **508/548-9400;** www.falmouthferry.com), operates a 1-hour passenger ferry, called the *Pied Piper,* from Falmouth Inner Harbor to Edgartown. The boat runs from late May to mid-October, and reservations are required. In season, there are five crossings a day (six on Fri). Round-trip fares are $30 for adults and $20 for children under 12. Bicycles are $8 round-trip. Parking is $15 per day.

From Hyannis, you can take the **Hy-Line,** Ocean Street Dock (© **888/778-1132** or 508/778-2602; www.hy-linecruises.com), to Oak Bluffs, May through October. They run four trips a day, fewer off season. Trip time is about 1 hour and 45 minutes; round-trip costs $30 for adults and $16 for children 5 to 12 ($10 extra for bikes). In July and August, it's a good idea to reserve a parking spot in Hyannis; the all-day fee is $10. From June to September, they also operate a 1-day cruise, called **Around the Sound,** with stops on the Vineyard and Nantucket ($45 adults; $24 children 4–12).

From Nantucket, Hy-Line runs three passenger-only ferries to Oak Bluffs on Martha's Vineyard from early June to mid-September (there is no car-ferry service between the Islands). The trip time is 2 hours and 15 minutes. The one-way fare is $15 for adults, $8 for children 5 to 12, and $5 extra for bikes.

Traveling to Martha's Vineyard from New Bedford, Massachusetts, is a great way to avoid Cape traffic (which can be severe) and enjoy a scenic ocean cruise. **New England Fast Ferry** (© **866/453-6800;** www.nefastferry.com) operates the M/V *Whaling City Express,* which travels from New Bedford to Martha's Vineyard in an hour. It makes six trips a day in season and is in service year-round, 7 days a week. A ticket costs $20 one-way and $40 round-trip for adults; $17 one-way and $34 round-trip for seniors and children under 12.

From **North Kingstown, Rhode Island,** to Oak Bluffs, **Vineyard Fast Ferry** (© **401/295-4040;** www.vineyardfastferry.com) runs its high-speed catamaran, *Millennium,* two to three round-trips daily from mid-June through October. The trip takes 90 minutes. The ferry leaves from Quonset Point, which is about 10 minutes from Route I-95, 15 minutes from T.F. Green Airport in Providence, and 20 minutes from the Amtrak station in Kingston. Rates are $28 one-way, $51 round-trip for adults; $21 one-way, $39 round-trip for children 4 to 12; and $4 one-way, $8 round-trip for bikes. Parking next to the ferry port is $10 per day.

BY AIR You can fly into **Martha's Vineyard Airport,** also known as Dukes County Airport (© **508/693-7022**), in West Tisbury, about 5 miles outside Edgartown.

Airlines serving the Vineyard include **Cape Air/Nantucket Airlines** (© **800/352-0714** or 508/771-6944; www.flycapeair.com), which connects the island year-round with Boston (with an hourly shuttle service in summer), Hyannis, Nantucket, New Bedford, and Providence; and **US Airways Express** (© 800/428-4322), which flies from Boston and also has seasonal weekend service from New York's La Guardia.

The only company offering year-round charter service is **Direct Flight** (© 508/693-6688). **Westchester Air** (© 800/759-2929) also runs some charters from White Plains, New York.

BY BUS   **Bonanza Bus Lines** (© 888/751-8800 or 508/ 548-7588 from 5am to 4:30pm only; www.bonanzabus.com) connects the Woods Hole ferry port with Boston (from South Station or Logan Airport), New York City, and Providence, Rhode Island. The trip from South Station in Boston takes about 1 hour and 35 minutes and costs from $17 to $18.50 one-way and from $29 to $31 round-trip (weekends cost slightly more). There are 11 buses per day. From Boston's Logan Airport, it's $42 round-trip and there are 8 buses per day. From New York City, it's about a 6-hour bus trip to Hyannis or Woods Hole, costing $49 to $52 each way or $89 to $95 round-trip. There are 5 buses per day from New York.

BY LIMO   **King's Coach** (© 800/235-5669 or 508/563-5669) picks you up at Boston's Logan Airport and takes you to meet your ferry in Woods Hole (or anywhere else in the Upper Cape area). The trip takes 90 minutes depending on traffic and costs $125 one-way plus a gratuity for a carload or a vanload of people. You'll need to book the service a couple of days in advance. **Falmouth Taxi** (© 508/ 548-3100) also runs limo service from Boston and the airport.

5 Tips on Accommodations

The listings in this book feature a range of summer rates for a double room. Keep in mind that this figure does not take into account the sales tax, which can go as high as 9.7%, depending on the town. Off-season prices are typically discounted by about 20% to 30%, sometimes more.

Both Nantucket and Martha's Vineyard have lodgings to suit every taste and budget. The essential trick is to secure reservations months—possibly as much as a year—in advance for the peak season of July through August (June and Sept are beginning to get crowded, too). You can't count on luck; in fact, unless you're just planning a day trip, you probably shouldn't even visit at the height of summer unless you've prearranged a place to stay.

Accommodations range from sprawling, full-facility resorts to cozy little B&Bs with room for only a handful of guests. The price differential, surprisingly enough, may not be that great. A room at a particularly exquisite inn might run more than a modern hotel room with every imaginable amenity.

There are lodging establishments of every stripe on the Islands, but I've focused only on those with special qualities: superb facilities, for example, or especially friendly and helpful hosts. I've personally visited every place listed in this guide, but worthy new inns—as well as resurrected old ones—are constantly popping up.

RESERVATIONS SERVICES   Several reservations services cover the region. A particularly good one is **Destination Insider** (© **866/ 829-1800** or 508/696-3223; http://nantucket.destinationinsider. com), a website and booking service for both Nantucket and Martha's Vineyard. The service is offered free to travelers 7 days a week 9am to 5:30pm.

Nantucket Accommodations, P.O. Box 217, Nantucket, MA 02554 (© **508/228-9559;** fax 508/325-7009; www.nantucket accommodation.com), is a private service that arranges advance reservations for inns, cottages, guesthouses, bed-and-breakfasts, and hotels. You can call until the day of arrival, and they will arrange a booking based on your preferences. A member of the Chamber of Commerce, Nantucket Accommodations has access to 95% of the island's lodging facilities, in addition to houses and cottages available to rent by the night or week (as opposed to most realtors, who will only handle rentals for 2 weeks or more). The charge for the service is $15—a fee assessed only when a reservation is made. The customer pays Nantucket Accommodations by any major credit card or check, and N.A. then pays the inn or hotel.

Last-minute travelers should keep in mind that the **Nantucket Visitor Services & Information Bureau** (© **508/228-0925**), a daily referral service for available rooms rather than a booking service, always has the most updated list of accommodations availability and cancellations. This town-run office can also recommend restaurants and attractions.

To avoid disappointment, always request a brochure, or check out the place online. Some inns and hotels offer special packages, which they may or may not list, so always inquire. Most require minimum stays which range from 2 to 5 nights. All provide free parking.

Remember: It's buyer beware when it comes to such promotional terms as "water view" or "beachfront."

FAMILY-FRIENDLY   Although all lodgings in the state are prohibited by law from discriminating on the basis of age, a lot of the
fancier, fussier B&Bs will be none too happy if you show up with a
young child or infant in tow. You may not be too happy either,
spending your entire vacation attending to damage control. It can't
hurt to inquire—perhaps anonymously, before calling to book—
about an establishment's attitude toward children and its suitability
for their needs. If you get the impression that your child won't be
welcome, there's no point in pushing it: The child, sensing correctly
that he/she is not wanted, is likely to exceed your worst expectations.
If, on the other hand, you know your child to be a reliable model of
"company behavior," you may want to risk an unannounced arrival.

It's probably easier from the outset, though, to seek out places
that like having kids around. Motels are always a safe bet (it's what
they're designed for), and the descriptions provided here should give
some indication of other likely spots.

A popular family option—but again, you must make plans as
much as a year in advance—is to rent a cottage or house by the
week, or even month (see below).

RENTING A COTTAGE OR HOUSE   Families planning an
Island vacation, especially families with young children, should consider renting a cottage or house rather than choosing an inn or
hotel. The trick to finding a great rental can be summed up in two
words: Book early. Start calling realtors in January and February (if
not sooner—some vacationers who return every summer book a
year in advance). If you can, visit earlier in the year to check out a
few places; if not, you may be able to view choices on a realtor's website or see photos that the realtor can mail to you.

Tell your realtor whether you will have a car. If you will not have
a car, you'll want to be in an area that's within easy walking or biking distance to supermarkets and beaches. Unless you are willing to
shell out big bucks for a rental, don't expect to have water
views—especially on Nantucket.

Prices on rentals vary, but they are always much lower off season.
Depending on the rental, off season could mean late June or even
late August, so ask what the cut-off dates are for high-season prices.
Location is the single biggest factor in determining price: A two-
bedroom cottage with a great location on Nantucket could cost
$8,000 a week. Tell your realtor your price range and what you are
looking for, and you'll get appropriate listings to choose from.

Each Island's chamber of commerce can put you in touch with
local realtors. You can also call the **Cape Cod and the Islands**

Tips **Hit the Pavement**

Sometimes the best way to find a good rental is to drive around the area you want to rent in and look for handwritten signs advertising rentals by owner. These rentals tend to be cheaper (no realtor commission), and you'll know just what you are getting into before you sign on the dotted line.

Board of Realtors, 450 Station Ave., South Yarmouth, MA 02664 (© **508/394-2277;** www.capeandislandsrealtors.com) for a complete list of realtors in the area.

Here is a list of good realtors with rentals on the Islands. On Nantucket, there's **Jordan Real Estate** (© 508/228-4449), **Heard Real Estate** (© 508/228-3838), or **Nantucket Real Estate Co.** (© 508/228-3131). On Martha's Vineyard, there's **Linda R. Bassett Vacation Rentals** (© 800/338-9201), **Ocean Park Rentals** (© 508/693-3037), **Sandpiper Rentals** (© 508/627-6070), and **Martha's Vineyard Home Rentals** (© 508/627-7890).

The website http://weneedavacation.com features listings of more than 650 rental properties on Cape Cod, Nantucket, and Martha's Vineyard. Vacationers state their needs, such as size of home, location desired, amenities, price range, and dates desired and a search engine presents them with pictures and complete descriptions of homes that are available and that suit their needs.

CAMPING INFORMATION   Camping is expressly forbidden on Nantucket. Seashore camping is not allowed on Martha's Vineyard either. The Vineyard has one campground, called **Martha's Vineyard Family Campground** on Vineyard Haven-Edgartown Road (© **508/693-3772**), which is in the middle of the island and not near a beach.

FAST FACTS: Nantucket & Martha's Vineyard

American Express The nearest **American Express Travel Service** office is at 1600 Falmouth Rd. in Centerville (© **877/645-6348** or 508/778-2310) and is open Monday to Friday from 9am to 6pm. Call © 800/221-7282 for other locations.

Area Code The telephone area code for the Cape and the Islands is **508**. You must always dial 1 and this area code first, even if you are making a call within the same town.

Business Hours Business hours in public and private offices are usually Monday to Friday from 8 or 9am to 4:30 or 5pm. Most stores are open Monday to Saturday from 9:30 or 10am to 6pm or later in the summer months; many are also open on Sunday from noon to 5pm—or earlier, now that Massachusetts's "blue laws" (intended to curb the sale of alcohol) have been relaxed. Virtually every town has some kind of convenience store carrying food, beverages, newspapers, and some household basics; and the larger communities have supermarkets, which generally stay open as late as 10 or 11pm.

Doctors For a referral, contact **Cape Medsource** at the Falmouth Hospital (© 800/243-7963 or 508/457-7963), **Ask-a-Nurse** at Cape Cod Hospital (© 800/544-2424), or the **Physician Referral Service** at Massachusetts General Hospital in Boston (© 617/726-5800). Physicians and surgeons are also listed by specialty in the Yellow Pages.

Drugstores All the larger towns have pharmacies that are open daily. The ones with the longest hours are likely to be located within a supermarket. A 24-hour **CVS** drugstore is located at 182 North St. in Hyannis (© 508/775-8346 pharmacy, or 508/775-8977 store phone).

Emergencies Phone © 911 for fire, police, emergency, or ambulance; be prepared to give your number, address, name, and a quick report. If you get into desperate straits—say, if your money is stolen and you need assistance arranging to get home—contact the **Travelers Aid** office in Boston (© 617/542-7286). Also see "Hospitals," below.

Fishing Licenses Contact the local town hall of the area in which you want to fish. Massachusetts residents pay $13.50 for a 3-day pass or $28.50 for a season pass; non-residents pay $24.50 for a 3-day pass or $38.50 for a season pass. On Nantucket, the **Marine and Coastal Resources Department,** 34 Washington St. (© 508/228-7261) is responsible for issuing all commercial and non-commercial permits for shell fishing. A permit for someone who is not a resident of Nantucket costs $100. (Residents pay $25.)

Hospitals The **Cape Cod Hospital** at 27 Park St., Hyannis (© 508/771-1800, ext. 5235), offers 24-hour emergency medical service and consultation, as does the **Falmouth Hospital** at 100 Ter Heun Dr. (© 508/457-3524). On the Islands, contact the **Martha's Vineyard Hospital** on Linton Lane in Oak Bluffs

(© 508/693-0410) or **Nantucket Cottage Hospital** on South Prospect Street (© **508/228-1200**).

Hot Lines   The **Poison Hot Line** is © **800/682-9211;** the **Samaritans Suicide Prevention line** is © **508/548-8900.** For a range of other hot lines related to social and health problems, check out the local phone book.

Information   See "Visitor Information," earlier in this chapter.

Internet Access   Most public libraries on the Islands have free terminals with Web access, allowing travelers to check their e-mail through a Web-based e-mail service such as Yahoo! or Hotmail. On Nantucket, you must book ahead to use the Internet terminals at the Atheneum, which is the public library. Internet cafes have come and gone in the last few years; it's best to ask around locally, or check www.netcafe guide.com or www.cybercafe.com.

Liquor Laws   The legal drinking age in Massachusetts is 21. Most bars are allowed to stay open until 1am every day, with "last call" at 12:30am. On Nantucket, beer, wine, and liquor are only available at package stores. On Martha's Vineyard, beer and wine are sold at grocery as well as package stores; hard liquor, at package stores only. Four towns on Martha's Vineyard (Chilmark, Aquinnah, West Tisbury, and Tisbury) are "dry" by choice or tradition (no alcohol can be sold or served), but at most establishments lacking a liquor license, you're welcome to bring your own wine or beer; if in doubt, call ahead. In Edgartown and Oak Bluffs, you will find plenty of bars and liquor stores.

Maps   Maps of the Cape and the Islands are available from the **Cape Cod Chamber of Commerce,** Routes 6 and 132, Hyannis, MA 02601 (© **888/332-2732** or 508/362-3225); the **Martha's Vineyard Chamber of Commerce,** P.O. Box 1698, Beach Rd., Vineyard Haven, MA 02568 (© **508/693-0085;** fax 508/696-0433; www.mvy.com); and the **Nantucket Island Chamber of Commerce,** 48 Main St., Nantucket, MA 02554 (© **508/228-1700**). For maps of Massachusetts, contact the **Massachusetts Office of Travel & Tourism,** 100 Cambridge St., 13th Floor, Boston, MA 02202 (© **617/727-3201;** fax 617/727-6525).

Newspapers & Magazines   The *Cape Cod Times* is published daily and runs regular supplements on arts and antiques, events and entertainment, and restaurants. Nantucket has two weeklies, the established paper, *The Inquirer and Mirror,* called the "Inky" for short, and the upstart, *The Nantucket Independent.* Martha's Vineyard also has two newspapers, *The Martha's Vineyard Times* and the *Vineyard Gazette,* each offering insight into regional issues. The *Gazette* is published twice a week in summer, once a week off season. *The Times,* which is free, is published once a week year-round. Each island has its own glossy magazine. In addition, a great many summer-guide magazines are available, and free booklets with discount coupons are ubiquitous.

Police For police emergencies, call © **911.**

Radio Of the local AM and FM radio stations, two can be counted on for local color (in the "alternative album" mode): WOMR (91.9 FM) out of Provincetown and WMVY (92.7 FM) from Martha's Vineyard. The classical choice is WFCC (107.5 FM), which also features twice-daily birding reports. All three stations come in clearly on the Cape and the Islands. The newest radio station in the area is WCAI/WNAN, a National Public Radio station that is broadcast on 91.1 FM in Nantucket and on 90.1 FM in Martha's Vineyard.

Safety Many people on the Cape and the Islands still don't even lock their houses, let alone their cars. However, the idyll may not last long: Real crime, from petty theft to rape, has made inroads everywhere, even on isolated Nantucket. So, all your city smarts should apply. Do lock up, keep a close hold on purses and cameras (especially in restaurants: don't just sling them over a chair), and don't frequent deserted areas alone, even in broad daylight.

Smoking In the past few years, 14 out of 15 Cape Cod towns and both Nantucket and Martha's Vineyard have gone "smoke-free" to some extent. All towns and islands have passed some variation on laws forbidding smoking in public places as a way to protect nonsmokers from secondhand smoke. This means that in most restaurants and even bars here, you cannot light up. A few bars have installed a ventilation system and/or a sep-arate area where smoking is allowed, but these are few and far between. While some large hotels have some rooms set aside for smokers, the vast majority of lodging establishments on Cape Cod and the Islands are completely nonsmoking.

The island of Nantucket, including all restaurants, is smoke-free. Smoking is allowed only on outdoor patios at the large Nantucket clubs, the Chicken Box, and the Muse.

On Martha's Vineyard, all restaurants are smoke-free except those in Oak Bluffs and Edgartown that have separately enclosed and ventilated bar areas. Since the other four towns on the Vineyard are "dry," meaning no alcohol can be sold, there are no bar areas in those towns and therefore no smoking at all in restaurants. There is also no smoking allowed in the common areas of inns on the Vineyard. There may be some inns where certain rooms are designated for smokers, and visitors wishing to smoke should inquire when they book their rooms.

Taxes In Massachusetts, the state sales tax is 5.7%. This tax applies to restaurant meals (but not food bought in stores) and all goods, with the exception of clothing items priced lower than $175. Nantucket's local hotel tax is 4%, bringing the total of state plus local to 9.7%.

Telephone Local pay-phone calls cost 50¢, and "local" typically means a small radius; a call to the next town over could cost a dollar or more. Beware of "slamming" (the usurpation of phone services by a small, overpriced carrier): Whatever the label on the phone, use the 800 number on your calling card. Smaller inns and B&Bs may not have in-room phones, but they generally provide a courtesy phone on which you can make local calls and charge long-distance calls. If you do have an in-room phone, check whether there's a per-call surcharge—they can quickly add up.

Tides If you have any question about the effect of the tides on beaches you plan to hike (they differ dramatically from town to town and could leave you stranded), check the tide chart in a local newspaper before heading out. Rip tides are particularly hazardous off Nantucket. Swim only where there are lifeguards.

Transit Information Both Islands have highly sophisticated public transportation systems. The phone number for **Nantucket Regional Transit Authority** is ℂ **508/228-7025,** and for **Martha's Vineyard Transit Authority** it's ℂ **508/627-7448.** The respective **chambers of commerce**—for Nantucket (ℂ **508/ 228-1700**) and Martha's Vineyard (ℂ **508/693-0085**)—can also provide maps and schedules for public transportation.

Weather For the latest reports and forecasts, call the WQRC (99.9 FM) **Forecast Phone** (ℂ **508/771-5522**), available around the clock.

3

Settling into Nantucket

In his classic, *Moby Dick*, Herman Melville wrote, "Nantucket! Take out your map and look at it. See what a real corner of the world it occupies; how it stands there, away off shore. . . ." More than 100 years later, this tiny island, 30 miles off the coast of Cape Cod, still counts its isolation as a defining characteristic. At only 3½×14 miles in size, Nantucket is smaller and more insular than Martha's Vineyard. But charm-wise, Nantucket stands alone—20th-century luxury and amenities wrapped in an elegant 19th-century package.

The island has long appealed to wealthy visitors, but in recent years higher-income families have tipped the scales in their favor. Locals shake their heads over the changing demographics. "If they can't get a reservation at a restaurant, they buy the restaurant," one islander said. Nevertheless, this is still a terrific spot for a family vacation or a romantic retreat. After all, window shopping at the island's exclusive boutiques and soaking up the sunshine on the pristine beaches are both free activities!

The Nantucket we see today is the result of a dramatic boom and bust that took place in the 1800s. Once the whaling capital of the world, the Nantucket of Melville's time was a bustling international port whose wealth and sophistication belied its size. But the discovery of crude oil put an end to Nantucket's livelihood, and the island underwent a severe depression until the tourism industry revived it at the turn of the 19th century. Stringent regulations preserved the 19th-century character of Nantucket Town, and today 36% of the island (and counting!) is maintained as conservation land. Nantucket has a year-round population of 14,000 and a summer population of about 50,000, not including short-term vacationers.

Nantucket Island has one town, also called Nantucket, which hugs the yacht-filled harbor. This sophisticated burg features bountiful stores, quaint inns, cobblestone streets, interesting historic sites, and pristine beaches. Strolling ensures you won't miss the scores of shops and galleries housed in wharf shacks on the harbor.

The rest of the island is mainly residential, but for a couple of notable villages. Siasconset (nicknamed 'Sconset), on the east side of the island, is a tranquil community with picturesque, rose-covered cottages and a handful of businesses, including a pricey French restaurant. Sunset aficionados head to Madaket, on the west coast of the island.

The lay of the land on Nantucket is rolling moors, heathlands, cranberry bogs, and miles of exquisite public beaches. The vistas are honeymoon-romantic: an operating windmill, three lighthouses, and a skyline dotted with church steeples. Although July and August are still the most popular times to visit, Nantucket's tourist season has lengthened considerably by virtue of popular festivals such as the **Daffodil Festival** in April and the month-long **Nantucket Noel,** the granddaddy of all holiday celebrations in the region. Off season, visitors enjoy a more tranquil and certainly less expensive vacation. While the "Grey Lady's" infamous fog may swallow you whole, frequent visitors learn to relish this moody, atmospheric touch.

1 Nantucket Orientation

For information on getting to Nantucket, see "Getting There," in chapter 2.

ARRIVING

Taxis wait at the airport and at all ferry ports; many are vans that can accommodate large groups or those traveling with bikes. During the busy summer months, I recommend reserving a taxi in advance to avoid a long wait upon arrival. If you don't have a reservation and are with at least two people, have someone run ahead to secure a cab. Be aware that you may have to share a cab with others; cabbies often do this to save time (though it won't save you any money). If you fail to get a cab at first, don't fret. After cabs drop off passengers, they'll be back for more, or a driver can radio another cab for you.

Rates are flat fees, based on one person riding before 1am, with surcharges for additional passengers, bikes, and dogs. A taxi from the airport to Nantucket Town will cost about $16 plus tip for two people. Reliable cab companies on the island include **A-1 Taxi** (© 508/228-3330), **Aardvark Cab** (© 508/728-9999), **All Point Taxi** (© 508/228-5779), **Bev's Taxi** (© 508/228-7874), **Lisa's Taxi** (© 508/228-2223), and **Val's Cab Service** (© 508/228-9410).

VISITOR INFORMATION

For information, contact the **Nantucket Island Chamber of Commerce** at 48 Main St., Nantucket, MA 02554 (*✆* **508/228-1700;** www.nantucketchamber.org). When you arrive, you should also stop by the **Nantucket Visitor Services & Information Bureau** in Nantucket Town at 25 Federal St. (*✆* **508/228-0925;** www. nantucket-ma.gov/departments/visitor.html), which is open daily June to September, and Monday to Saturday October to May. Information booths are also at Steamboat Wharf and Straight Wharf. Always check the island's newspapers for information on current events. *The Inquirer and Mirror* is Nantucket's main paper, published weekly. *Yesterday's Island* is a free weekly newspaper that covers everything to do on Nantucket for that week, plus features articles, restaurant reviews, and recipes. *The Nantucket Independent* is a relatively new weekly newspaper with a fresh viewpoint.

NEIGHBORHOODS IN BRIEF

Nantucket Town, fronting the harbor and bisected by the wide, cobblestoned Main Street, has everything a visitor needs for a perfect island vacation. There are many inns in the center of town, from large luxury resorts to tiny B&Bs, and a slew of restaurants from exquisite fine-dining establishments to sandwich shops. The streets are lined with a wide range of shops selling everything from luxury goods to essentials. Beachgoers can walk or take the shuttle to Jetties Beach or the small Children's Beach, both geared to families.

If you want some variety, venture to the village of **Siasconset,** nicknamed 'Sconset, on the east side of the island. Its narrow streets and lanes are lined with tiny cottages framed by climbing roses. A couple of fine-dining restaurants are here, as well as a cafe, a sandwich shop, and a general store. The beach features rough surf with a strong riptide. You can ride your bike to 'Sconset on one of two scenic bike paths: the Milestone Road path (about 7 miles long) or the Polpis Road path (about 9 miles long).

Madaket, on the west side of the island, is the place to see the best sunsets. The 6-mile bike path from Nantucket Town to Madaket is one of the most scenic on the island. Madaket has a restaurant and a general store, but this is mainly a residential neighborhood. The beach at Madaket features heavy surf but lifeguards are stationed.

Fun Fact **An Island Steeped in History**

News travels fast on the tiny island of Nantucket, and in 1821, everyone on the island was talking about the shocking story of what happened to the whaleship *Essex*.

The ship had sailed out of Nantucket Harbor in 1819 on a routine whale-hunting voyage with a crew of motley sailors, many of them Nantucket locals. While in the middle of the South Pacific, the ship was rammed and sunk by an 80-ton sperm whale. For 3 months, the 20 men who had escaped the sinking ship tried to make the 3,000-mile trip to South America, but only 8 men survived. Perhaps most shocking of all, the men had to resort to cannibalism when they ran out of their sparse provisions.

The story is known as one of the most harrowing marine disasters of the time. A first-hand account of the tragedy was written by the ship's first mate, just months after being rescued. When news of the *Essex* reached author Herman Melville, he used parts of it in his classic novel, *Moby Dick*.

In 1980, Nantucket historian Edouard Stackpole discovered a notebook written by the cabin boy of the *Essex*, Thomas Nickerson, a Nantucket local who was 14 years old when he sailed aboard the *Essex* and who later ran a Nantucket boarding house. He wrote the account in 1876, at the urging of one of his guests.

GETTING AROUND

You can easily navigate Nantucket on bike, moped, or on foot, as well as by shuttle bus or taxi. If you're staying outside of Nantucket Town, however, or if you simply prefer to explore by car, you may want to bring your own or rent one when you arrive. Adventure-minded travelers may even want to rent a Jeep or other four-wheel-drive vehicle, which you can take out on the sand—a unique Island experience—on certain sections of the coast (a permit is required—see "By Car & Jeep," below). Keep in mind that if you opt to travel by car, in-town traffic can reach gridlock in the peak season, and parking can be a nightmare.

The most recent account of the story is the bestselling *In the Heart of the Sea: The Tragedy of the Whaleship Essex*, by Nathaniel Philbrick. Using the first-hand accounts by Chase and Nickerson, and exhaustive research, Philbrick weaves an adventure story that is part history, part thriller.

For visitors intent on reliving the 19th-century life outlined in the book, Nantucket's cobbled streets and old-time storefronts serve as a perfect backdrop for time-travel. The last of the old boarding houses (which used to be an island staple but have since been replaced by luxury lodging) is **The Nesbitt Inn** (p. 56) at 21 Broad St. (✆ **508/228-0156**). The Nesbitt offers basic accommodations, with shared bathrooms, but you can't beat the hospitality shown by native Nantucket innkeepers Dolly and Nobby Noblit.

From the Nesbitt, walk next door to **The Brotherhood of Thieves** (p. 69), 23 Broad St. (no phone), the classic Nantucket whaling bar. Generations of sailors and their yachting progeny have bellied up to the bar here for a pint of brew and a steaming plate of shoestring french fries.

But no visit to Nantucket would be complete without a visit to the **Nantucket Whaling Museum** (p. 81) at 13 Broad St. (✆ **508/228-1984**), which has an ongoing exhibition of the few surviving materials from the ill-fated *Essex*, including maps, charts, manuscripts, and artifacts.

BY BICYCLE & MOPED   If you are only here for a few days, biking should be your preferred mode of transportation. The island itself is relatively flat, and paved bike paths abound—they'll get you from Nantucket Town to Siasconset, Surfside, and Madaket. With many unpaved back roads to explore, mountain bikes are a wise choice when pedaling around Nantucket.

A word of warning for bikers: One-way street signs apply to you, too! This law is enforced in Nantucket Town, and don't be surprised if a tanned but stern Island policeman requests that you get off your bike and walk. Helmets are required for children under 12. Mopeds are also prevalent, but watch out for sand on the roads. Be aware that local rules and regulations are strictly enforced. Mopeds are not allowed on sidewalks or bike paths. You'll need a driver's license to rent a moped, and state law requires that you wear a helmet.

The following shops rent bikes and scooters; all are within walking distance of the ferries: **Cook's Cycle Shop, Inc.,** 6 S. Beach St. (© **508/228-0800**); **Holiday Cycle,** 4 Chester St. (© **508/228-3644**), rents just bikes; **Nantucket Bike Shops,** at Steamboat Wharf and Straight Wharf (© **508/228-1999**); and **Young's Bicycle Shop,** at Steamboat Wharf (© **508/228-1151**), which also does repairs. Bike rentals average around $18 to $25 for 24 hours.

If you've rented a house, call **Island Bike Co.,** 25 Old South Rd. (© **877/228-4070** or 508/228-4070), which offers all types of bikes for children and adults, as well as Get-A-Long child trailers, Tag-A-Long tandem trailers, and Run-A-Long strollers/joggers. The friendly staff delivers and picks up your rentals. Island Bike Co. can get busy, so you should make reservations before you arrive on the island.

BY CAR & JEEP I recommend a car if you'll be here for more than a week, or if you're staying outside Nantucket Town (or if you simply prefer to drive). However, with no in-town parking lots, parking, although free, is limited to Nantucket's handful of narrow streets, which can be a problem in the busy summer months. Also, gas is much more expensive on Nantucket than it is on the mainland.

Four-wheel-drives are your best bet, as many beaches and nature areas are off sandy paths; be sure to reserve at least a month in advance if you're coming in summer. If you plan on doing any four-wheeling in the sand, you need to get an **Over-Sand Permit** ($100 for nonresident vehicles; $100 for rental vehicles) from the **Nantucket Police Department** (20 South Water St.; © **508/228-1212**). To drive in the Coskata-Coatue nature area, you need a separate permit from the **Trustees of Reservations,** at the gatehouse (© **508/228-0006**), which costs about $100 for a season pass, or a $20 gate fee for rental cars.

The following on-island rental agencies offer cars, Jeeps, and other four-wheel-drive vehicles: **Affordable Rentals of Nantucket,** 6 S. Beach Rd. (© 508/228-3501); **Budget,** at the airport (© 800/527-0700 or 508/228-5666); **Don Allen Auto Service,** 24 Polpis Rd. (© 800/258-4970 or 508/228-0134), which specializes in Ford Explorers; **Hertz,** at the airport (© 800/654-3131 or 508/228-9421); **Nantucket Windmill Auto Rental,** at the airport (© 800/228-1227 or 508/228-1227); **Thrifty Car Rental,** at the airport (© 508/325-4616); and **Young's 4 × 4 & Car Rental,**

Steamboat Wharf (© 508/228-1151). A standard car costs about $90 per day in season; a four-wheel-drive rental is about $180 per day (including an Over-Sand Permit).

BY SHUTTLE BUS From June to September, inexpensive shuttle buses, with bike racks and accessibility for those with disabilities, loop through Nantucket Town and to a few outlying spots; for routes and stops, contact the **Nantucket Regional Transit Authority** (© **508/228-7025**) or pick up a map and schedule at the Visitor Services & Information Bureau on Federal Street or the Chamber Office on Main Street (see "Visitor Information," above). The shuttle permits you to bring your clean, dry dog along, too. The cost is 50¢ to $1 for each ride, and exact change is required. You can purchase a 3-day pass for $10 at the Visitor Bureau.

Shuttle routes and fares are pretty simple. Downtown shuttle stops are located on the corner of Salem and Washington streets (for South and Miacomet loops), Broad Street in front of the Foulger Museum (for Madaket loop and Beach Express), and at the corner of Washington and Main streets (for 'Sconset loops).

- **South Loop** services Surfside Beach, Hooper Farm Road, and Pleasant Street area; every 15 minutes from 7am to 11:30pm; 50¢.
- **Miacomet Loop** services Fairgrounds Road, Bartlett Road, and Hummock Pond area; every 30 minutes from 7am to 11:30pm; 50¢.
- **Madaket Route** services Madaket (from Broad St. downtown) via Cliff Road and New Lane; every 30 minutes from 7:30am to 11:30pm; $1 each way.
- **'Sconset Route 1** services 'Sconset via Polpis Road; every 30 minutes from 8:20am to 11pm; $1 each way.
- **'Sconset Route 2** services 'Sconset via Old South Road/ Nobadeer Farm Road and Milestone Road; every 30 minutes from 7:40am to 10:30pm; $1 each way. This route makes a stop about ⅓ mile from the airport. If you don't have a lot of bags, this is the cheapest way to go.
- **Beach Express** services Surfside and Jetties Beach. Downtown stop on Broad Street. $1 each way to Surfside; 50¢ each way to Jetties; every 30 minutes for Jetties Beach and every hour for Surfside Beach from 10:15am to 5:45pm.

BY TAXI See the "Arriving" section earlier in this chapter for local taxi companies and fares.

FAST FACTS: Nantucket

Airport See "Getting There," in chapter 2.

Area Code The telephone area code for Nantucket is **508**. You must always dial 1 and this area code first, even if you are making a call to another Nantucket number.

Banks **Automated teller machines (ATMs)** are available in several locations in Nantucket. **Nantucket Bank** (© **800/533-9313** or 508/228-0580) has three locations: 2 Orange St., 104 Pleasant St., 1 Amelia Dr., all open 24 hours, plus an ATM at the airport that's open during airport hours. **Pacific National Bank** (© **508/228-1917**) has seven locations: Pacific National Bank lobby at the top of Main Street (open during bank hours only), the branch at 15 Sparks Ave. (24-hr. drive-up ATM), the Stop & Shop on Pleasant Street (open 24 hr. seasonally), the Pacific Club on lower Main Street (open 24 hr.), the Steamship Authority at Steamboat Wharf (open during business hours), Grand Union Supermarket (next to the wharves, open store hours), and at the airport (open during airport hours).

Emergencies Phone © **911** for fire, police, emergency, or ambulance; be prepared to give your number, address, name, and a quick report. The following are non-emergency numbers: **police department** (© 508/228-1212); **fire department** (© 508/228-2324); and **Coast Guard** (© 508/228-0388). If you get into desperate straits—if, for example, your money is stolen and you need assistance arranging to get home—contact the **Travelers Aid** office in Boston (© 617/542-7286).

Hospital In case of a medical emergency, **Nantucket Cottage Hospital,** 57 Prospect St. (© 508/228-1200), is open 24 hours.

Liquor Laws The legal drinking age in Massachusetts is 21. Most bars are allowed to stay open until 1am every day, with "last call" at 12:30am. Beer, wine, and liquor are sold at package stores only.

Newspaper & Magazines Nantucket's newspaper is *The Inquirer and Mirror,* fondly known as the "Inky," which has been published since 1821. A relatively new weekly newspaper with a fresh viewpoint is *The Nantucket Independent. Yesterday's Island* is a free weekly newspaper available all over the island. *Nantucket Magazine* is a glossy published by the Inky staff. In addition, several summer-guide magazines are available, as well as free booklets. The two major ones on

Nantucket are the *Nantucket Guide and Travel Planner* published by Anderson Publishing, and the *Official Guide to Nantucket,* published by the Nantucket Chamber of Commerce. Both are thick, glossy guides with comprehensive listings and lots of Island information.

Public Restrooms In Nantucket Town, public restrooms are located at the Visitor Services & Information Bureau, 25 Federal St., and on Straight Wharf where the Hy-Line boats dock. You'll also be able to find public restrooms at the Nantucket Memorial Airport and at the following beaches: Children's, Jetties, Dionis, and Surfside.

Smoking The island, including all restaurants, is smoke-free. Smoking is allowed only on outdoor patios at two large Nantucket clubs: The Chicken Box and The Muse.

Time Zone Though it feels a world apart, Nantucket is in the Eastern Time zone and goes on daylight saving time in the summer.

2 Where to Stay

Most visitors to Nantucket wish to stay in the center of town. You have no need for a car here; in fact, parking can be a real problem in season. Everything is within walking distance, including beaches, restaurants, and the finest shopping in the region. Unless otherwise stated, hotels are open year-round.

VERY EXPENSIVE

Cliffside Beach Club ✯✯✯ *(Finds* Right on the beach and within walking distance (about a mile) of town, this is the premier lodging on the island. It may not be as fancy as some, but there's a sublime beachy-ness to the whole setup: simply decorated rooms; cheerful, youthful staff; a sea of antique wicker in the clubhouse; and of course, blue, yellow and green umbrellas lined up on the beach. All rooms have such luxuries as French milled soaps, thick towels, and exceptional linens. Turndown service is provided. Guests receive an umbrella, chairs, and beach towels. A very good continental breakfast is served in the large clubhouse room, its beamed ceilings draped with colorful quilts. Lucky guests on the Fourth of July get a front-row seat for the fireworks staged at Jetties Beach nearby.

46 Jefferson Ave. (about 1 mile from town center), Nantucket, MA 02554. © 800/932-9645 or 508/228-0618. Fax 508/325-4735. www.cliffsidebeach.com.

Accommodations & Dining Outside of Town

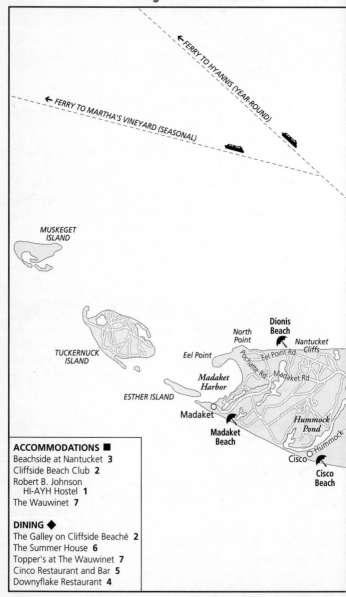

FERRY TO HYANNIS (YEAR-ROUND)

FERRY TO MARTHA'S VINEYARD (SEASONAL)

MUSKEGET ISLAND

TUCKERNUCK ISLAND

ESTHER ISLAND

Eel Point

Madaket Harbor

Madaket

Madaket Beach

North Point

Dionis Beach

Nantucket Cliffs

Pochattie Rd.

Eel Point Rd.

Madaket Rd.

Hummock Pond

Cisco

Cisco Beach

ACCOMMODATIONS ■
Beachside at Nantucket **3**
Cliffside Beach Club **2**
Robert B. Johnson
  HI-AYH Hostel **1**
The Wauwinet **7**

DINING ◆
The Galley on Cliffside Beaché **2**
The Summer House **6**
Topper's at The Wauwinet **7**
Cinco Restaurant and Bar **5**
Downyflake Restaurant **4**

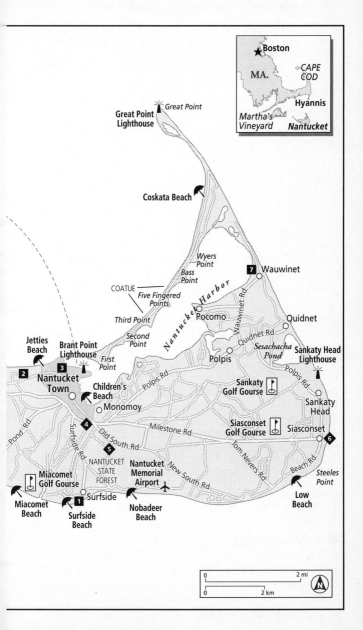

25 units, 1 cottage. Summer $395–$625 double; $755–$1,535 suite; $785 3-bedroom apt; $955 cottage. Rates include continental breakfast. AE. Closed mid-Oct to late May. **Amenities:** Restaurant (elegant French bistro); exercise facility (Cybex equipment and on-staff trainer); indoor hydrotherapy spa; steam saunas; concierge; climate-controlled massage room; babysitting. *In room:* A/C, TV/VCR, fridge, coffeemaker, hair dryer.

The Wauwinet 🎖🎖🎖 This ultra-deluxe beachfront retreat, the most luxurious lodging choice on the island, is Nantucket's only Relais & Châteaux property. The inn is at the tip of a wildlife sanctuary, nestled between the Atlantic Ocean and Nantucket Bay. With 25 rooms in the main building (which started out as a restaurant in 1850), and 10 more in 5 modest-looking shingled cottages, the complex holds about 80 decorously spoiled guests, outnumbered by 100 staffers. Each of the lovely rooms—all with a cozy nook from which to gaze out across the water—has a unique decorating scheme, with pine armoires, plenty of wicker, exquisite Audubon prints, handsome fabrics, and a lovely array of antique accessories. Extras include Egyptian cotton bathrobes and bottled water. Additional perks include a personalized set of engraved note cards. (Don't tell them I told you; it's supposed to be a surprise.) All rooms have CD players and VCRs, and if you order up a video from the extensive library (400 videos), it is delivered on a tray by a steward with a couple of boxes of complimentary hot popcorn. The staff goes to great lengths to please, ferrying you into town, for instance, in a 1946 "Woody" (12 trips daily), or dispatching you on a 21-foot launch across the bay to your own private strip of beach in season. There are also free guided nature tours on weekdays in season.

120 Wauwinet Rd. (P.O. Box 2580, about 8 miles east of Nantucket center), Nantucket, MA 02554. (℃) **800/426-8718** or 508/228-0145. Fax 508/325-0657. www.wauwinet.com. 30 units (all with tub/shower), 5 cottages. Summer $700 double; $800–$1,025 cottage. Rates include full breakfast and afternoon wine and cheese. AE, DC, MC, V. Closed late Oct to mid-May. Families with children ages 12–18 in cottages only; no children under 12. **Amenities:** Fine-dining restaurant; 2 clay tennis courts w/pro shop and teaching pro; croquet lawn; rowboats, sailboats, sea kayaks, and mountain bikes to borrow; concierge; room service (8am–9pm). *In room:* A/C, TV/VCR, CD player, hair dryer, iron.

White Elephant 🎖🎖🎖 This luxury property on the harbor is the ultimate in-town lodging and has been newly renovated by the owners of The Wauwinet (see above). Rooms (distributed among one building and 12 cottages) are big and airy (the most spacious on Nantucket), with country-chic decor and most with harbor views. A small private beach on the harbor is reserved for hotel guests. All

Accommodations in Town

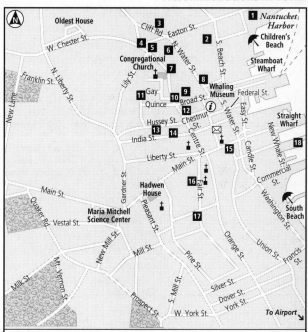

Anchor Inn **7**

Centerboard **4**

Cliff Lodge **3**

The Cottages/Woof Cottages **18**

Harbor House Village **2**

Jared Coffin House **10**

Martin House Inn **5**

Nantucket Whaler Guesthouse **8**

The Nesbitt Inn **9**

The Pineapple Inn **13**

Sherburne Inn **11**

The Ship's Inn **16**

Summer House at India Street **14**

Union Street Inn **15**

The Veranda House **6**

VNH (Vanessa Noel Hotel) **12**

White Elephant **1**

The Woodbox Inn **17**

Beach 🏖

Ferry ----

Information ⓘ

Post Office ✉

rooms have DVD players, and about half have working fireplaces. The two-bedroom cottage features a fireplace, kitchenette, and dining area. Guests can borrow from an extensive collection of new and old movies. The hotel has pleasant commons rooms, including a cozy library with a large fireplace, and it welcomes "sail-in" guests.

50 Easton St. (P.O. Box 1139), Nantucket, MA 02554. © **800/475-2637** or 508/228-2500. Fax 508/638-2327. www.whiteelephanthotel.com. 54 units, 12 cottages (64 with tub/shower, 2 shower only). Summer $450–$900 double; $470–$540 1-bedroom cottage; $1,250–$1,400 2-bedroom cottage; $800–$950 3-bedroom cottage. Rates include full breakfast. AE, DC, DISC, MC, V. Closed Oct–Mar. **Amenities:** Restaurant (lobster and steak house, lunch and dinner daily); outdoor heated pool; fitness center; concierge; full room service; laundry and dry-cleaning service; business lounge; newspapers. *In room:* A/C, TV/VCR, DVD player, dataport, fridge, hair dryer, iron, safe.

EXPENSIVE

Beachside at Nantucket 🏖 No ordinary motel, the Beachside's 90 air-conditioned bedrooms and lobby have been lavished with Provençal prints and handsome rattan and wicker furniture; the patios and decks overlooking the central courtyard with its heated pool have been prettified with French doors and latticework. If you prefer the laissez-faire lifestyle of a motel to the sometimes-constricting rituals of a B&B, this may be an ideal base.

30 N. Beach St. (about ¾ mile west of the town center), Nantucket, MA 02554. © **800/322-4433** or 508/228-2241. Fax 508/228-8901. www.thebeachside.com. 90 units (all with tub/shower). Summer $280–$335 double; $650–$675 suite. Rates include continental breakfast. AE, DC, DISC, MC, V. Closed early Dec to late Apr. **Amenities:** Heated outdoor pool. *In room:* A/C, TV, fridge, hair dryer.

Centerboard 🏖🏖 Nantucket actually has very little in Victorian housing: The island was just too poor (and under-populated) to build much in those days. The few to be found tend to be dolled up like this updated 1886 home, replete with parquet floors, Oriental rugs, lavish fabrics, and lace-trimmed linens. The overall look is light, airy, and less cluttered than the original Victorian look. Innkeeper Debbie Wasil has large-resort experience and is most hospitable. Of the inn's seven bedrooms—each with plush feather mattresses—the first-floor suite is the most romantic, with a green-marble Jacuzzi and a private living room with fireplace. Other rooms and bathrooms are small, but all have bathrobes and minifridges.

8 Chester St. (in the center of town), Nantucket, MA 02554. © **508/228-9696**. Fax 508/325-4798. www.centerboardguesthouse.com. 7 units. Summer $255 double; $425 suite. Rates include continental breakfast. AE, MC, V. Closed Nov–Apr. *In room:* A/C, TV, fridge, hair dryer, iron.

The Cottages/Woof Cottages ★★ *(Finds)* Formerly known as the Wharf Cottages, these small apartments have the best location on the island, stacked up on a wharf that juts out into Nantucket Harbor. If you are looking for a place on Nantucket where you can bring your pooch, these one- and two-bedroom cottages are the perfect choice. All cottages have been newly renovated—floors polished, walls painted—and each has an eat-in kitchen and cozy living room area. Dogs get a welcome basket of treats and a Nantucket bandana.

One Old South Wharf (P.O. Box 1139, in the center of town), Nantucket, MA 02554. ℂ 866/838-9253 or 508/325-1499. Fax 508/325-1173. www.harborviewcottages.com. 33 units. Summer $280–$630 studio and 1-bedroom; $430–$840 2-bedroom; $570–$940 3-bedroom. AE, MC, V. Closed mid-Oct to mid-May. *In room:* TV, VCR/CD, hair dryer.

Harbor House Village ★★ This resort has recently undergone a multi-million dollar freshening-up. The main building, the 35-room historic Harbor House, was built in the 1870s, but the property is now one of Nantucket's most full-service lodging options. It is located just a short walk from the center of Nantucket Town, as well as Children's Beach, Jetties Beach, and Brant Point Lighthouse. The rooms are decorated with pine and wicker furniture and feature new mattresses and bedding. Some are spacious and have balconies. The Hearth Bar offers live entertainment some nights in season and doubles as a sports bar in the fall. The resort's restaurant, Harbor Wok, which is open in July and August, is the island's only gourmet Chinese food restaurant. Lunch is available poolside.

South Beach St., Nantucket, MA 02554. ℂ 866/325-9300 or 508/228-1500. Fax 508/228-7639. www.harborhousevillage.com. 104 units. Summer $360–$410 double. AE, DC, DISC, MC, V. Closed early Dec to mid-Apr. **Amenities:** Restaurant (Chinese, summer only); breakfast cafe; bar/lounge; outdoor heated pool (in season); free children's program in summer; concierge; babysitting; laundry service; dry cleaning; free shuttle from Steamship Authority ferry. *In room:* A/C, TV, dataport, hair dryer, iron. VCR or fridge available on request.

Jared Coffin House ★★ *(Kids)* This classic hotel gets two stars for its central location and status on Nantucket. The hotel is now owned by the same organization that owns the deluxe Wauwinet, the White Elephant, and Harbor House Village. Major renovations are expected in 2005. The grand brick manse was built in 1845 to the specs of the social-climbing Mrs. Coffin, who abandoned Nantucket for the big city after 2 years and left the house to boarders. Lovingly renovated to its original splendor by the Nantucket Historical Trust, it is the social center of town, as well as a mecca for visitors. Accommodations range from well-priced singles (rare in these parts) to spacious doubles. Rooms in the neighboring annex houses are equally grand. Most have air-conditioning. The concierge, Mrs. K., can't do enough to help, and refuses tips! The central location does have a drawback: The front rooms can be quite noisy. Locals appreciate the best breakfast in town (not included with your room rate, and 20-min. waits are not unusual. It's a good idea to call down and put your name on the list before heading to breakfast.)

29 Broad St. (at Centre St.), Nantucket, MA 02554. © **800/248-2405** or 508/228-2400. Fax 508/228-8549. www.jaredcoffinhouse.com. 60 units (52 with tub/shower, 8 shower only). Summer $150–$320 double. AE, DC, DISC, MC, V. Open year-round. **Amenities:** 2 restaurants (family and tavern); concierge. *In room:* TV, dataport, fridge, coffeemaker, iron.

Nantucket Whaler Guesthouse ☆☆   This lodging option, an 1850s Greek Revival sea captain's house, is unique in that all of the rooms are suites with their own entrance and kitchen facilities. Compared to other B&Bs on the island, this one has a particularly private feel, almost like having your own apartment. Many rooms have decks or patios. The building has been recently restored and all rooms are comfortably outfitted with cottage-y furnishings, including overstuffed couches and stacks of games and books. Guests who prefer not to whip up their own breakfast can order up a continental breakfast basket that ranges in cost depending on your order.

8 North Water St. (in the center of town), Nantucket, MA 02554. © **800/462-6882** or 508/228-6597. Fax 508/228-6291. www.nantucketwhaler.com. 12 units. Summer $325–$450 double; $575–$650 2-bedroom suite. AE, DC, MC, V. Closed mid-Dec to mid-Mar. No children under 12. *In room:* A/C, TV/VCR, CD player, dataport, hair dryer, iron.

The Pineapple Inn ☆☆   This beautifully renovated historic inn is one of the premier places to stay on the island. The graceful Quaker entrance of this 1838 home bespeaks the hospitality. The inn is owned by the people who own The Summer House in 'Sconset, as well as several other inns on Nantucket, and guests have use of the 'Sconset property pool, which overlooks the Atlantic Ocean (a complimentary jitney takes guests to 'Sconset). Rooms are spacious and decorated in a Colonial style with fine reproductions and antiques, including handmade Oriental rugs, marble bathrooms, and many four-poster canopy beds. Five large king bedrooms have beds of tiger maple. Smaller, less expensive rooms are on the third floor. All rooms are equipped with goose-down comforters, voice mail, and cable TV. The extra-deluxe continental breakfast has fresh baked goods, espresso, cappuccino, and freshly squeezed orange juice among the offerings. The garden patio with climbing roses is a fine place to enjoy an afternoon cocktail and contemplate dinner plans.

10 Hussey St. (in the center of town), Nantucket, MA 02554. © 508/228-9992. Fax 508/325-6051. www.pineappleinn.com. 12 units (8 with tub/shower, 4 shower only). Summer $195–$325 double. Rates include continental breakfast. AE, MC, V. Closed early Dec to mid-Apr. No children under 8. *In room:* A/C, TV, dataport, hair dryer, iron.

Sherburne Inn ⭐ You'd never guess from the gracious foyer of this 1835 house that it was once the headquarters of the Atlantic Silk Company, a short-lived 19th-century enterprise. Now this elegant and comfortable inn offers quiet lodging in the heart of Nantucket village. Rooms vary in size, with smaller rooms a good value. Ask for one on the sunny side of the inn. Two parlors with fireplaces offer plenty of space for relaxing. Innkeepers Dale Hamilton and Susan Gasparich bought the inn in 1994. Susan's recipes for baked goods such as butterscotch coffeecake have been featured in *Gourmet* magazine. Guests have complimentary access to wireless Internet service.

10 Gay St. (in the center of town), Nantucket, MA 02554. © 888/577-4425 or 508/228-4425. Fax 508/228-8114. www.sherburneinn.com. 8 units (2 with tub/shower, 6 shower only). Summer $185–$310 double. Rates include continental breakfast. AE, DISC, MC, V. Open year-round. No children under 6. *In room:* A/C, TV/VCR, DVD/CD, hair dryer.

Summer House at India Street ⭐ The Summer House management now owns four properties: the very expensive cottages overlooking the beach in Siasconset, an inn on Fair Street, the Pineapple Inn on Hussey Street, and this property on India Street. This India Street property is a handsome historic house, fully renovated with all new furnishings and top-notch amenities. All rooms are equipped with robes and deluxe toiletries. Guests have access to complimentary jitney service to The Summer House beachfront property in 'Sconset and use of the pool there.

31 India St. (in the center of town), Nantucket, MA 02554. © 508/257-4577. Fax 508/257-4590. www.thesummerhouse.com. 10 units. Summer $200–$350 double. Rates include continental breakfast. AE, MC, V. Closed Jan–Apr. *In room:* A/C, TV, hair dryer.

Union Street Inn ⭐⭐⭐ *(Finds* This wins my vote as the best B&B on Nantucket. Sophisticated innkeepers Deborah and Ken Withrow have a terrific location for their historic 1770s property, just steps from Main Street yet in a quiet, residential section. Ken's experience in big hotels shows in the inn's amenities and full concierge service. The Withrows have completely restored the inn, highlighting its period charms and updating all amenities. Many rooms have canopied or four-poster beds; half have working wood-burning fireplaces. All rooms are decorated with antique furniture and fixtures, some with toile wallpaper and Oriental rugs. The comfortable beds are made up with Egyptian cotton linens. Bathrooms are equipped with pique-woven bathrobes and large terry bath towels. Unlike many Nantucket inns that are forbidden by zoning laws to serve a full breakfast, this inn's location allows a superb complete breakfast on the garden patio. If you are hanging around in the afternoon, you can usually find home-baked cookies or other goodies to sample as well.

7 Union St. (in the center of town), Nantucket, MA 02554. © **800/225-5116** or 508/228-9222. Fax 508/325-0848. www.unioninn.com. 12 units (1 with tub/shower, 11 shower only). Summer $260–$395 double; $495 suite. Rates include full breakfast. AE, MC, V. Closed Jan–Mar. *In room:* A/C, TV, CD player, hair dryer, no phone.

VNH (Vanessa Noel Hotel) ⭑ This is Nantucket's trendiest inn; think Ian Schraeger–style wrapped in a historic package. Vanessa Noel, a shoe designer whose shoe store is on the first floor, has decorated the eight rooms in this historic building with boutique hotel features such as Philippe Starck fixtures, queen-size feather beds with custom Frette linens, Bulgari toiletries, 15-inch flatscreen plasma televisions, and minibars stocked with the hotel's bottled water. Most of the rooms are tiny, though two, including a fun attic space, are comfortably spacious. Bathrooms are small but luxurious. This lodging house has no lobby, just the upstairs rooms. The Vanno Bar, a caviar and champagne bar on the first floor, has novelties such as leopard-print calfskin banquettes, swings, and food imported from Caviarteria, the New York City caviar emporium.

5 Chestnut St. (in the center of town), Nantucket, MA 02554. © **508/228-5300.** Fax 508/228-8995. www.vanessanoel.com/vnh.htm. 8 units. Summer $340–$480 double. AE, DISC, MC, V. Open year-round. **Amenities:** Vanno Bar, a hip gathering spot. *In room:* A/C, TV, minibar, hair dryer, iron upon request, robes and slippers.

MODERATE
Anchor Inn ⭑ *Value* Innkeepers Ann and Charles Balas have two historic gems. The main inn house is an 1806 sea captain's home located next to the Old North Church; three doors down is another captain's house from the same period. Authentic details can be found throughout the houses in the antique hardware and paneling, wide-board floors, and period furnishings. As in many historic inns, some of the rooms in the main inn are quite small. The rooms in the second property are, for the most part, larger. All rooms are equipped with air-conditioning (in season) and voice mail. Guests

enjoy continental breakfast with home-baked muffins at individual tables on the enclosed porch of the main house.

66 Centre St. (P.O. Box 387, in the center of town), Nantucket, MA 02554. ℭ 508/228-0072. www.anchor-inn.net. 16 units (2 with tub/shower, 1 tub only, 13 shower only). Summer $185–$235 double; $265 suite. Rates include continental breakfast. AE, MC, V. Closed Jan–Feb. *In room:* A/C, TV, hair dryer.

Cliff Lodge ★★ *(Finds* This property, managed by the same people who own the Martin House (see below) is a freshened-up, charming 1771 whaling captain's house with its own countrified style. It's located about a block from the center of town and has sunny, cheerful interiors featuring colorful quilts and splatter-painted floors. Rooms range from a first-floor beauty with king-size bed, paneled walls, and fireplace, to the tiny third-floor rooms tucked into the eaves. All are spotlessly clean and blessed with quality beds and linens. The spacious apartment in the rear of the house is a sunny delight. The continental breakfast, serving home-baked breads and muffins on the garden patio, is congenial. Chat with Debby for a wealth of island info and the latest goings-on, then climb up to the widow's walk for a bird's-eye view of the town and harbor.

9 Cliff Rd. (a few blocks from the center of town), Nantucket, MA 02554. ℭ 508/228-9480. Fax 508/228-6308. www.clifflodgenantucket.com. 11 units, 1 apt. Summer $140 single; $195–$260 double; $450 apt. Rates include continental breakfast. MC, V. Open year-round. No children under 12. *In room:* A/C, TV.

Martin House Inn ★★ *(Value* This is one of the lower-priced B&Bs in town, but also one of the most stylish, with a formal parlor, dining rooms, and a spacious side porch. This historic 1803 mariner's home is kept shipshape. The garret single rooms with a shared bathroom are a bargain. Higher-priced rooms have four-posters and working fireplaces. The suite has a flatscreen TV and a CD/DVD player. The extensive continental breakfast, served at the long dining room table, includes home-baked breads, muffins, and fresh fruits.

61 Centre St. (between Broad and Chester sts., a couple blocks from town center), Nantucket, MA 02554. ℭ 508/228-0678. Fax 508/325-4798. www.martinhouseinn.net. 13 units, 4 with shared bathroom (4 with tub/shower, 5 shower only). Summer $110 single; $180–$300 double; $350 suite. Rates include continental breakfast. AE, MC, V. Open year-round. *In room:* A/C, no phone.

The Ship's Inn ★★ *(Value* This pretty, historic inn is on a quiet side street, just 3 blocks removed from Nantucket's center. Rooms are comfortable, spacious, charming, and offer a good variety of bedding situations such as single rooms and twin beds. The restaurant downstairs holds its own (see "Where to Dine," below).

13 Fair St. (a few blocks from town center), Nantucket, MA 02554. ⓒ **888/872-4052** or 508/228-0040. Fax 508/228-6524. 12 units, 2 with shared bathroom. Summer $110 single with shared bathroom; $225 double. Rates include continental breakfast. AE, DISC, MC, V. **Closed late Oct to mid-May. Amenities:** Fine-dining restaurant located in the basement. *In room:* A/C, TV, fridge, hair dryer, iron.

The Veranda House 🏃🏃 *(Finds)* One of the most recent of the Island's B&Bs to receive a major remodeling job, this stand-out classic guesthouse, formerly known as the Overlook Hotel, has been in the same family for generations. The inn is located in a quiet neighborhood, a short walk from the center of town. It is perched on a hill, so rooms on the third floor have distant harbor views. Wraparound porches surround the inn and serve as a comfortable communal area. Inn rooms are on the small side, but are smartly decorated with antique photos. It's a minimalist look, but it works. Some of the more deluxe rooms have private balconies. All rooms have extras such as robes, Frette linens, and goose-down comforters. On the top floor, seven rooms share bathrooms. Breakfast, which features hot delicacies such as quiches and frittatas, is served with great hospitality on the ample front porch. The entire property is covered by wireless Internet service.

3 Step Lane (a few blocks from town center), Nantucket, MA 02554. ⓒ **508/ 228-0695.** Fax 508/374-0406. www.theverandahouse.com. 20 units, 7 with shared bathroom. Summer $135–$165 double with shared bathroom; $175–$225 double; $250–$350 2-bedroom suite. Rates include continental breakfast. AE, MC, V. Closed mid-Oct to late May. *In room:* Hair dryer.

The Woodbox Inn 🏃 Built in 1709, this atmospheric place is Nantucket's oldest inn. Located in a residential section of the historic district, the inn is a short walk to Main Street. The well-regarded restaurant on-site serves breakfast and dinner and is famous for popovers. The rooms, decorated with canopy beds and period antiques and reproductions, range from cozy to spacious. Some rooms have refrigerators and phones. There are also one- and two-room suites with working fireplaces.

29 Fair St., Nantucket, MA 02554. ⓒ **508/228-0587.** Fax 508/228-7527. www. woodboxinn.com. 9 units. Summer $185–$210 double; $210 1-room suite; $310 2-room suite. (Unusual in the area, a 10% "service" fee is added to your bill here, in addition to the 9.7% room tax.) MC, V. Closed early Jan to Mar. **Amenities:** Fine-dining restaurant serving breakfast and dinner. *In room:* TV, hair dryer.

INEXPENSIVE

The Nesbitt Inn *(Value)* This Victorian-style inn located in the center of town has been run by the same family for 95 years. It's quite old-fashioned and a bargain for Nantucket. All rooms have sinks and share bathrooms, which are in the hall. There's a friendly, family atmosphere to the inn, and beloved innkeepers Dolly and Nobby Noblit are salt-of-the-earth Nantucketers who will cheerfully fill you in on Island lore.

21 Broad St. (P.O. Box 1019), Nantucket, MA 02554. ✆ **508/228-0156** or 508/228-2446. 13 units (all with shared bathroom), 2 apts. Summer $75 single; $95–$125 double; $1,200 weekly apts. Rates include continental breakfast. MC, V. Open year-round. *In room:* No phone.

Robert B. Johnson HI-AYH Hostel   This youth hostel has an almost perfect location. Set beside Surfside Beach, the former "Star of the Sea" is an authentic 1873 lifesaving station, Nantucket's first. Where seven Surfmen once stood ready to save shipwrecked sailors, 49 backpackers now enjoy gender-segregated bunk rooms; the women's quarters, upstairs, still contain a climb-up lookout post. The usual Hostel lockout (10am–5pm) and curfew (11pm) rules prevail.

31 Western Ave. (on Surfside Beach, about 3 miles south of Nantucket Town), Surfside, MA 02554. ✆ **508/228-0433**. Fax 508/228-5672. www.hiusa.org. 49 beds. $19 for members, $24 for non-members. MC, V. Closed mid-Oct to mid-Apr.

3 Where to Dine

Nantucket is filled with outrageously priced restaurants where star chefs create dazzling meals served in high style. Obviously, you don't need this kind of treatment every night, but you'll probably want to try at least one deluxe place here. Many of the best restaurants serve terrific lunches at half the price of their dinner menus. Thankfully, a number of cafes scattered around town serve reasonably priced lunches and dinners. Nantucket also has two old-fashioned drugstore soda fountains, **Nantucket Pharmacy** and **Congdon's Pharmacy,** right next to each other on upper Main Street serving breakfast and lunch—definitely the best dining deal on the Island. Congdon's has the best sandwiches, with favorites such as the Yard Sale, which is a smoked turkey panini. If you dine in town, you may enjoy an evening stroll afterwards; many stores stay open late.

VERY EXPENSIVE

Brant Point Grill 🏷🏷 NEW AMERICAN   Recent renovations to the entire White Elephant complex on the harbor have converted this pretty dining room into a lobster, steak, and chops house. Many of the signature dishes, such as the cedar planked Atlantic salmon and rotisserie of prime rib, are prepared on the Fire Cone grill, a 21st-century interpretation of a Native American cooking technique that cooks foods by radiant heat and imparts a smoky mesquite flavor. If you can't sit on the terrace, try to snag a seat near one of the windows where you can watch the twilight fade over the harbor. The candlelight and white, airy dining room make for a perfectly romantic setting. Dinner at this establishment is an expensive proposition. The raw bar is open July through Labor Day from 4 to 7pm for a light snack.

At the White Elephant Hotel (Easton and Willard sts.). ℂ **508/325-1320.** Reservations strongly recommended. Jacket requested for gentlemen. Main courses $26–$39. AE, DISC, MC, V. Daily noon–2:30pm and 6–9:30pm. (An all-day light menu is served 2:30–11pm.) Closed early Dec to mid-Apr.

The Club Car 🍴🍴🍴 CONTINENTAL   One of the top restaurants on Nantucket for decades, this posh venue is popular with locals, many of whom particularly enjoy beef-Wellington night on autumn Sundays. Executive chef Michael Shannon was influenced by a friend and colleague, the late Julia Child, and the menu shows it with its classic French influences. Interesting offerings include a first course of Japanese octopus in the style of Bangkok (with mixed hot peppers, tiparos fish sauce, mint, cilantro, lime, and tomato concassee) and an entree of roast rack of lamb Club Car (with fresh herbs, honey-mustard glaze, and minted Madeira sauce). Some nights, seven-course tasting menus are available for $65 per person. The lounge area is within an antique first-class car from the old Nantucket railroad; you'll want to have a drink while cuddled in the red leather banquettes before or after dinner.

1 Main St. ℂ **508/228-1101.** Reservations recommended. Main courses $24–$45. AE, MC, V. July–Aug daily 11am–3pm and 6–10pm; call for off-season hours. Closed late Oct to Apr.

The Galley on Cliffside Beach 🍴🍴🍴 NEW AMERICAN Offering the best setting of any restaurant on the island, The Galley is set on a private beach, close to Jetties Beach, about a mile from town on the property of the beautiful Cliffside Beach Club,. The restaurant offers a particularly chic yet beachy fine-dining experience, as fragrant ocean breezes perfume the air and guests relax on white wicker chairs. Given the setting, it's no surprise that the Galley specializes in seafood, caught locally by island fishermen. Produce comes from the restaurant's own organic garden. The menu changes often, but noteworthy menu choices include the restaurant's signature New England clam chowder with smoked bacon, or the shrimp tempera served with Asian slaw. Or you may see a luscious lobster risotto, native halibut with forest mushroom strudel,

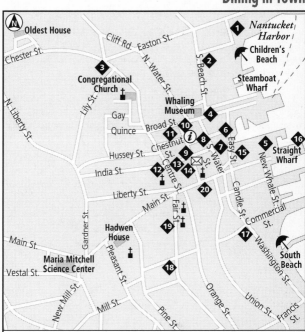

21 Federal **9**

American Seasons **3**

Arno's **20**

The Atlantic Cafe **7**

Black Eyed Susan's **12**

Bluefin **2**

Boarding House **14**

Brant Point Grill **1**

The Brotherhood of Thieves **11**

Cap'n Tobey's Chowder House **5**

Centre Street Bistro **12**

Cioppino's **10**

Club Car **15**

Company of the Cauldron **13**

DeMarco **13**

The Even Keel Café **20**

Fog Island Cafe **7**

Le Languedoc Cafe **11**

Nantucket Lobster Trap **17**

Òran Mór **4**

The Pearl **14**

Queequeg's **6**

Ropewalk **16**

Schooner's at Steamboat Wharf **6**

The Ship's Inn Restaurant **19**

Straight Wharf **5**

Sushi by Yoshi **8**

The Woodbox Inn Restaurant **18**

Beach

Ferry

Information

Post Office

Black Angus filet, or a 2-pound lobster with all the fixings. Desserts are made on-site by one of the island's finest pastry chefs.

54 Jefferson Ave., Nantucket. 📞 508/228-9641. Reservations suggested. Main courses $29–$39. AE, MC, V. July–Aug daily 11:30am–2pm and 6–10pm; call for off-season hours. Closed Oct to late May.

The Pearl 🐾🐾 NEW AMERICAN   It's Miami Beach on Nantucket at the swankiest fine-dining establishment on the island. The contemporary look here features bluish lighting and large fish tanks; it's definitely a different look for Nantucket. There are numerous stylish touches: appetizers and desserts served in martini glasses, local seafood prepared in innovative ways, an extensive champagne list. It's all very festive. Skip the *grande deluxe plateau de mer;* it's not a lot of shellfish for a lot of money. But do choose the wild mushroom galette with white-truffle cream. As a main course, look no further than the pan-roasted striped bass with citrus tomato infusion and local lobster.

12 Federal St. 📞 **508/228-9701.** Reservations recommended. Main courses $33–$45. AE, MC, V. July–Aug daily 6–9:30pm; call for off-season hours. Closed Jan to late May.

Straight Wharf 🐾🐾 NEW AMERICAN   This is fine and very expensive dining on the waterfront in the center of town. Make your reservation for 8pm on the outside deck so that you can watch the sunset over the harbor. Straight Wharf has long been known for its creative cuisine, and it's also the place where the island's top chefs hang out after their shifts. As befits a harborside restaurant, the focus here is seafood. On the regular menu, you'll find fancy appetizers such as seared beef carpaccio with white-truffle oil, and main courses such as native lobster "a la nage," which is prepared with a champagne sauce. In addition to the regular menu, a "summer grill" menu is served in the bar area and is more reasonably priced. On this grill menu, you'll find simpler fare such as Nantucket clam chowder and Maine crab cake BLT. Devoted regulars, of which there are many, swear by the smoked bluefish pâté served with herb focaccia.

Straight Wharf. 📞 **508/228-4499.** Reservations recommended. Main courses $31–$38; summer grill menu $34–$38 (food minimum of $29 per person). AE, MC, V. July–Aug Tues–Sun 6–10pm; call for off-season hours. Closed late Sept to May.

The Summer House 🐾🐾 *Finds* NEW AMERICAN   The classic Nantucket atmosphere, 'Sconset-style, distinguishes this fine-dining experience from others on the island: wicker and wrought-iron, roses and honeysuckle. A pianist plays nightly—often Gershwin standards. The pounding Atlantic Ocean is just over the bluff. Service is wonderful, and the food is excellent, if expensive. Specialties of the house include fresh, locally caught seafood with local vegetables delicately prepared and stylishly presented. Tempting appetizers include the grilled portobello mushrooms served with a pungent Stilton-basil terrine, and the house-smoked salmon frisée with avocado salsa. The distinctive main courses are roast saddle of lamb with rosemary caponatina port and feta mashed potatoes; the unusual and tasty lobster cutlets with coconut-jasmine risotto timbale and mint-tomato relish; and the grilled rib-eye with wild mushrooms, foie gras, and cabernet. Desserts are bountiful. Order the blueberry pie if it's in season. The Summer House Beachside Bistro, which is poolside, across from the restaurant is a great place to eat lunch, or even dinner on a sultry midsummer night.

17 Ocean Ave., Siasconset. ℭ **508/257-9976.** Reservations recommended. Main courses $30–$42. AE, MC, V. July–Aug daily 6–11pm; mid-May to June and Sept to mid-Oct Wed–Sun 6–10pm. Beachside Bistro (ℭ **508/257-4542**): daily 11:30am–3pm and 5:30-9pm. Closed mid-Oct to Apr.

Topper's at The Wauwinet 𝘢𝘢𝘢 REGIONAL/NEW AMERICAN This 1850 restaurant—part of a secluded resort—is a tastefully subdued knockout, with wicker armchairs, splashes of chintz, and a two-tailed mermaid to oversee a chill-chasing fire. Try to sit at one of the cozy banquettes if you can. The menu features the finest regional cuisine: Lobster is a major event (it's often sautéed with champagne beurre blanc), and be on the lookout for unusual delicacies such as arctic char. Those are Gruyère-and-chive biscuits in the breadbasket, and you need to try one. Other recommendable house specialties include the lobster and crab cakes appetizer and the roasted Muscovy duck breast. Desserts are fanciful and fabulous: Consider the toasted brioche with poached pears and caramel sauce. The Wauwinet runs a complimentary round-trip launch service from mid-June to mid-September to the restaurant for lunch and dinner; it leaves from Straight Wharf at 11am and 5pm and takes 1 hour.

120 Wauwinet Rd. (off Squam Rd.), Wauwinet. ℭ **508/228-8768.** Reservations required for dinner and the launch ride over. Jacket requested. Main courses $34–$56. AE, DC, MC, V. May–Oct Mon–Sat noon–2pm and 6–9:30pm, Sun 11:30am–2pm and 6–9:30pm. Closed Nov–Apr.

21 Federal 𝘢𝘢 NEW AMERICAN This restaurant, a veritable institution with locals, is popular particularly for the happening bar scene. With multiple years of *Wine Spectator* awards to its credit, 21 Federal features 11 carefully selected wines available by the glass each night. Chef Russell Jaehnig seems to get better and more refined every year. Don't fill up on the cheddar-cheese bread sticks:

There's a lot of good food to come. For melt-in-your-mouth pleasure, try the appetizer tuna tartare with wasabi crackers and cilantro aioli. Order a side of mashed potatoes if they don't come with your entree—not that you'll need more food; portions are generous. The fish entrees are most popular here, although you might opt for the fine breast of duck accompanied by pecan wild rice and shiitake mushrooms. I prefer the pan-crisped salmon with champagne cabbage and beet-butter sauce, which has been a staple on the menu for years. Desserts are tantalizing and sinful.

21 Federal St. (in the center of town). ✆ **508/228-2121**. Reservations recommended. Main courses $28–$39. AE, MC, V. May-Sept daily 6–10pm; call for off-season hours. Closed mid-Dec to Mar.

EXPENSIVE

American Seasons 𝕽𝕽 REGIONAL AMERICAN   This romantic little restaurant has a great theme: Choose your region (New England, Pacific Coast, Wild West, or Down South) and select creative offerings. You can mix or match your appetizers and main courses. For instance, begin with the Louisiana crawfish risotto with fire-roasted onion and fried parsnips in a sweet-corn purée from Down South; then from the Pacific Coast, an aged beef sirloin with caramelized shallot and Yukon potato hash served with an Oregon blue-cheese salad with white-truffle oil and fried onions. A light tapas menu is available at the bar in the evenings.

80 Centre St. (2 blocks from the center of town). ✆ **508/228-7111**. Reservations recommended. Main courses $24–$30. AE, MC, V. June–Sept daily 6–9:30pm; call for off-season hours. Closed early Dec to mid-Apr.

Boarding House 𝕽𝕽 NEW AMERICAN   This centrally located fine-dining restaurant doubles as one of the most popular bars in town. It is in the same building as The Pearl (see above) and owned by the same couple, hostess Angela Raynor and chef Seth Raynor. You can dine in the romantic lower-level dining room or upstairs in the hopping bar area, but on clear summer nights, try to get one of the tables outside on the patio. The menu has definite Asian and Mediterranean influences in dishes like the seared yellow fin tuna with sesame sushi rice cake and wasabi aioli. One of the best soups on Nantucket is the luxe double lobster chowder with fresh corn and truffle mousseline. But the signature dish is the classic grilled lobster tails with grilled asparagus, mashed potatoes, and champagne beurre blanc. The wine list is award-winning with a range of prices.

12 Federal St. ✆ **508/228-9622**. Reservations recommended. Main courses $24–$35. AE, MC, V. July–Aug daily 5:30–10pm; call for off-season hours. Open year-round.

Moments **Biking to The Summer House**

For athletic gourmands, a perfect Nantucket afternoon could be spent biking the 18-mile loop from town to the picturesque village of 'Sconset on the east end of the island. At 'Sconset, take a break at The Summer House. There you can enjoy a glass of wine and perhaps a thin-crust pizza by the pools, where you are eye-level with the Atlantic Ocean.

Cinco Restaurant and Bar ★★ TAPAS   Nantucket's newest dining venue is a sophisticated tapas restaurant. It is the place to see and be seen on Nantucket this season. Because it is a few miles outside of town, you will need a car or a taxi to get to Cinco. From the towering bull sculpture at the entrance to the soft lighting and abstract artwork inside, you'll know immediately that you are in for a special treat. The menu lists 23 different tapas dishes, from fish tacos to marinated beef shoulder, to chile relleno tart. All are small portions with big flavors. The best way to dine here is for each person to choose three or four tapas, then share. This is not the place to come with a big appetite; Cinco is all about grazing and socializing.

5 Amelia Dr. (¼ mile past the rotary). ✆ 508/325-5151. Reservations recommended. Tapas $5–$12. AE, MC, V. June–Sept daily 6–10pm; call for off-season hours. Closed Jan to mid-Apr.

Company of the Cauldron ★★★ CONTINENTAL   With an intimate candlelit dining room where, several nights a week in season, a classical harpist plays, this is one of the island's most romantic restaurants. Chef/owner All Kovalencik offers an intricate and distinct three- to four-course fixed-price meal each night, so would-be patrons must check the menu out front or telephone and then choose which evening's menu is most appealing. Dietary preferences, such as vegetarianism, can be accommodated if you call ahead. The menu, with classic American and Continental influences, changes nightly and portions are generous. Don't miss the soft-shell crab appetizer when it is offered in season. The main course could be seafood, a special swordfish preparation for instance, or a meat dish, such as rack of lamb or beef Wellington. Dessert could be chocolate soufflé cake: exquisite.

5 India St. (between Federal and Centre sts.) ✆ 508/228-4016. Reservations required. Fixed-price menu $48–$50. MC, V. Early July to early Sept Tues–Sun, 2 seatings 6:45 and 8:45pm; call for off-season hours. Closed late Oct to mid-May, except Thanksgiving weekend and the first 2 weeks of Dec.

DeMarco ☆☆ NORTHERN ITALIAN   This frame house carved into a cafe/bar and loft is the place to get the best Northern Italian food on the island. A forward-thinking menu and attentive service ensure a superior meal, which may include *antipasto di salmone* (house-smoked salmon rollantini, lemon-herb cream cheese, cucumber-and-endive salad with chive vinaigrette) and the delicate *capellini con scampi* (capellini with rock shrimp, tomato, black olives, capers, and hot pepper).

9 India St. (between Federal and Centre sts.). ℂ **508/228-1836.** Reservations recommended. Main courses $19–$31. AE, MC, V. Mid-June to Sept daily 6–10pm; call for off-season hours. Closed mid-Oct to late May.

Le Languedoc Cafe ☆☆ NEW AMERICAN   This is Nantucket's most authentic French cafe. The atmosphere in this historic building is wonderful and the prices are reasonable. There's also an expensive dining room upstairs, but locals prefer the casual bistro atmosphere downstairs and out on the terrace. There's a clubby feel here as diners come and go, greeting each other and enjoying themselves. Soups are superb, as are the Angus-steak burgers with garlic french fries. More elaborate dishes include the roasted tenderloin of pork stuffed with figs and pancetta, berlotti bean stew, and the napoleon of grilled tuna, tapenade, and roasted vegetables with pesto sauce. As expected at a French bistro, desserts, like crème brûlée and chocolate pot de crème, are standouts.

24 Broad St. ℂ **508/228-2552.** www.lelanguedoc.com. Reservations not accepted for cafe and garden; reservations recommended for main dining room. Main courses $22–$38. AE, MC, V. June–Sept daily 5:30–10pm, Tues–Sun noon–5pm; call for off-season hours. Closed mid-Dec to mid-May.

Òran Mór ☆☆☆ *(Finds* INTERNATIONAL   Renowned Chef Peter Wallace runs this second-floor waterfront venue, which has quickly become the premier restaurant on the island. The unusual name is Gaelic and means "great song"; it's the name of Wallace's favorite single-malt scotch. Climb up the stairs of this historic building, and prepare yourself for a somewhat extravagant dining experience. The menu changes nightly, always with some surprising and unusual choices, as well as local seafood specials. Standouts recently include crisp veal sweetbreads and organic salmon gravlax. Intriguing entrees include pan-roasted sea scallops with whole grain mustard (a perfect early fall dish) and roast Colorado rack of lamb with sausage. Some say the grilled breast of duck with savory tapioca and local nectar jus is the best duck dish on the island. An excellent sommelier is on hand to assist wine lovers.

2 S. Beach St. (in the center of town). © **508/228-8655.** Reservations recommended. Main courses $26–$36. MC, V. July–Aug Thurs–Tues 6–9:30pm; Sept–June Thurs–Sat and Mon–Tues 6–9pm. Closed mid-Dec to mid-April.

Ropewalk ☆ SEAFOOD   This open-air restaurant on the harbor is Nantucket's only outdoor raw bar, and it's where the yachting crowd hangs out after a day on the boat. While the food is a bit overpriced, the location is prime. The raw bar, serving littlenecks, oysters, and shrimp, is open daily in high season from 3 to 10pm, and is a good place to enjoy a light meal or appetizers, such as fried calamari, crab cakes, or fried oysters. Lunch prices for sandwiches and burgers are fairly reasonable; dinner prices are expensive. The dinner menu includes grilled swordfish with ratatouille and grilled breast of chicken with roasted garlic and rosemary jus.

1 Straight Wharf. © **508/228-8886.** Reservations not accepted. Main courses $24–$34. AE, MC, V. July–Aug daily 11:30am–3pm and 5-10pm; call for off-season hours. Closed mid-Oct to Apr.

The Ship's Inn Restaurant ☆☆ NEW AMERICAN   This intimate restaurant in the brick-walled basement of a 12-room inn is one of the island's most romantic dining options. The restaurant is a short walk from Main Street down a quiet side street. The restaurant, with its candlelit alcoves, is a cozy hideaway. The waitstaff here is professional and entertaining, a real treat. The menu features a variety of fresh fish, meat, and pasta dishes including several lighter options made without butter or cream. The lengthy wine list, which has a number of well-priced options, has won awards. A flavorful starter here is the Roquefort and walnut terrine with Asian pear. As a main course, popular dishes include the pan-roasted Muscovy duck breast and the grilled yellowtail flounder. For a festive dessert, there's always the Grand Marnier soufflé.

13 Fair St. © **508/228-0040.** Reservations recommended. Main courses $19–$34. AE, DISC, MC, V. July–Sept Wed–Mon 5:30–9:30pm; call for off-season hours. Closed Nov to mid-May.

Sushi by Yoshi ☆ JAPANESE   This tiny place is Nantucket's best source for great sushi. The incredibly fresh local fish is artfully presented by Chef Yoshihisa Mabuchi, who also dishes up such healthy, affordable staples as miso or udon (noodle) soup. It's tempting to order a raft of Rhoda rolls (with tuna, avocado, and caviar), especially when a portion of the proceeds goes toward AIDS support, but prices can add up. Be prepared for spotty service during the high season, however. In fact, this is an excellent place for takeout, but you'll want to allow an hour in season.

2 E. Chestnut St. ⒞ **508/228-1801.** Reservations not accepted. Main courses $12–$28; sushi $5–$15 per roll, most $6–$9. V. May to mid-Oct daily 11:30am–10pm; mid-Oct to Apr Thurs–Sat 11:30am–10pm, Sun–Wed 5–10pm.

The Woodbox Inn Restaurant ⭐⭐ NEW AMERICAN/ FRENCH   The Woodbox, a short stroll from Main Street in the historic district, is a romantic fine-dining restaurant. Entering the restaurant, with its low-beamed ceilings and wide pine floors, transports you to the era of the whaling captains. The small dining rooms are decorated with antique tables, Oriental rugs, and bone china. As befits the setting, the food features fancy ingredients in classic preparations. For example, appetizer choices include beef carpaccio and sautéed foie gras, and a special main course is the beef Wellington. You can also find innovative offerings such as a slowly cooked crispy salmon filet with cucumber vermicelli and salmon caviar. The Woodbox is most famous for its homemade popovers, light and buttery treats that accompany both breakfast and dinner.

29 Fair St., Nantucket. ⒞ **508/228-0587.** Main courses $22–$32. MC, V. Tues–Sun 8:30–10:30am and 6:30–9pm; call for off-season hours. Closed early Jan to late Mar.

MODERATE

Black Eyed Susan's ⭐⭐ ETHNIC ECLECTIC   This is supremely exciting food in a funky bistro atmosphere. It's small, popular with locals, and packed. Reservations are accepted for the 6pm seating only, and these go fast. Others must line up outside the restaurant (the line starts forming around 5:30pm), and the hostess will assign you a time to dine. If you don't mind sitting at the counter, you'll have a better choice. Inside, it may seem a bit too cozy, but that's all part of the charm. The menu is in constant flux, as chef Jeff Worster's mood and influences change every 3 weeks. I always enjoy the spicy Thai fish cake when it is on the menu, and also the tandoori chicken with green mango chutney. There's usually a southwestern touch such as the Dos Equis beer-battered catfish quesadilla with mango slaw, hoppin' johns, and jalapeño. You'll mop up the sauce with the delectable organic sourdough bread. There's no liquor license, but you can BYOB. The corking fee is $1 per person.

10 India St. (in the center of town). ⒞ **508/325-0308.** Reservations accepted for 6pm seating only. Main courses $15–$25. No credit cards. Apr–Oct daily 7am–1pm, Mon–Sat 6–10pm; call for off-season hours. Closed Nov–Mar.

Bluefin ⭐⭐ *Finds* ASIAN/INTERNATIONAL   This restaurant, an intimate and romantic spot a short walk from the center of town, offers great prices and tasty food, including sushi and tapas. The melt-in-your-mouth crispy crab rangoon comes with the perfect hot and sour sauce, and shrimp lo-mein is served with wok crisp vegetables. The lobster ravioli served with sweet basil cream is the ultimate in wretched excess. Each choice on an extensive sushi menu (more than 30 items) costs $5 to $7 and comes with six pieces (for example, if you order the tuna roll, you get six pieces of tuna roll). Keep in mind, there is a bar scene here too, so if you are sitting near the bar area, it can be loud.

15 South Beach St. ☎ **508/228-2033**. Main courses $18–$28. AE, MC, V. June–Aug daily 5:30–10pm; call for off-season hours. Open year-round.

Centre Street Bistro 🍴🍴 NEW AMERICAN This tiny fine-dining restaurant in the center of Nantucket Town is owned and operated by Ruth and Tim Pitts, who are considered top chefs on the island. The dining room only has about eight tables and a few bar seats inside, though in the summer there is extra seating on the front patio. This cozy place features wonderful, creative cuisine at reasonable prices, especially compared to other island fine-dining restaurants. The menu is in constant flux, but recent high points included the warm goat cheese tart to start, and the Long Island duck breast with pumpkin and butternut squash risotto as a main course. If the sautéed Nantucket Bay scallops are on the menu, you won't want to miss whatever clever preparation the Pitts have dreamed up. One dish featured these world-famous local scallops with wontons and a citrus soy and spice glaze. This is a particularly good spot for lunch.

29 Centre St., Nantucket. ☎ **508/228-8470**. www.nantucketbistro.com. No reservations. Main courses $19–$25. No credit cards. May–Sept Wed–Sat 7–11am, 11:30am–2pm, and 6–9pm, Sun 8am–1pm and 6–9pm; call for off-season hours. Open year-round.

Cioppino's 🍴 NEW AMERICAN Sometimes it's the hosts that can make a restaurant stand out. Susie and Tracy Root want to be sure all their guests are enjoying themselves, and they are likely to stop by your table to see how you are doing. Ask Tracy Root for a wine recommendation because that's his specialty. The service is attentive and the food is hearty. On a clear night, you'll want to sit out on the patio and watch the strollers. The menu features simple, hearty dishes. Portions are generous; service is swift and friendly. Favorites on the menu include the Nantucket lobster bisque, scaloppini of pork picatta with lemon and capers, and Italian herb-crusted sea bass with a light citrus sauce. The signature dish, Cioppino's cioppino is a rich, chunky seafood stew served over linguini. For the finale, try the peach and blueberry cobbler served warm with vanilla-bean ice cream.

20 Broad St. (between Federal and Centre sts.). ☎ **508/228-4622**. Reservations accepted. Main courses $20–$32. AE, DC, DISC, MC, V. May–Oct daily 5:30–10pm. Closed Nov–Apr.

Nantucket Lobster Trap ✿ SEAFOOD When only a bowl of chowder and a giant lobster roll will do, bring the whole family to this quintessential clam shack where the big game is usually on the TV behind the bar. Seating is on large picnic tables, and lobsters and other shellfish come straight from local waters, as are the world-renowned Nantucket bay scallops. The prices are kept relatively affordable here. There's also a kid's menu.

23 Washington St. ⓒ **508/228-4200.** Reservations for parties of 6 or more only. Main courses $12–$30. AE, MC, V. June–Sept daily 5–10:30pm; call for off-season hours. Closed late Oct to early May.

Queequeg's ✿ NEW AMERICAN A cozy bistro atmosphere and good value are the hallmarks of this small restaurant, which is tucked along a side street behind the Atheneum. Outside seating is available on the patio in good weather. As befits the Moby Dick reference in the name, the specialty here is seafood. The menu offers a range from basics to fancier fare. For example, as an appetizer, you could have New England clam chowder or tuna tartare. The rich and flavorful pan-seared halibut with Parmesan risotto is becoming a favorite with locals. Meat-lovers may enjoy chargrilled New Zealand lamb or New York strip sirloin, and vegetarians have options as well.

6 Oak St. ⓒ **508/325-0992.** Reservations recommended. Main courses $18–$25. MC, V. June–Sept daily 5–10:30pm; call for off-season hours. Closed Nov–Apr.

Schooner's at Steamboat Wharf ✿ AMERICAN This casual family-friendly restaurant near the Steamship Authority dock is noteworthy for the outdoor dining on the screened-in porch. Diners who sit on the second floor have views of the harbor. Prices are reasonable and portions are generous in this casual pub. The most popular dishes are the fajitas, fried clams, fish and chips, and the lobster salad. A lively late-night bar scene here includes live acoustic music some nights in season.

31 Easy St. ⓒ **508/228-5824.** Reservations accepted. Main courses $18–$24. AE, MC, V. Apr–Dec daily 11am–10pm. Closed Jan–Mar.

INEXPENSIVE

Arno's ✿ ECLECTIC A storefront facing the passing parade of Main Street, this institution packs surprising style between its bare-brick walls (Molly Dee's mostly monochrome paintings, like vintage photographs, are especially nice). The internationally influenced menu yields tasty, bountiful platters for breakfast, lunch, and dinner. Specialties include grilled sirloin steaks and fresh grilled fish.

Generous servings of specialty pasta dishes such as shrimp and scallop scampi Florentine are featured nightly.

41 Main St. ⓒ **508/228-7001.** Reservations recommended. Main courses $9–$17. AE, DC, DISC, MC, V. Apr–Dec daily 8am–9pm. Closed Jan–Mar.

The Atlantic Cafe *(Kids)* AMERICAN   The A.C. is a casual, local favorite with a friendly staff who seem to remember the patrons summer to summer (or at least they make you feel that way). The menu is extensive: You can find anything from salads to burgers to quesadillas to fried scrod to New York sirloin. The clam chowda' is one of the best on the island. Your little ones can choose from a menu with all the kiddie favorites—chicken fingers, grilled cheese, mozzarella sticks, hot dogs, PB&J, and hamburgers. The bar here is well stocked and offers a good list of beers. Don't hesitate to try one of the special cocktails—the French Orchid and the Bloody Marys are popular. During scallop season—if you're lucky—you'll find a fried scallop roll offered as a daily special—don't pass it up!

15 South Water St. ⓒ **508/228-0570.** Reservations not accepted. Main courses $7.95–$25. AE, DISC, MC, V. Mar–Jan 11:30am–1am.

The Brotherhood of Thieves *(R)* PUB   This classic whaling bar housed in the basement of an early-19th-century brick building in the center of town is a Nantucket institution. After a fire almost destroyed the building, its future was uncertain, but new investors came in to save it. In July and August, tourists line up for a table in the dark tavern to chow on burgers and hand-cut curly shoestring fries. The specialty drink menu here is longer than the food menu and includes such playful concoctions as the "Goombay Smash," a fruity rum punch, and a wide selection of coffee and liquor drinks. In the fall and winter, locals enjoy the decently priced dinner offerings such as chicken teriyaki and fried Cajun shrimp while sitting beside the cozy brick hearth.

23 Broad St. No phone. Reservations not accepted. Main courses $9–$18. No credit cards. Mid-May to mid-Oct Mon–Sat 11:30am–12:30am, Sun noon–12:30am; mid-Oct to mid-May Mon–Sat 11:30am–10:30pm, Sun noon–10pm. Closed Feb.

Cap'n Tobey's Chowder House *(R)* *(Kids)* SEAFOOD   The specialty at this convenient eatery close to the harbor is seafood, obtained on a daily basis from local fishermen. Diners can choose between halibut, yellowfin tuna, swordfish, and salmon, and have it grilled, baked, or blackened. The raw bar features oysters, littlenecks and shrimp. Options range from a Nantucket bluefish sandwich ($10) to a surf and turf platter ($30). A less-expensive fried-fish menu is an alternate choice for families. Upstairs, Off Shore at Cap'n Tobey's has live music in season.

20 Straight Wharf. © **508/228-0836.** Reservations accepted. Main courses $10–$30. AE, MC, V. Late June to Sept daily 11:30am–10pm; call for off-season hours. Closed Jan–Apr.

Downyflake Restaurant ☆ (Kids) DINER   Serving breakfast and lunch only, this popular mid-island eatery has the best breakfast and prices around. It's the closest establishment to a diner that you'll find on Nantucket. Downyflake doughnuts are famous around these parts, and once you taste one you'll know why (my favorite is the chocolate frosted). During the summer you'll always find yourself waiting in line, but the turnover is fast, so grab a newspaper to bide your time and you'll be sitting down enjoying breakfast with your family in no time at all. Coffee, doughnuts, and other fresh-baked breakfast delights are available at the takeout counter.

18 Sparks Ave (across from the Fire Department). © **508/228-4533.** Main courses $5–$10. No credit cards. Daily 7am–1pm. Closed Wed in Jan and Feb.

The Even Keel Café ☆ AMERICAN   This low-key cafe in the heart of town serves breakfast, lunch, and dinner both indoors and outside on a patio in the back. Unlike much of Nantucket's dining scene, you'll find reasonable prices and non-exotic fare such as burgers and sandwiches. The menu has vegetarian choices, as well as meat and fish dishes such as grilled salmon or veal *osso buco*. There's also a kid's menu, a hearty Sunday brunch, and even high-speed Internet access. This place has lots of off-season dining deals, such as half-price weekday breakfasts and two-for-one dinners. There is no alcohol for sale here, but you can BYOB.

40 Main St. © **508/228-1979.** Reservations not accepted. Main courses $10–$25. AE, MC, V. July–Aug daily 7am–10pm; call for off-season hours. Open year-round.

Fog Island Cafe ☆☆ NEW AMERICAN   You'll be wowed by the creative breakfasts and lunches at this sassy cafe; they're reasonably priced, with super-fresh ingredients. Homemade soups and salads are healthy and yummy. The dinner menu, served June through August only, features fresh seafood, pasta dishes, and a vegetarian alternative among the specialties. There is also a kid's menu. This local joint also has their cookbook for sale on-site.

7 S. Water St. © **508/228-1818.** Reservations not accepted. Main courses at dinner $15–$20. MC, V. July–Aug Mon–Sat 7am–noon, 11am-2pm, and 5–9pm, Sun 7am–1pm; call for off-season hours. Open year-round.

Nantucket's Best Sweets & Baked Goods

Daily Breads ⋒⋒: Coffee, fresh-baked breads, pastries, croissants, muffins, cookies, desserts, and so on. Try a slice of gourmet pizza here—it's delicious. 147 Orange St. ✆ **508/228-8961**. Call for hours.

The Juice Bar ⋒⋒: This humble hole-in-the-wall scoops up some of the best homemade ice cream and frozen yogurt around, complemented by superb homemade hot fudge. Waffle cones are homemade, too. And, yes, you can also get juice—from refreshing lime rickeys to healthful carrot cocktails. 12 Broad St. ✆ 508/228-5799. June–Aug daily 10am–11pm; Apr–May and Sept to mid-Dec 11am–9pm. Closed mid-Oct to mid-Apr.

Nantucket Bake Shop ⋒⋒⋒: This place has wonderful breakfast treats, breads (the Portuguese bread is a stand-out), gorgeous cakes (if you need a wedding cake, this is *the* place), and pies. With an extensive catalog, they ship off-island year-round. 79 Orange St. ✆ **800/440-BAKE** or 508/228-2797. www.nantucketbakeshop.com. Open seasonally Mon–Sat 6:30am–5pm.

Something Natural ⋒⋒: Besides its delicious sandwiches (see the "Takeout & Picnic Fare" section, below), Something Natural is first a bakery, selling loaves of fresh-baked bread on-site and at grocery stores around the island. You'll want to take a couple of loaves with you when you leave the island. 50 Cliff Rd. ✆ **508/228-0504**. Apr to mid-Oct 7am–5:30pm. Closed mid-Oct to Mar.

TAKEOUT & PICNIC FARE

Bartlett's Ocean View Farm ⋒⋒   You can get fresh-picked produce (in season, the tomatoes are incomparable) in town from Bartlett's traveling market, or head out to this seventh-generation farm where, in June, you may get to pick your own strawberries. They also sell sandwiches, quiches, pastries, pies, and more.

33 Bartlett Farm Rd. ✆ **508/228-9403**. www.bartlettsfarm.com. MC, V. Apr–Dec Mon–Sat 8am–6pm. Truck parked on Main St. in season.

Henry's Sandwich Shop 𝒦   Andrew Fee's classic sandwich shop, which opened in 1969, is set a block away from Steamboat Wharf, where the ferries dock. They bake their own sub rolls from scratch every morning, as well as their chocolate-chip cookies. Bring the family for a cheap and easy lunch.

Steamboat Wharf. ℭ **508/228-0123.** July–Aug 8am–8pm; call for off-season hours. Closed Nov–May.

Nantucket Gourmet   Besides an enticing array of kitchen items, Jonathan and Patty Stone have set up a deli full of scrumptious sandwiches, fixin's, and salads to take out.

4 India St. ℭ **508/228-4353.** Daily 10am–5pm. Open year-round.

Provisions 𝒦   Before you bike out of town to the beach, stop by this gourmet sandwich shop for picnic staples including salads, soups, and muffins.

3 Harbor Sq., Straight Wharf. ℭ **508/228-3258.** Apr to early Nov daily 8am–6pm. Closed early Nov to Mar.

Something Natural 𝒦𝒦   This sandwich shop is a bit far from town to walk to, unless you're in the mood for a hike. But it's a great stop on a bike or car ride from town to the beach. A local institution and a terrific value, Something Natural turns out gigantic sandwiches, with fresh ingredients piled atop fabulous bread. Plan on sharing, so you'll have room for their addictive chocolate-chip cookies. It's a great place to stock up for a day at the beach, or you can eat your lunch right on the grounds, where there are picnic tables.

50 Cliff Rd. ℭ **508/228-0504.** Apr to mid-Oct daily 7am–5:30pm. Closed mid-Oct to Mar.

Exploring Nantucket

Nantucket is steeped in history. Just walking down the streets in town and looking at the architecture can take up days. The island has much to offer: Whether you want to shop, fish, sail, golf, run, sightsee, or just relax, this chapter tells you where to find the best of everything.

1 Beaches & Recreational Pursuits

BEACHES   In distinct contrast to Martha's Vineyard, virtually all of Nantucket's 110-mile coastline is open to the public. Though the pressure to keep people out is sometimes intense (especially when four-wheel-drivers insist on their right to go anywhere, anytime), islanders are proud that they've managed to keep the shoreline in the public domain.

Each of the following areas tends to attract a different crowd.

- **Children's Beach** ⋒: This small beach is a protected cove just west of busy Steamship Wharf. Appealing to families, it has a park, playground, restrooms, lifeguards, snack bar (the beloved Downyflake, famous for its homemade doughnuts), and even a bandstand for free weekend concerts.

- **Cisco Beach** ⋒⋒: About 4 miles from town, in the southwestern quadrant of the island (from Main St., turn onto Milk St., which becomes Hummock Pond Rd.), Cisco enjoys vigorous waves—great for the surfers who flock here, not so great for the waterfront homeowners. Restrooms and lifeguards are available.

- **Coatue** ⋒: This fishhook-shaped barrier beach, on the northeastern side of the island at Wauwinet, is Nantucket's outback, accessible only by four-wheel-drive vehicles, watercraft, or the very strong-legged. Swimming is strongly discouraged because of fierce tides.

- **Dionis Beach** ⋒⋒⋒: About 3 miles out of town (take the Madaket bike path to Eel Point Rd.) is Dionis, which enjoys gentle-sound surf and steep, picturesque bluffs. It's a great spot

Exploring Nantucket

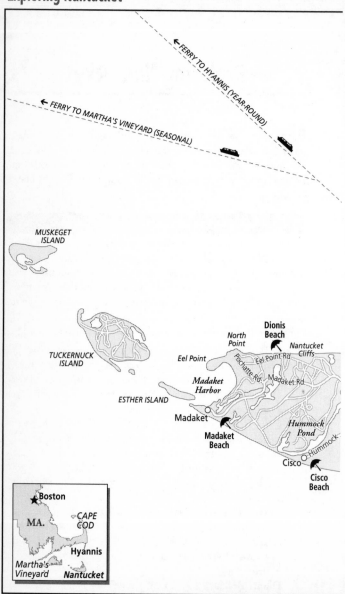

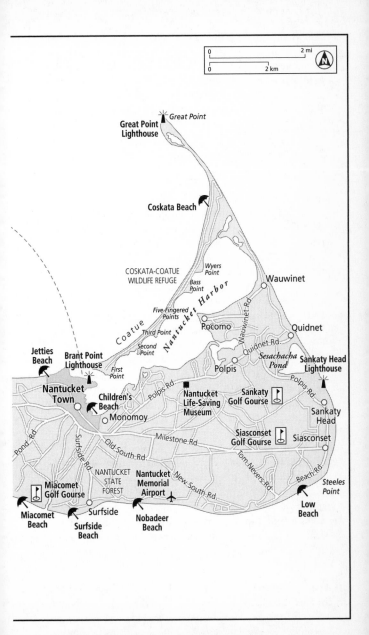

0   2 mi
0   2 km

Great Point
Great Point
Lighthouse

Coskata Beach

COSKATA-COATUE
WILDLIFE REFUGE

Wyers
Point

Bass
Point

Nantucket Harbor

Five-Fingered
Points

Coatue

Third Point

Wauwinet

Pocomo

Quidnet

Quidnet Rd.

Second
Point

Sesachacha
Pond

Sankaty Head
Lighthouse

Jetties
Beach

Brant Point
Lighthouse

First
Point

Polpis

Polpis Rd.

Nantucket
Town

Children's
Beach

Polpis Rd.

Nantucket
Life-Saving
Museum

Sankaty
Golf Gourse

Sankaty
Head

Monomoy

Milestone Rd.

Siasconset
Golf Gourse

Siasconset

Pond Rd.

Surfside Rd.

Old South Rd.

Tom Nevers Rd.

Beach Rd.

Steeles
Point

Miacomet
Golf Gourse

NANTUCKET
STATE
FOREST

Nantucket
Memorial
Airport

New South Rd.

Miacomet
Beach

Surfside

Nobadeer
Beach

Low
Beach

Surfside
Beach

75

for swimming, picnicking, and shelling, and you'll find fewer children than at Jetties or Children's beaches. Stick to the established paths to prevent further erosion. Lifeguards patrol here, and restrooms are available.

- **Jetties Beach** ★★★: Located about ½ mile west of Children's Beach on North Beach Street, Jetties is about a 20-minute walk, or even shorter bike ride, shuttle bus ride, or drive, from town (a large parking lot fills up early on summer weekends). This beach is a family favorite because of its mild waves, lifeguards, bathhouse, restrooms, and relatively affordable restaurant, **The Jetties Cafe & Grille** (© **508/325-6347**). Facilities include the town tennis courts, volleyball nets, a skate park, and a playground; watersports equipment and chairs are also available to rent. Every August, Jetties hosts an intense sandcastle competition, and Fourth of July fireworks are held here.

- **Madaket Beach** ★★★: Accessible by Madaket Road, the 6-mile bike path that runs parallel to it, and by shuttle bus, this westerly beach is narrow and subject to pounding surf and sometimes serious crosscurrents. Unless it's a fairly tame day, you may content yourself with wading. It's the best spot on the island for admiring the sunset. Facilities include restrooms, lifeguards, and mobile food service.

- **Siasconset (known as 'Sconset) Beach** ★★: The easterly coast of 'Sconset is as pretty as the town itself and rarely, if ever, crowded, perhaps because of the water's strong sideways tow. You can reach it by car, shuttle bus, or by a less scenic and somewhat hilly (at least for Nantucket) 7-mile bike path. Lifeguards are usually on duty. The closest facilities (restrooms, grocery store, and cafe) are back in the center of the village.

- **Surfside Beach** ★★★: Three miles south of town via a popular bike/skate path, broad Surfside—equipped with lifeguards, restrooms, and a surprisingly accomplished little snack bar—is appropriately named and commensurately popular. It draws thousands of visitors a day in high season, from college students to families, but the free parking lot fits only about 60 cars—you do the math, or better yet, ride your bike or take the shuttle bus.

BICYCLING   Several lovely, paved bike paths radiate out from the center of town to outlying beaches. The **bike paths** run about 6 miles west to Madaket, 3½ miles south to Surfside, and 8 miles east to Siasconset. To avoid backtracking from Siasconset, continue

north through the charming village, and return on the **Polpis Road
bike path** 🚲. Strong riders could do a whole circuit of the island in
a day, but most will be content to combine a single route with a few
hours at a beach. You'll find picnic benches and water fountains at
strategic points along all the paths.

On the way back to town, lighthouse enthusiasts will want to
stop by Brant Point Light at the end of Easton Street. Located next
to the Coast Guard station, this squat lighthouse is still used by
boats maneuvering in and out of the harbor. It's a scenic spot to take
a break and enjoy the view; you'll see ferries chugging by and
immense yachts competing for prize berths along the wharves.

BOATING   If your idea of a perfect afternoon is to rent a small
motorboat and putter around Nantucket Harbor and out into Nantucket Sound, stop by **Nantucket Boat Rentals** on the harbor, Slip
1 at Straight Wharf (✆ **508/325-1001**). A small powerboat for a
couple of hours will cost you about $140.

FISHING   For shellfishing, you'll need a permit from the **harbor-
master's office** at 34 Washington St. (✆ **508/228-7261**). You'll see
surf-casters all over the island (no permit is required). Deep-sea
charters heading out of Straight Wharf include Captain Pete Kaizer's
Althea K. (✆ **508/325-2167**), Captain Bob DeCosta's *The Alba-
core* (✆ **508/228-5074**), and Captain Josh Eldridge's *Monomoy*
(✆ **508/228-6867**). There's also **Capt. Tom's Charters** specializing
in fly and plug casting with Tom Mleczko (✆ **508/228-4225**). On
the *Flicka,* 2½-hour trips for bluefish cost $350 for six people and
5-hour trips for bass cost $700.

FITNESS   **Nantucket Health Club,** at 10 Youngs Way (✆ **508/
228-4750**), offers all the usual equipment and classes. Non-members
pay $20 a day.

GOLF   Two pretty 9-hole courses are open to the public: **Miacomet Golf Club,** 12 W. Miacomet Rd. (✆ **508/325-0333**), and
the **Siasconset Golf Club,** off Milestone Road (✆ **508/257-6596**).
You'll pay $26 for 9 holes and $48 for 18 holes.

NATURE TRAILS   Through preservationist foresight, about one-
third of Nantucket's 42 square miles are protected from development. Contact the **Nantucket Conservation Foundation** at 118
Cliff Rd. (✆ **508/228-2884**) for a map of their holdings ($4), which
include the 205-acre **Windswept Cranberry Bog** (off Polpis Rd.),
where bogs are interspersed amid hardwood forests, and a portion of
the 1,100-acre **Coskata-Coatue Wildlife Refuge,** comprising the

barrier beaches beyond Wauwinet (see "Organized Tours," below). The **Maria Mitchell Association** (see "Museums & Historic Landmarks," below) also sponsors guided birding and wildflower walks in season.

TENNIS   The town courts are located next to Jetties Beach, a short walk west of town; call the **Nantucket Park and Recreation Commission** (© 508/325-5334) for information. Nine clay courts are available for rent nearby at the **Brant Point Racquet Club,** on North Beach Street (© **508/228-3700**), for $34 an hour. Though it's not generally open to the public, the grand, turn-of-the-20th-century **Siasconset Casino,** New Street, Siasconset (© **508/257-6585**), occasionally has courts open for rent from 1 to 3pm for $20 an hour.

WATERSPORTS   **Nantucket Community Sailing** manages the concession at **Jetties Beach** (© **508/228-5358**), which offers lessons and rents out kayaks, sailboards, sailboats, and more. Rental rates for single kayaks are $15 per hour; Windsurfers $25 per hour; Sunfish $30 per hour. **Sea Nantucket** (© **508/228-7499**), on tiny Francis Street Beach off Washington Street, also rents kayaks; it's a quick sprint across the harbor to beautiful Coatue. Single kayaks rent for $35 and tandems rent for $60 for 4½ hours. They also rent sailboats. **Nantucket Island Community Sailing** (© **508/228-6600**) gives relatively low-cost private and group lessons from the Town Pier for adults (16 and up) and families; a seasonal adult membership covering open-sail privileges costs $150. One 3-hour lesson costs $100.

Gear for scuba-diving, fishing, and snorkeling are readily available at the souvenir shop **Sunken Ship** on South Water and Broad streets near Steamboat Wharf (© **508/228-9226**). Fishing gear costs $15 per day; snorkeling gear costs $15 a day; scuba diving gear costs $30 to $40. Scuba diving lessons are $450.

2 Museums & Historic Landmarks

Hadwen House 🏛🏛   During Nantucket's most prosperous years, whaling merchant Joseph Starbuck built the "Three Bricks" (93, 95, and 97 Main St.) for his three sons. His daughter married successful businessman William Hadwen, owner of the candle factory that is now the Whaling Museum, and Hadwen built this grand Greek revival home across the street from his brothers-in-law in 1845. Although locals (mostly Quakers) were scandalized by the opulence, the local outrage spurred Hadwen on, and he decided to make the

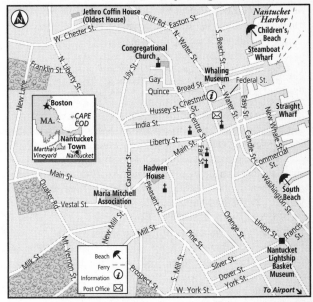

home even grander than he had first intended. The home soon became a showplace for entertaining the Hadwens' many wealthy friends. Soon after, Hadwen built the matching home next door for his niece, and it is assumed that he enjoyed using its grand ballroom for his parties, too. The Historical Association has done a magnificent job restoring the home and furnishing it with period furniture, fabrics, porcelains, wallpapers, and other decorative accessories thought to be original. The gardens are maintained in period style by the Nantucket Garden Club.

96 Main St. (at Pleasant St., a few blocks southwest of the town center). ☎ 508/ 228-1894. www.nha.org. Admission included in Nantucket Historical Association's History Ticket ($15 adults, $8 children, $35 families). AE, MC, V. Apr–Nov Mon–Sat 10am–5pm, Sun noon–5pm. Closed Dec–Mar.

Jethro Coffin House 🐿🐿 Also known simply as The Oldest House, this late-17th-century saltbox is the oldest building left on the island. A National Historical Landmark, the brick design on its central chimney has earned it the nickname "The Horseshoe House." It was struck by lightning and severely damaged (in fact, nearly cut in two) in 1987, prompting a long-overdue restoration. Dimly lighted by leaded glass diamond-pane windows, it's filled with period furniture such as lathed ladder-back chairs and a clever trundle bed on wooden wheels. Nantucket Historical Association docents will fill you in on all the related lore.

Sunset Hill Rd. (off W. Chester Rd., about ½ mile northwest of the town center). ℭ 508/228-1894. www.nha.org. Admission included in Nantucket Historical Association's History Ticket ($15 adults, $8 children, $35 families). AE, MC, V. Late May to mid-Oct Mon–Sat 10am–5pm, Sun noon–5pm. Closed mid-Oct to late May.

The Maria Mitchell Association 🕏🕏 *Kids*   This is a group of six buildings organized and maintained in honor of distinguished astronomer and Nantucket native Maria Mitchell (1818–89). The science center consists of astronomical observatories, with a lecture series, children's science seminars, and stellar observation opportunities (when the sky is clear) from the **Loines Observatory** at 59 Milk St. (ℭ **508/228-8690**) and the **Vestal Street Observatory** at 3 Vestal St. (ℭ **508/228-9273**). The Vestal Street Observatory is open June to September on Saturdays at 11am for a 1-hour tour. The Loines Observatory is open July and August on Monday, Wednesday, and Friday at 9pm; September through June on Fridays at 8pm. The cost is $10 adults, $6 children.

The **Hinchman House Natural Science Museum** (ℭ **508/ 228-0898**), at 7 Milk St., houses a visitor center and offers evening lectures, bird-watching, wildflower and nature walks, and discovery classes for children and adults. The **Mitchell House** (ℭ **508/ 228-2896**) at 1 Vestal St., the astronomer's birthplace, features a children's history series, adult-artisan seminars, and has wildflower and herb gardens. The **Science Library** (ℭ **508/228-9219**) is at 2 Vestal St., and the tiny, child-oriented **aquarium** (ℭ **508/228-5387**) is at 28 Washington St.

4 Vestal St. (at Milk St., about ½ mile southwest of the town center). ℭ **508/ 228-9198**. www.mmo.org. Admission to each site: $4 adults, $3 children. Museum pass (for birthplace, aquarium, science museum, and Vestal Street Observatory) $10 adults, $7 children ages 6–14. MC, V. Early June to late Aug Tues–Sat 10am–4pm; call for off-season hours.

Nantucket Life-Saving Museum 🕏🕏 *Finds*   Housed in a replica of the Nantucket Lifesaving Station (the original serves as the island's youth hostel), the museum has loads of interesting exhibits, including historic photos and newspaper clippings, as well as one of the last remaining Massachusetts Humane Society surf boats and its horse-drawn carriage.

158 Polpis Rd. ℭ **508/228-1885**. Admission $5 adults, $2 children. Mid-June to mid-Oct daily 9:30am–4pm.

Nantucket Lightship Basket Museum Nantucket Lightship Baskets were first made by bored but talented sailors aboard lightships (scrimshaw was another popular craft). The popularity of the baskets led locals to churn them out beginning around the 1950s. These are now considered rarities and when they turn up at auctions in New York, they sell for thousands of dollars. Nantucket's newest museum is dedicated to preserving the art of basket-making. One unique exhibit is a replica of the workshop of the legendary Nantucket basket-maker Jose Formoso Reyes. The baskets displayed go back to the 1850s.

49 Union St. © 508/228-1177. Admission $4 adults, $2 children. Late May to mid-Oct Tues–Sat 10am–4pm.

Whaling Museum 🦈🦈🦈 *Kids* Housed in a former spermaceti-candle factory (candles used to be made from a waxy fluid that's extracted from sperm whales), this museum is a must-visit; if not for the awe-inspiring skeleton of a 43-foot finback whale (stranded in the 1960s), then for the exceptional collections of scrimshaw and nautical art (check out the action painting, *Ship Spermo of Nantucket in a Heavy Thunder-Squall on the Coast of California 1876*, executed by a captain who survived the storm). A wall-size map depicts the round-the-world meanderings of the *Alpha*, accompanied by related journal entries. Admission includes daily lectures on the brief and colorful history of the industry, such as the beachside "whalebecue" feasts that natives and settlers once enjoyed. Pursued to its logical conclusion, this booming business unfortunately led to the near-extinction of some extraordinary species, but that story must await its own museum; this one is full of the glories of the hunt. Don't miss the gift shop on the way out.

The Whaling Museum is scheduled to reopen in the spring of 2005 after a major renovation. Visitors can see some of the Whaling Museum exhibits at the Friends Meeting House at 7 Fair St., an 1838 former Quaker school, during the renovations. Call the Nantucket Historical Association (© **508/228-1985**) for updates.

13 Broad St. (in the center of town). © **508/228-1894**. www.nha.org. Admission $10 adults, $6 children 5–14. Admission is also included in the Nantucket Historical Association's History Ticket ($15 adults, $8 children, $35 families). AE, MC, V. Apr–Nov Mon–Sat 10am–5pm, Sun noon–5pm. Closed Dec–Mar.

3 Organized Tours

Christina 🦈🦈 *Value* Built in 1926, the *Christina* is a classic solid mahogany cat boat. The boat makes six 1½-hour trips daily in season, and the sunset trips tend to sell out a day or two in advance.

Price-wise, a sail around the harbor on the *Christina* is probably the best entertainment bargain on Nantucket. Bring your own drinks and picnic supplies.

Slip 1016, Straight Wharf. ✆ **508/325-4000.** Day sails $25 per person; sunset sails $35 per person. Reservations recommended. Closed Nov–Apr.

Coskata-Coatue Wildlife Refuge Natural History Tour 🐾🐾🐾 *Kids*

The Trustees of Reservations, a private statewide conservation organization that oversees the bulk of the Coskata-Coatue Wildlife Refuge, offers 3-hour naturalist-guided tours. The trip is over sand dunes via Ford Expedition out to the **Great Point Lighthouse,** a partly solar-powered replica of the 1818 original. Those interested can also tour the inside of the light. During the trip through this rare habitat, you may spot snowy egrets, ospreys, terns, and oystercatchers. Call to make a reservation and meet the group at the Wauwinet Inn parking lot.

✆ **508/228-6799.** www.thetrustees.org. $30 adults, $15 children 15 and under. Call for reservations. Mid-May to mid-Oct daily 9:30am and 1:30pm. Closed mid-Oct to mid-May.

Endeavor Sailing Excursions 🐾🐾

The Endeavor is a spirited 31-foot replica Friendship sloop, ideal for jaunts across the harbor into Nantucket Sound. Skipper James Genthner will gladly drop you off for a bit of sunbathing or beachcombing.

Slip 15, Straight Wharf. ✆ **508/228-5585.** www.endeavorsailing.com. Rates are $25–$35 for a 1½-hr. sail (highest rates are July–Aug); reservations recommended. Closed Nov–Apr.

Gail's Tours 🐾🐾 *Value*

If you want to get some dirt on the island's colorful residents, Gail Nickerson Johnson—a seventh-generation native whose mother started a tour business back in the 1940s—has the inside track, and the charm, to keep a captive van-load rapt throughout a 1½-hour circuit of Island highlights, including lots of celebrity info.

Departs from the Nantucket Visitor Services & Information Bureau at 25 Federal St., and from pre-arranged pickup sites. ✆ **508/257-6557.** Reservations required. Rates $13 adults, free for children 3 and under. July–Aug departures at 10am, 1pm, and 3pm; call for off-season hours.

Nantucket Harbor Cruises 🐾🐾 *Kids*

The *Anna W. II,* a lobster-boat-turned-pleasure-barge, offers lobstering demos in summer (passengers sometimes get to take home the proceeds). Captain Bruce Cowan also takes groups out just to view the lovely shoreline. There's also the Marine Life Discovery Cruise, a 1½-hour trip that costs $25 per person. In season, a 1-hour ice-cream cruise leaves at 1:30 and 3:30pm daily and costs $15 per person. Sunset cruises take 1¼ hours and cost $25 per person.

Slip 11, Straight Wharf. ℂ 508/228-1444. Rates $25 adults, $20 for children 4–12; call for reservations. MC, V. Closed mid-Oct to June.

Nantucket Historical Association Guided Walking Tours ⌀
Stroll along downtown's cobblestone streets on this Historical Society tour that spotlights the history and architecture of Nantucket. The tours are led by Nantucket Historical Society docents trained in Nantucket history.

Sign up for tour at the Whaling Museum. ℂ 508/228-1894. www.nha.org. Admission included with Historical Association's History Ticket ($15 adults, $8 children, $35 families). AE, MC, V. Apr–Nov Mon–Sat 10:15am and 2:15pm. Closed Dec–Mar.

4 Kid Stuff

The **Nantucket Park and Recreation Commission** (ℂ 508/228-7213) organizes various free and low-cost activities for kids, like tennis clinics, a concert series, and tie-dye workshops (bring-your-own-T-shirt). The **Artists' Association of Nantucket** (ℂ 508/325-5251) sponsors a variety of classes for children in different media, and the **Nantucket Island School of Design and the Arts** (ℂ 508/228-9248) offers all sorts of summer courses. The **Nantucket Atheneum** (ℂ 508/228-1110) holds readings in its spiffy new children's wing, and the **Nantucket Historical Association** (ℂ 508/228-1894) sponsors **Living History for Children,** 2-hour adventures for ages 6 to 10, which include grinding flour at the Old Mill, baking bread at the Jethro Coffin House, and trying your hand at knots and sailors' valentines. The cost is $25.

The **Actor's Theatre of Nantucket** at the Methodist Church, 2 Centre St. (ℂ 508/228-6325), performs theater for children, by children, from late July to mid-August, Tuesday to Saturday at 5pm; tickets are $10. **Nobadeer Minigolf,** at 12 Nobadeer Farm Rd., near the airport (ℂ 508/228-8977), offers 18 fancily landscaped holes laced with lagoons; there's a great little Mexican restaurant, **Patio J,** on the premises. Little kids may like to get their hands on (and into) the touch tanks at the modest little **Maria Mitchell Aquarium** at 28 Washington St. (ℂ 508/228-5387), which overlooks the harbor from whence the creatures came; the cost is only $1. It's open June through September, Tuesday to Saturday from 10am to 4pm. For a real seafaring adventure, consider embarking on a treasure hunt aboard *The Endeavor* (ℂ 508/228-5585).

Fun Fact A Peachy Idea

It was just over 13 years ago, on a cold December night on Nantucket, that two college buddies concocted a sweet peach drink in a blender. Nowadays, the hip and popular juices of Nantucket Nectars are available coast to coast, and the privately held company racked up sales of $70 million last year.

Juice Guys Tom First and Tom Scott, both in their 30s, are the photogenic chief operating officer and chief executive officer, respectively, of a thriving business they started on the island. They make frequent trips year-round to Nantucket and sponsor many local events. But these poster boys of entrepreneurship are quick to point out that success was neither easy nor immediate.

Their roots on Nantucket go back to childhood; both Toms vacationed on the island with their families. They first met at Brown University and continued to spend summers on the island working and playing. In the summer of 1989, while still in college, they started a harbor delivery service called Allserve, which catered to wealthy yacht owners.

With their Allserve business up and running, the two moved to Nantucket after college. Their juice epiphany occurred soon after. The two Toms were at a party and Tom First was fooling around with a blender, trying to duplicate a peach drink he had enjoyed in Spain. When their friends raved about the new drink, Tom and Tom christened it "Peach Nectar" and started selling it at Allserve. Soon local businesses were selling the hand-bottled drinks. Sales grew from 8,000 cases the first year to 20,000 the second year.

The Toms knew they were onto something, and invested their savings in the start-up, researched the juice business, and studied mass production. The business really picked up

5 Shopping

Nantucket shopping is so phenomenal you'll be tempted to rent a U-Haul. It's as if all the best big-city buyers, from Bendel's to Brooks Brothers, got together and gathered up their favorite stuff. True, some tourist dreck has managed to drift in, but most of what you'll find for sale is as high in quality as it is in price—everything from

around 1993, when the Toms persuaded an investor they had met through their yacht delivery business—rent-a-car magnate Michael Egan, now pictured in the background of the bottles' label—to provide much-needed capital. That $50,000 allowed them to expand, and revenues soon broke the $1 million mark.

Today, Ocean Spray, a juice company owned by a cooperative of growers, owns an undisclosed portion of Nantucket Nectars, which expects sales of $80 million next year. But Tom and Tom are still running the show with their trademark humor and charisma.

A few Juice Guy tidbits:

Deciphering the label: That's Tom and Tom in their Allserve boat with their devoted dogs. Becky is part lab, part springer spaniel, and part shortstop, according to owner Tom Scott. Pete, the black dog, is Tom First's Portuguese water dog.

Visitors to Nantucket hoping to live out the complete Juice Guy experience should make a beeline to **Juice Guys Juice Bar,** 4 Easy St. (② 508/228-4464), where high-tech blenders mix potent combinations of fresh juice with vitamins, sorbet, yogurt, nuts, fruit, and holistic enhancers. Open 9am to 5pm, spring through Christmas.

If you're hoping to spot the Juice Guys, try one of their hangouts, such as the bar at **The Boarding House,** 12 Federal St. (② 508/228-9622), or **Straight Wharf,** Straight Wharf (② 508/228-4499), where they were employed one summer shucking scallops. The Juice Guys also participate in local athletic competitions, such as the annual Ironman triathlon in early summer. Juice Guy pilgrims can poke their heads into **Allserve,** Straight Wharf (② 508/228-8170), the wharf-side general store where it all started.

$6 boxes of chocolate-covered dried cranberries to $900 cashmere sweaters.

ANTIQUES/COLLECTIBLES Most tourists aren't looking to return home with a new living-room set, but **Lynda Willauer Antiques,** at 2 India St., between Federal and Centre streets (② 508/228-3631), has such an exquisite selection of American,

French, and English furniture that it's worth stopping by just to gawk. All pieces are painstakingly tagged as to provenance and state of repair, and most are quite pricey. The shop also stocks paintings, Chinese export porcelain, Staffordshire china, samplers, ship wool works, majolica, and brass and tortoise-shell boxes.

An island fixture since 1971, **Tonkin of Nantucket,** 33 Main St. (© 508/228-9697), specializes in English and French antiques. Antiques hounds will be in heaven browsing through the 9,000 square feet of showrooms, featuring such finery as silver, china, marine paintings, ship models, fireplace equipment, Quimper, and majolica.

ART & CRAFTS   The Artists' Association of Nantucket has the widest selection of work by locals, and the gallery at 19 Washington St. (© 508/228-0294; www.nantucketarts.org) is impressive. Open daily in spring from noon to 5pm and daily in summer 10am to 6pm.

The Golden Basket, 44 Main St. (© 877/453-2758 or 508/228-4344; www.thegoldenbasket.com), also known as **The Golden Nugget** at Straight Wharf (© 508/228-1019), introduced widely copied, miniaturized jewelry versions of Nantucket's trademark lightship baskets. Artisan Glenaan Elliott Robbins' rendition is still the finest. The baskets, complete with gold penny, represent a small portion of the inventory, all of which is exquisite.

The celebrated sculptor **David L. Hostetler** exhibits his work at his gallery on Old South Wharf, 2 Old South Wharf (© 508/228-5152). Private viewing appointments are also available in his large showroom. His work in various media appears as spiritual icons expressed in the female form.

Exquisite art glass pieces, as well as ceramics, jewelry, and basketry, can be found at **Dane Gallery,** 28 Centre St. (© 508/228-7779), where owners Robert and Jayne Dane show top-quality work. You'll be amazed at the colors and shapes of the glassware.

You'll definitely want to poke your head into **Sailor's Valentine** in the Macy Warehouse on lower Main Street (© 508/228-2011), which houses an international collection of contemporary fine art, sculpture, folk art, and "outsider art." There are also new versions of the namesake craft, a boxed design of colorful shells, which 19th-century sailors used to bring back from the Caribbean for their sweethearts at home.

BOOKS   At **Mitchell's Book Corner,** 54 Main St. (© 508/228-1080), Mimi Beman handpicks her stock, with an astute sampling of general-interest books and an entire room dedicated to regional and maritime titles.

Nantucket Bookworks, 25 Broad St. (© **508/228-4000**), is a charming bookstore, with a central location and strong customer service.

COSMETICS   Bella, 44 Centre St. (© **508/228-7642**), stocks handmade soaps from Nantucket Soap Company and all manner of luxurious lotions and bath products. **Crush** at 4 E. Chestnut St. (© **508/228-0170**) is a cosmetic shop where you can get a personalized make-over or just shop for top-of-the-line cosmetics by Paula Dorf, Sue Devitt Studio, Flygirl, and others.

Resembling an old-fashioned pharmacy, **The Fragrance Bar,** 5 Centre St. (© **800/223-8660** or 508/325-4740), is run by a colorful fellow who goes by the solo sobriquet of Harpo. A self-professed "nose," he has assembled some 400 essential oils with which he can duplicate designer scents or customize blends. Uncut by alcohol (unlike their commercial counterparts), these perfumes linger on the skin and do not cause associated problems such as allergies and headaches. Harpo won't discuss his clientele, but admits to creating a custom scent for a certain recording megastar who also goes by a single name, starting with an "M."

FASHION   Martha's Vineyard may have spawned "Black Dog" fever, but this island boasts the inimitable "Nantucket reds"— cotton clothing that starts out tomato-red and washes out to salmon-pink. The fashion originated at **Murray's Toggery Shop,** 62 Main St. (© **800/368-2134** or 508/228-0437; www.nantucketreds.com). Legend has it that the original duds were colored with an inferior dye that washed out almost immediately, but customers so liked the thick cottons and instant aged look that the proprietor was forced to search high and low for more of the same fabric. Roland Hussey Macy, founder of Macy's, got his start here in the 1830s—his shop shows no signs of fading (no pun intended)—although today's management also manages to keep up with current trends.

Preppy patterns and bright colors are back! You'll find **Lilly Pulitzer**'s latest, including sensational minidresses, at 5 S. Water St. (© **508/228-0569**).

Beautiful People, 13 Centre St., (© **508/228-2001**), a lovely high-ceilinged shop, has the largest selection of hand-knit sweaters made on Nantucket plus a full line of women's clothing.

Ralph Lauren's new store at 16 Main St. (© **508/228-9451**) scandalized Nantucketers when it first opened last year, but now everyone is used to it. The store is stocked with high-end resort wear, featuring very bright—or what one Nantucketer called "intense"—colors.

Zero Main, at 0 Main St. (© **508/228-4401**), has a limited but fine selection of elegant yet casual women's clothes, shoes, and accessories.

GIFTS/HOME DECOR   A casual counterpart to its Madison Avenue boutique, **Erica Wilson Needle Works,** 25–27 Main St. (© **508/228-9881**), features the designs of its namesake, an Islander since 1958 and author of more than 2 dozen books on needlepoint. The shop offers hands-on guidance for hundreds of grateful adepts, as well as kits and handiwork of other noteworthy designers.

The also eponymous **Claire Murray,** 11 S. Water St. (© **508/228-1913**), is famous for elaborate hand-hooked rugs. As a New York transplant running a Nantucket B&B in the late 1970s, Murray took up the traditional art of hooking rugs to see her through the slow season. Her retail company now grosses millions a year and is so busy creating new collections that hundreds of "hookers" (probably an old profession, but not the oldest) from around the world work for her. Do-it-yourself kits ($100–$500) are sold here for about two-thirds the price of finished rugs and come with free lessons.

Although certain influences are evident (from Queen Anne to Shaker), the hand-fashioned furniture at **Stephen Swift,** 34 Main St. (© **508/228-0255**), is far too individualized to pass as reproduction. Such is its classicism, though, that Swift's work would blend into the most traditional of homes, or just as easily adapt to a modern setting. Among his signature pieces are wavy-backed Windsor chairs and benches (as sturdy as the original but more comfortable), and delicate, pared-down four-poster beds.

JEWELRY   **Diana Kim England, Goldsmiths** (© **508/228-3766**) is a team of six goldsmiths that have over 70 years of combined experience in making jewelry. You'll find gold baskets and pearls, as well as unique custom pieces.

NEWSSTAND   **The Hub,** 31 Main St. (© **508/325-0200**), offers a good selection of newspapers, magazines, and books, as well as greeting cards by local artists and gift wrap.

PET STORES   **Sandy Paws,** 20 Centre St. (© **508/228-0708**), is a new pet-gift store offering biscuits, bowls, and toys, as well as artwork and calendars featuring dogs.

Distinctly Nantucket

Cisco Brewers, on 5 Bartlett Farm Rd. ((C) **800/324-5550** or 508/325-5929; www.ciscobrewers.com), is Nantucket's only brewery and a favorite with locals. The beer here is produced year-round in small batches. Stop by to pick up some of the fresh stuff on your way out for picnic goodies at Bartlett's Farm further down the road. Call for hours.

SEAFOOD   Sayle's Seafood, Washington Street Extension ((C) 508/228-4599), sells fresh seafood from Nantucket waters and has a new menu of takeout seafood platters. This is a great place to get a huge, steaming plate of fried clams to go.

TOYS   The Toy Boat, Straight Wharf #41 ((C) **508/228-4552**), is keen on creative and educational toys. In addition to the top commercial lines, owner Loren Brock stocks lots of locally crafted, hand-carved playthings, such as "rainbow fleet" sailboats, part of the Harbor Series that includes docks, lighthouses, boats, and everything your child needs to create his or her own Nantucket Harbor. There are also stackable lighthouse puzzles replicating Nantucket's beams.

6 Nantucket After Dark

The Nantucket Arts Alliance ((C) **800/228-8118** or 508/228-8118) operates Box Office Nantucket, offering tickets for all sorts of cultural events around town. They operate out of the Macy Warehouse on Straight Wharf in season, daily from 10am to 4pm.

Nantucket usually has an attractive crowd of barhoppers making the scene around town. The best part is that everything is within walking distance, so you don't have to worry about driving back to your inn. You'll find good singles scenes at **The Boarding House, 21 Federal,** or **The Club Car.** Live music comes in many guises on Nantucket, and a number of good itinerant performers play at different venues. For instance, the talented P. J. Moody sings all your favorite James Taylor, Cat Stevens, and Van Morrison tunes; he usually plays at **Jared Coffin House's Tap Room** or **Schooner's.** Meanwhile, it may be Reggae Night at **The Chicken Box,** when the median age of this rocking venue rises by a decade or two.

PUBS, BARS, DANCE CLUBS & LIVE MUSIC

If body boarding, bike riding, and windsurfing coupled with sun and salt air haven't taken their toll, several nightspots offer live music and dancing, while others cater to those content with toe tapping. The Grey Lady can kick up her heels after dark.

A car or taxi ride is necessary to visit the two other large, live-band venues, The Muse and The Chicken Box. **The Muse,** 44 Atlantic Ave., about 1½ miles south of the town center (✆ **508/228-6873**), is where you'll find college-age kids and the island's summer employees wolfing pizza and subs, downing beer and exotic shots, and dancing to local and regional rock bands plus a scattering of name acts (George Clinton, Burning Spear, 10,000 Maniacs, and Maceo Parker are among recent headliners). The cover charge varies from $3 to the steep $50 required to lure George Clinton and his P-Funk All-Stars over from the mainland. Pool tables round out this 20-year-old club, which is open 365 days a year—there's a drastic upward shift in its demographics during the winter.

Pipe-smoking owner "Cap'n Seaweed" will tell you that **The Chicken Box,** 12 Dave St. (✆ **508/228-9717**), has been jumping since the mid-1970s, and if you want to work up a sweat on the dance floor, the Box is a good bet most any night. Beer, shots, mixed drinks, and pool tables draw a crowd slightly older than Muse's; the cover charge runs from $4 to $15, and ska bands, a staple of what might be called New England Beach Music, are a favorite, along with reggae, funk, and rock. NRBQ and The Dirty Dozen Brass band have both dropped anchor here.

At the end of the day (when else?), it comes down to which of these clubs has booked the best band on a given night. Check *The Inquirer and Mirror*'s "Music Beat" column to find out who is playing where.

You can find live jazz Wednesday to Saturday at the **Tap Room,** downstairs at the Jared Coffin House, 29 Broad St. (✆ **508/228-2400**). Listen for folk, blues, and low-key acoustic performers down the street at **The Brotherhood of Thieves,** 23 Broad St. (no phone); closed February. **The Beach Club at Cap'n Tobey's** at 20 Straight Wharf (✆ **508/228-0836**) is a dance club with theme nights such as karaoke, salsa night, and '80s night. None of these three venues charges a cover.

Piano bars are numerous, including **The Club Car** ⟨, 1 Main St. (✆ **508/228-1101**), **The Ropewalk,** 1 Straight Wharf (✆ **508/228-8886**), **The Regatta,** at the White Elephant, Easton and

Willard streets (℃ **508/228-5500;** closed Oct–Apr), and **The Summer House,** 17 Ocean Ave., Siasconset (℃ **508/228-9976**). The latter, a fine restaurant on the east end of the island, fills whatever need there is on Nantucket for the Manhattan martini-and-cigar-bar experience, complete with fabulous people. The Ropewalk is where the rich and famous yachting crowd meets for drinks, and it's a major social scene in July and August. In addition, it's one of the only outdoor raw bars on the island.

THEATER

Theatre Workshop of Nantucket   This venerable company (℃ **508/228-4305;** www.theatreworkshop.com) puts on plays—including children's theater in the spring, summer, and fall—and offers acting classes year-round. The theater is based in the Methodist Church on Centre Street, just steps from the intersection with Main Street. 2 Centre St. ℃ **508/228-6325.** Tickets $20.

MOVIES

Nantucket has two first-run movie theaters: **Dreamland Theatre,** 19 S. Water St. (℃ **508/228-5356**), and **Gaslight Theatre,** 1 N. Union St. (℃ **508/228-4435**). The **Siasconset Casino,** 10 New St., Siasconset (℃ **508/257-6661**), also shows films in season.

NANTUCKET LITERATI

Continuing a 160-year tradition, the **Nantucket Atheneum,** 1 India St. (℃ **508/228-1110;** www.nantucketatheneum.org), offers free readings and lectures for general edification year-round, with such local literati as David Halberstam, Frank Conroy, and Nathaniel Philbrick filling in for the likes of Henry David Thoreau and Herman Melville. The summer events are often followed by a charming garden reception. Hours are Monday, Wednesday, Friday, and Saturday 9:30am to 5pm, Tuesday and Thursday 9:30am to 8pm. Closed Sunday year-round and Monday in winter.

5

Settling into
Martha's Vineyard

Martha's Vineyard is a picturesque New England island with captain's houses and lighthouses, white picket fences and ice-cream shops, an authentic fishing village and a Native American community, and miles of pristine beaches and rolling farmland. Unfortunately, it has been discovered, in a big way. If you can survive the hassles of getting to the island, and the crowds and traffic once you arrive, you may just have the perfect vacation. Better yet, visit the island in the off season, during May or October, when the weather is often mild and the crowds have cleared out.

When the former First Family, the Clintons, chose to vacation on the island several years in a row, it only served to increase the worldwide fascination with this popular place. In fact, the island is loaded with celebrities, but you are unlikely to see them, as they prefer private house parties. But don't come to this island for the celebrities; it's considered impolite to gawk, and, like jaded New Yorkers, the locals barely seem to notice the stars in their midst.

Instead, visit the Vineyard to bicycle the shaded paths hugging the coastline. Admire the regal sea captain's houses in Edgartown, and stop by the Edgartown Scrimshaw Gallery for a memento of the sea. Stroll down Circuit Avenue in Oak Bluffs with a Mad Martha's ice-cream cone and then ride the Flying Horses Carousel, said to be the oldest working carousel in the country. Don't miss the cheerful "gingerbread" cottages behind Circuit Avenue, where the echoes of 19th-century revival meetings still ring out from the imposing tabernacle. Marvel at the red-clay cliffs of Gay Head, now known as Aquinnah, a national historic landmark and home to the Wampanoag Tribe. Travel the country roads of West Tisbury and Chilmark, stopping at Allen Farm for sweaters made from the wool of their flock of over 200 sheep. Buy a lobster roll in the fishing village of Menemsha.

Unlike much of New England, Martha's Vineyard has long been a melting pot in which locals, homeowners, and summer people coexist in an almost effortless comfort, united in their disapproval of traffic, their criticism of the Steamship Authority, and their protective attitude toward the island. The roots of Martha's Vineyard's diversity go back more than 100 years. In the late 19th century, Oak Bluffs, with its religious roots, was one of the first spots where African Americans of means went on vacation. Today, this community includes such notable celebrities as film director Spike Lee and Washington power broker Vernon Jordan. In the tiny town of Aquinnah, the Wampanoags are the only Native American tribe in the region to have official status in Washington, D.C. Twelfth-generation Vineyarders farm the land in Chilmark and rub shoulders at Cronig's Market with posh Yankees from Edgartown.

There's always a lot of "hurry up and wait" involved in ferry travel, so allowing yourself just a weekend on the Vineyard may be less than you need. If you're traveling from New York, take an extra day off, allowing a minimum of 3 days for this trip. Four days will feel more comfortable. From Boston, a couple days is fine (the drive from Boston to Woods Hole takes 1½ hr. with no traffic), but beware of summer weekend bottlenecks (never aim for the last ferry). You really don't need to bring a car to get around this small island, but if you absolutely have to be accompanied by four wheels, you'll need a car reservation for the ferry (see "Getting Around," below, for details).

Savor the 45-minute ferry ride to and from this pastoral place. The Vineyard's pace is decidedly laid-back, and your biggest chore should be to try to blend in with the prevalent, ultra-cool attitude.

Fun Fact **Going Native on Martha's Vineyard**

Down-island: If you must buy a Black Dog T-shirt, wait until you get home to wear it. Don't loiter at the Charlotte Inn. Have cocktails on the porch of the Harborview Hotel. In Oak Bluffs, don't ask when Illumination Night is (it's a secret). Experience Edgartown on a snowy winter weekend or in spring when the lilacs are in bloom.

Up-island: When in doubt, don't wear shoes. Sail a boat to a remote beach for a picnic. Don't view the rolling farmlands from a tour bus. By all means, bike. Canoe. Rent a cottage for a week or two. Don't be a day-tripper.

1 Martha's Vineyard Orientation

For information on getting to Martha's Vineyard, see "Getting There," in chapter 2.

ARRIVING

Upon arrival, you'll find taxis at all ferry terminals and at the airport, and there are permanent taxi stands in Oak Bluffs (at the Flying Horses Carousel) and Edgartown (next to the Town Wharf). Most taxi outfits operate cars as well as vans for larger groups and travelers with bikes. Cab companies on the island include **Adam Cab** (© 800/281-4462 or 508/693-3332), **Accurate Cab** (© 888/557-9798 or 508/627-9798; the only all-night service); **All Island Taxi** (© 800/693-TAXI or 508/693-2929); **Atlantic Taxi** (© 508/693-7110); **Martha's Vineyard Taxi** (© 508/693-9611 or 508/693-8660); **Mario's Taxi** (© 508/693-8399); and **Marlene's Taxi** (© 508/693-0037). Rates from town to town in summer are generally flat fees based on where you're headed and the number of passengers on board. A trip from Vineyard Haven to Edgartown would probably cost around $15 for two people. Late-night revelers should keep in mind that rates are double from midnight until 7am.

VISITOR INFORMATION

Contact the **Martha's Vineyard Chamber of Commerce** at Beach Road, Vineyard Haven, MA 02568 (© **508/693-0085;** fax 508/693-7589; www.mvy.com). Their office is 2 blocks up from the ferry terminal in Vineyard Haven and is open Monday to Friday from 9am to 5pm year-round plus weekends in season. There are also information booths at the ferry terminal in Vineyard Haven, across from the Flying Horses Carousel in Oak Bluffs, and on Church Street in Edgartown. The Edgartown info booth is particularly convenient. It offers a free phone to call taxis, as well as an ATM, post office, and sundry store. You'll want to poke your head into these offices to pick up free maps, tourist handbooks, and flyers on tours and events, or to get answers to any questions you may have. Most inns also have tourist handbooks and maps available for guests.

Always check the two local newspapers, the *Vineyard Gazette* (www.mvgazette.com) and the *Martha's Vineyard Times* (www.mvtimes.com), for information on current events.

In case of an emergency, call © **911** and/or head for the **Martha's Vineyard Hospital,** Linton Lane, Oak Bluffs (© **508/693-0410**), which has a 24-hour emergency room.

NEIGHBORHOODS IN BRIEF: DOWN-ISLAND, UP-ISLAND

The six towns on Martha's Vineyard have distinct identities, but they can be divided into "down-island," referring to Vineyard Haven (officially called Tisbury), Edgartown, and Oak Bluffs; and "up-island," made up of West Tisbury, Chilmark, and Aquinnah.

Vineyard Haven, where the majority of ferry passengers disembark, tends to be a quieter community than the other down-island towns of Edgartown and Oak Bluffs, perhaps because of its "dry" status. Nevertheless, several fine restaurants, as well as some wonderful shops and galleries, are along Main Street. The town's Vineyard Playhouse hosts a full season of plays every summer. Vineyard Haven has several inns within walking distance of the center of town, as well as a small public beach on the harbor.

To many visitors, prim and proper **Edgartown** is Martha's Vineyard. It's certainly the Vineyard's fanciest community, where regal historic captain's houses are lined up behind picket fences. Most of the island's B&Bs and inns are in Edgartown, as well as many fine restaurants, bars, shops and galleries. Katama Beach is a short bike ride away, and State Beach lies between Edgartown and Oak Bluffs. You can also take a short ferry to the island of Chappaquiddick from Oak Bluffs.

Oak Bluffs feels like a more casual community than Edgartown: It has a touch of honky-tonk. This is where you find the famous gingerbread houses, which are elaborately decorated Carpenter Gothic summer cottages originally built in the late 19th century. The cottages surround a huge wrought-iron tabernacle, which hosts live concerts as well as church services in the summer. The Flying Horses Carousel nearby is one of the oldest in the country. Most of the island's bars, as well as live music, are in Oak Bluffs. Several fine restaurants are on Circuit Avenue, which is Oak Bluffs' main street. More casual restaurants, as well as shops, are along the harbor. Oak Bluffs has a range of lodging accommodations, from historic waterfront B&Bs to inexpensive motels and lodging houses.

West Tisbury is a rural community in the center of the island. The center of the community is Alley's General Store, which operates much the same as it must have 100 years ago. The town has several fine art galleries, and the area features miles of beautiful countryside with rolling farmland and forests.

Chilmark, a rural community next to West Tisbury, is mainly residential, though it contains the charming fishing village of Menemsha on the coast. Menemsha, with its fishing boats lined up along the pier, as well as a small selection of shops and restaurants, is worth a half-day trip.

Aquinnah, formerly known as Gay Head, is the headquarters for the Wampanoag Indian Tribe. Here you'll find beautiful coastal scenery and beaches, as well as the famous red-clay cliffs.

GETTING AROUND

The down-island towns of Vineyard Haven, Oak Bluffs, and Edgartown are fairly compact, and if your inn is located in the heart of one of these small towns, you'll be within walking distance of shopping, beaches, and attractions in town. Frequent shuttle buses can whisk you to the other down-island towns and beaches in 5 to 15 minutes. To explore the up-island towns, you'll need to bike; it's possible to tour the entire island—60 some-odd miles—in a day. In season, you can also take the shuttle bus up-island. Otherwise, you have to take a cab.

BY BICYCLE & MOPED   You shouldn't leave without exploring the Vineyard on two wheels, even if only for a couple of hours. There's a little of everything for cyclists, from paved paths to hilly country roads (see "Beaches & Recreational Pursuits," in chapter 6, for details on where to ride), and you don't have to be an expert rider to enjoy yourself. Plus, biking is a relatively hassle-free way to get around the island.

Mopeds are also a way to navigate Vineyard roads, but remember that some roads tend to be narrow and rough—the number of accidents involving mopeds seems to rise every year, and many islanders are opposed to these vehicles. The renting of mopeds is banned in Edgartown. You need a driver's license to rent a moped. If you rent a moped, be aware that they are considered quite dangerous on the island's busy, narrow, winding, and sandy roads.

Bike-, scooter-, and moped-rental shops are clustered throughout all three down-island towns. Bike rentals cost about $15 to $30 a day (the higher prices are for suspension mountain bikes), scooters and mopeds $30 to $80. In Vineyard Haven, try **Strictly Bikes,** Union Street (© 508/693-0782); **Martha's Bike Rentals,** Lagoon Pond Road (© 508/693-6593); or **Adventure/Thrifty Rentals,** Beach Road (© 508/693-1959), which rents mopeds only. In Oak Bluffs, there's **Anderson's,** Circuit Avenue Extension (© 508/693-9346), which rents bikes only; **DeBettencourt's Bike Shop,** 31 Circuit Ave. Extension (© 508/693-0011); **Ride-On Mopeds,** Circuit Avenue Extension (© 508/693-2076); **Sun 'n' Fun,** Lake Avenue (© 508/693-5457); and **Vineyard Bike & Moped,** Oak

Bluffs Avenue (© 508/693-4498). In Edgartown, you'll find **R. W. Cutler Bike,** 1 Main St. (© 508/627-4052); **Edgartown Bicycles,** 190 Upper Main St. (© 508/627-9008); and **Wheel Happy,** 204 Upper Main St. and 8 S. Water St. (© 508/627-5928), which rents bikes only.

BY CAR & JEEP   If you're coming to the Vineyard for a few days and you're going to stick to the down-island towns, I think it's best to leave your car at home, since traffic and parking on the island can be brutal in summer. Also, it's easy to take the shuttle buses (see below) from town to town, or simply bike your way around. If you're staying for a longer period of time or you want to do some exploring up-island, you should bring your car or rent one on the island—my favorite way to tour the Vineyard is by Jeep. Keep in mind that car-rental rates can soar during peak season, and gas is also much more expensive on the island. Off-road driving on the beaches is a major topic of debate on the Vineyard, and the most popular spots may be closed for nesting piping plovers at the height of the season. If you plan to do some off-road exploration, check with the Chamber of Commerce to see if the trails are open to vehicles before you rent. To drive off-road at Cape Pogue or Cape Wasque on Chappaquiddick, you'll need to purchase a permit from the **Trustees of Reservations** (© **508/627-7260**); the cost is $70 to $110.

National car-rental chains are at the airport and in Vineyard Haven and Oak Bluffs. Local agencies also operate out of all three port-towns, and many of them also rent Jeeps, mopeds, and bikes. The national chains include **Budget** (© 800/527-0700 or 508/693-1911), **Hertz** (© 800/654-3131), and **Thrifty** (© 800/874-4389).

In Vineyard Haven, you'll find **Adventure Rentals,** Beach Road (© 508/693-1959), where a Jeep will run you about $130 per day in season; **Atlantic/Consumer Car Rental,** 15 Beach Rd. (© 508/693-0480), which rents small cars for about $60 per day; and **Holmes Hole Car Rentals,** Water Street (© 508/693-8838), where a four-wheel-drive vehicle rents for about $120 per day in season. In Edgartown, try **AAA Island Rentals,** 141 Main St. (© 508/627-6800; also at Five Corners in Vineyard Haven (© 508/696-5300). Another recommendable Island company that operates out of the airport is **All Island Rent-a-Car** (© 508/693-6868).

BY SHUTTLE BUS & TROLLEY   In season, shuttle buses run often enough to make them a practical means of getting around. The **Martha's Vineyard Transit Authority** (© **508/693-9440;**

www.vineyardtransit.com) provides the cheapest, quickest, and easiest way to get around the island during the busy summer season and in the off season too. Connecting Vineyard Haven (near the ferry terminal), Oak Bluffs (near the Civil War statue in Ocean Park), and Edgartown (Church St., near the Old Whaling Church), the transit authority buses cost $2 to $4 per trip, depending on distance. The price is $1 per town. So, if you are going from Vineyard Haven to Oak Bluffs, the price is $2. If you are going from Vineyard Haven past Oak Bluffs to Edgartown, that trip will cost $3. A 1-day pass with unlimited trips is $6, a 3-day pass is $15, and a 7-day pass is $25. Seniors over 70 years old pay half-price and children under 6 years old ride free.

From early May to early October, buses run from 5:30am to 1am every half-hour or hour. Hours are reduced in spring, fall, and winter. From late June through August, buses go out to Aquinnah (via the airport, West Tisbury, and Chilmark), leaving every couple of hours from down-island towns and looping about every hour through up-island towns. The Edgartown Downtown Shuttle and the South Beach buses circle throughout town or out to South Beach every 30 minutes in season. They also stop at the free parking lots just north of the town center—this is a great way to avoid circling the streets in search of a vacant spot on busy weekends.

THE CHAPPAQUIDDICK FERRY The **On-Time ferry** (© 508/627-9427) runs the 5-minute trip from Memorial Wharf on Dock Street in Edgartown to Chappaquiddick Island from June to mid-October, every 5 minutes from 7am to midnight. Passengers, bikes, mopeds, dogs, and cars (three at a time) are all welcome. The one-way cost is $1 per person, $4 for one car/one driver, $2.50 for one bike/one person, and $3.50 for one moped or motorcycle/one person.

FAST FACTS: Martha's Vineyard

Area Code The telephone area code for the Vineyard is **508**. You must always dial 1 and this area code first, even if you are making a call to another Vineyard number.

Banks Automated teller machines (ATMs) are in a number of locations on Martha's Vineyard. In Edgartown, ATMs are located at the Church Street visitors center; 2 South Water St. (near the corner of Main St.); and 19 Main St. (just west of

North Water St.). In Oak Bluffs, there are ATMS on Oak Bluffs Avenue, at the Park Avenue Mall, and next to the Flying Horses. In Vineyard Haven, ATMs are at 75 Main St.; 53 Main St.; and 40 South Main St.

Emergencies Phone 🕾 **911** for fire, police, emergency, or ambulance; be prepared to give your number, address, name, and a quick report. If you get into desperate straits—if, for example, your money is stolen and you need assistance arranging to get home—contact the **Travelers Aid office** in Boston (🕾 **617/542-7286**).

Hospital In case of a medical emergency, **Martha's Vineyard Hospital,** Linton Lane, Oak Bluffs (🕾 **508/693-0410**), has a 24-hour emergency room.

Liquor Laws The legal drinking age in Massachusetts is 21. Most bars are allowed to stay open until 1am every day, with "last call" at 12:30am. Beer, wine, and liquor are sold at package stores only. On Martha's Vineyard, alcohol is only allowed to be served in the towns of Edgartown and Oak Bluffs. The other four towns, Aquinnah, Chilmark, West Tisbury, and Tisbury (Vineyard Haven) are "dry," meaning no alcohol can be served or purchased. Many restaurants in those towns allow you to bring your own alcoholic beverages to accompany your dinner. Some charge a corking fee. Call ahead to be sure.

Newspapers & Magazines Martha's Vineyard has two newspapers, the long-established *Martha's Vineyard Gazette,* and the upstart, the *Martha's Vineyard Times.* The *Gazette* is published twice a week in the summer and once a week in the off season. The *Times,* which is free, is published once a week year-round. The two newspapers have dueling editorial pages and it's fun to compare and contrast the two, especially on big island issues.

Public Restrooms The Vineyard has numerous public restrooms. In Vineyard Haven, you'll find them in the ferry terminals and in the A&P parking lot (open seasonally). In Oak Bluffs, bathrooms are next to the ferry terminal, on Kennebec Avenue, and beside the harbor next to Our Market. In Menemsha, public bathrooms are located on the pier across from the fish markets; and in Aquinnah, they are near the cliffs parking lot. In Edgartown, public bathrooms are at the Church Street Visitor Center and in Town Hall (weekdays only), as well as at Katama Beach. In West Tisbury, restrooms are in the Grange Hall next to Town Hall.

> *Smoking* On Martha's Vineyard, all restaurants and bars are smoke-free. There is also no smoking allowed in the commons areas of inns on the Vineyard. There may be some inns where certain rooms are designated for smokers, and visitors wishing to smoke should inquire when they book their rooms.
>
> *Time Zone* Martha's Vineyard is in the Eastern Time zone and goes on daylight saving time in the spring.

2 Where to Stay

When deciding where to stay on Martha's Vineyard, you'll need to consider the type of vacation you prefer. The down-island towns of Vineyard Haven, Oak Bluffs, and Edgartown provide shops, restaurants, beaches, and harbors all within walking distance, and frequent shuttles to get you all over the island. But all three can be overly crowded on busy summer weekends. Vineyard Haven is the gateway for most of the ferry traffic; Oak Bluffs is a raucous town with most of the Vineyard's bars and nightclubs; and many visitors make a beeline to Edgartown's manicured Main Street. Up-island inns provide more peace and quiet, but you'll probably need a car to get around, including going to the beach. Nevertheless, you'll find some wonderful places to stay on the Vineyard, and all of the following choices have something special to offer.

EDGARTOWN
VERY EXPENSIVE

Charlotte Inn 𝔸𝔸𝔸 Ask anyone to recommend the best inn on the island and this is the name you're most likely to hear—not just because it's the most expensive, but because it's easily the most refined. Owners Gery and Paula Conover have been tirelessly fine-tuning this cluster of 18th- and 19th-century houses (five in all, counting the Carriage House, a replica) since 1971. Linked by formal gardens, each house has a distinctive look and feel, though the predominant mode is English country, with fascinating antiques, hunting prints, and quirky decorative accents. All but one room have televisions, and some have VCRs. Bathrooms are luxurious, and some are enormous (bigger than most hotel rooms). In the elegant 1860 Main House, the common rooms double as the Edgartown Art Gallery and feature Ray Ellis's wonderful oil paintings. This is one of only two Relais & Châteaux properties on the Cape and Islands—a world-class distinction that designates excellence in hospitality. The inn's restaurant, L'étoile, is the island's best fine-dining restaurant (see "Where to Dine," later in this chapter).

27 S. Summer St. (in the center of town), Edgartown, MA 02539. *©* **508/ 627-4751.** Fax 508/627-4652. 25 units (all with tub/shower). Summer $325–$695 double; $695–$895 suite. Rates include continental breakfast; full breakfast offered for extra charge ($15). AE, MC, V. Open year-round. No children under 14. **Amenities:** Restaurant; turndown service; newspapers available at breakfast. *In room:* A/C, TV (all rooms but 1), VCR (in some), hair dryer.

Harbor View Hotel ✿ This is the Vineyard's version of a grand hotel. It has the most amenities, including outdoor pool, tennis courts, a very fine restaurant (The Coach House; see "Where to Dine," later in this chapter), and a cozy bar that serves lunch and dinner (you can ask to be served by the pool, if you like). Enjoying a drink on one of the rocking chairs on the hotel's expansive wrap-around porch has to be one of the ultimate Vineyard experiences. The view is one of the Vineyard's best, Edgartown Lighthouse, Edgartown Harbor, and across to the island of Chappaquiddick. The rooms at the Harbor View are mostly standard, but front rooms that overlook that terrific view are very expensive and some would say well worth the price. In back of the hotel, a large pool is surrounded by newer annexes, where some rooms and suites have kitchenettes. The hotel is located just far enough from "downtown" to avoid the traffic hassles, but close enough for a pleasant walk past impressive captain's houses.

131 N. Water St. (about ½ mile northwest of Main St.), Edgartown, MA 02539. *©* **800/255-6005** or 508/627-7000. Fax 508/627-8417. www.harbor-view.com. 124 units (all with tub/shower). Summer $345–$615 double; $575–$695 1-bedroom suite; $750–$775 2-bedroom suite; $925 3-bedroom suite. AE, DC, MC, V. Open year-round. **Amenities:** Restaurant; bar; heated outdoor pool; 2 tennis courts; concierge; room service (seasonal only: breakfast, lunch, and dinner); babysitting; same-day laundry service. *In room:* A/C, TV, fridge, hair dryer, iron, safe.

Hob Knob Inn ✿✿✿ Owner Maggie White has reinvented this 19th-century Gothic revival inn as an exquisite destination now vying for honors as one of the Vineyard's best places to stay. Her style is peppy/preppy, with crisp floral fabrics and striped patterns creating a clean and comfortable look. Sure, it's meticulously decorated, but nothing is overdone. All rooms are equipped with bathrobes and fine toiletries. Returning guests get little extras, such as a small box of Chilmark Chocolates. Maggie and her attentive staff will pack a splendid picnic basket or plan a charter fishing trip on Maggie's 27-foot Boston Whaler. The full farm breakfast is a

Martha's Vineyard

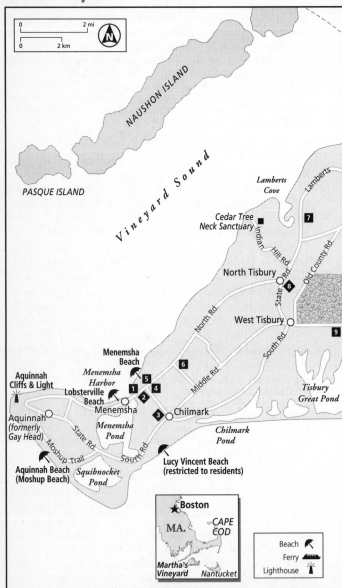

0   2 mi

0   2 km

N

NAUSHON ISLAND

PASQUE ISLAND

Vineyard Sound

Lamberts Cove

Lamberts

Cedar Tree
Neck Sanctuary

7

Indian Hill Rd

North Tisbury

State Rd

8

Old County Rd.

West Tisbury

North Rd.

9

Menemsha
Beach

6

South Rd.

Menemsha
Harbor

5

Middle Rd.

Tisbury
Great Pond

Aquinnah
Cliffs & Light

Lobsterville
Beach

1

2

4

Menemsha

3

Chilmark

Aquinnah
(formerly
Gay Head)

State Rd.

Menemsha
Pond

Chilmark
Pond

Aquinnah Beach
(Moshup Beach)

Moshup Trail

South Rd.

Squibnocket
Pond

Lucy Vincent Beach
(restricted to residents)

Boston

MA.

CAPE
COD

Martha's
Vineyard

Nantucket

Beach

Ferry

Lighthouse

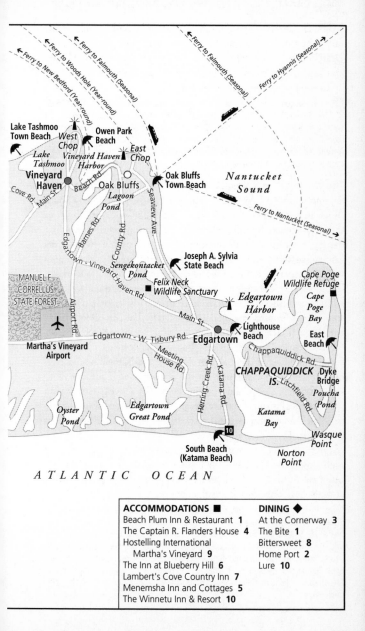

ACCOMMODATIONS ■

Beach Plum Inn & Restaurant **1**
The Captain R. Flanders House **4**
Hostelling International
   Martha's Vineyard **9**
The Inn at Blueberry Hill **6**
Lambert's Cove Country Inn **7**
Menemsha Inn and Cottages **5**
The Winnetu Inn & Resort **10**

DINING ◆

At the Cornerway **3**
The Bite **1**
Bittersweet **8**
Home Port **2**
Lure **10**

delight and is served at beautifully appointed individual tables in the sunny, brightly painted dining rooms. Bovine lovers will enjoy the agrarian theme, a decorative touch throughout the inn. The Thaxter House across the street, which is rented by the week, accommodates up to eight people in four bedrooms.

128 Main St. (on upper Main St., in the center of town), Edgartown, MA 02539. ℂ 800/696-2723 or 508/627-9510. Fax 508/627-4560. www.hobknob.com. 24 units, 4-bedroom cottage. Summer $275–$550 double; $7,500 per week for cottage. Rates include full breakfast and afternoon tea. AE, MC, V. Open year-round. **Amenities:** Exercise room; rental bikes ($20 per day); limited room service; massage (extra charge). *In room:* A/C, TV, hair dryer.

The Winnetu Inn & Resort ☆☆☆ *Kids* This is the island's newest lodging option, a large luxury hotel on 11 acres overlooking South Beach in Katama. Guests can walk down a 250-yard path to get to the private beach. A 3-mile bike path links the inn to Edgartown, but the inn also runs a shuttle service that can pick up inn guests at the Edgartown ferry. Most rooms are two- and three-bedroom suites with kitchenettes, and there is one deluxe cottage with a four-person hot tub and a roof deck. Some have ocean views and conveniences such as a washer/dryer. Many have private decks or patios. The rooms are decorated in a modern, cozy style. The inn offers a number of amenities at an extra charge, including rental of beach cabanas, bicycle delivery service, grocery delivery service, and Wednesday evening family-style clambakes in season. For kids, the inn hosts children's programs and has such on-site amusements as outdoor Ping-Pong, foosball, a pool, and a putting green. For active guests, the inn staff arranges "island adventure day trips" that include fishing, kayaking, and beach buggy rides for an extra charge. The inn's fine-dining restaurant, Lure, is top-notch (see "Where to Dine," later in this chapter). A general store is on-site for snacks and sun-dried items. In high season, late June to early September, there is a 3-night minimum stay during the week and a 4-night minimum stay on weekends. Several wheelchair-accessible rooms are available.

South Beach, Edgartown, MA 02539. ℂ 978/443-1733 (reservations line), or 508/627-4747. www.winnetu.com. 48 units, 1 deluxe cottage. Summer $305 double; $570–$630 1-bedroom suite; $1,255 3-bedroom suite. MC, V. Closed Dec to mid-Apr. **Amenities:** Restaurant; outdoor heated pool; pro putting green; tennis courts (6 Har-Tru, 4 all-weather); fitness room; children's program (late June to early Sept, complimentary 9am–noon, charge in evenings, for 3-year-olds through preteens); concierge; laundry facilities. *In room:* A/C, TV/VCR, fridge, coffeemaker, iron, microwave.

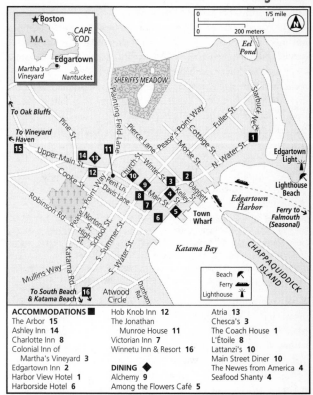

Inset map: ★Boston, CAPE COD, MA., Edgartown, Martha's Vineyard, Nantucket

0 — 1/5 mile
0 — 200 meters

Eel Pond

SHERIFFS MEADOW

To Oak Bluffs

To Vineyard Haven

Painting Field Lane
Pierce Lane
Pease's Point Way
Morse St.
Fuller St.
Starbuck Neck
N. Water St.

Pine St.
Upper Main St.
Cooke St.
Robinson Rd.
Pease's Point Way
Norton St.
High St.
School St.
S. Summer St.
S. Water St.
Summer St.
Davis Lane
Pent Ln.
Church St.
Winter St.
Kelley St.
Daggett
Main St.

Edgartown Light

Lighthouse Beach

Edgartown Harbor

Ferry to Falmouth (Seasonal)

Town Wharf

Katama Bay

CHAPPAQUIDDICK ISLAND

Mullins Way
Katama Rd.

To South Beach & Katama Beach **16**
Atwood Circle
Dunham Rd.

Beach
Ferry
Lighthouse

15 **14** **13** **11** **12** **10** **9** **8** **7** **6** **5** **4** **3** **2** **1**

ACCOMMODATIONS
The Arbor **15**
Ashley Inn **14**
Charlotte Inn **8**
Colonial Inn of
  Martha's Vineyard **3**
Edgartown Inn **2**
Harbor View Hotel **1**
Harborside Hotel **6**

Hob Knob Inn **12**
The Jonathan
  Munroe House **11**
Victorian Inn **7**
Winnetu Inn & Resort **16**

DINING
Alchemy **9**
Among the Flowers Café **5**

Atria **13**
Chesca's **3**
The Coach House **1**
L'Étoile **8**
Lattanzi's **10**
Main Street Diner **10**
The Newes from America **4**
Seafood Shanty **4**

EXPENSIVE

Ashley Inn 🐾 *(Value* Located on Main Street in Edgartown, this attractive B&B is just a short walk to the many shops and restaurants on Main Street, and the picturesque harbor. Innkeepers Fred and Janet Hurley have decorated the bedrooms in this 1860 captain's house with period antiques and quilts, and some have canopy or four-poster beds. There are thoughtful extras at this B&B, like a little box of Chilmark Chocolates left on your pillow. In the morning, breakfast is served on individual tables in the dining room.

129 Main St., Edgartown, MA 02539. ☎ **508/627-9655.** Fax 508/627-6629. www.ashleyinn.net. 10 units. Summer $215–$305 double. Rates include continental breakfast. MC, V. Open year-round. *In room:* TV, A/C.

Colonial Inn of Martha's Vineyard 🐾🐾 *Kids* This four-story, 1911 inn in the center of Edgartown has been transformed into a fine modern hotel, and recent extensive renovations have elevated it to what can accurately be described as "affordable luxury." Its lobby serves as a conduit to the Nevins Square shops beyond, and two fine restaurants are on the premises. The 43 rooms, decorated in soothing, contemporary tones (with pine furniture, crisp fabrics, hardwood floors, beadboard wainscoting, and four-poster beds), offer all one could want in the way of conveniences. Guests whose rooms lack harbor views can wander onto one of the four common harbor view decks to have a cocktail and enjoy the scenery. Suites have VCRs (complimentary videos) and kitchenettes. Many rooms have gas fireplaces. Be sure to visit the roof deck, ideally around sunset, or, if you're up for it, sunrise over the water.

38 N. Water St., Edgartown, MA 02539. © 800/627-4701 or 508/627-4711. Fax 508/627-5904. www.colonialinnmvy.com. 28 units (27 with tub/shower, 1 shower only). Summer $225–$325 double; $355–$435 suite or efficiency. Rates include continental breakfast. AE, MC, V. Closed Dec–Mar. Pets allowed in designated rooms. **Amenities:** 2 restaurants; fitness room; spa; shopping arcade. *In room:* A/C, TV, dataport, hair dryer, iron, 2 rooms for those w/limited mobility.

Harborside Inn 🐾 This large hotel complex overlooking Edgartown Harbor has a great location in the center of town, just off Main Street. The rooms are fairly generic, but if you get one with a harbor view, you'll be delighted. Among the seven buildings that make up the inn are restored whaling captain's cottages from the 1700s. Some rooms have private balconies. A large heated pool is in the center of the courtyard, as well as a whirlpool tub and sauna.

3 S. Water St., Edgartown, MA 02539. © 800/627-4009 or 508/627-4321. Fax 508/627-7566. www.theharborsideinn.com. 89 units. Summer $180–$355 double; $415 suite. AE, MC, V. Closed mid-Nov to mid-Apr. **Amenities:** Heated outdoor pool; whirlpool tub; sauna. *In room:* A/C, TV, fridge.

The Jonathan Munroe House 🐾🐾 *Finds* With its graceful wraparound, colonnaded front porch, the Jonathan Munroe House stands out from the other inns and captain's homes on this stretch of upper Main Street. Inside, the formal parlor has been transformed into a comfortable gathering room with European flair. Guest rooms are immaculate, antiques-filled, and dotted with clever details. Many rooms have fireplaces and bathtubs with whirlpool jets. All have sitting areas, perfect for curling up with a bestseller (provided) or matching wits over a game of chess (also provided). At breakfast, don't miss the homemade waffles and pancakes, served on the sunny porch. Wine and cheese are served in the evening.

Request the garden cottage, with its flowering window boxes, if you are in a honeymooning mood.

100 Main St., Edgartown, MA 02539. (C) 877/468-6763 or 508/627-5536. Fax 508/627-5536. www.jonathanmunroe.com. 8 units, 1 cottage (5 with tub/shower, 2 shower only, 1 tub and shower). Summer $190–$250 double; $290 cottage. Rates include full breakfast. AE, MC, V. Open year-round. No children under 12. *In room:* A/C, hair dryer.

Victorian Inn 🐾🐾 Do you ever long to stay at a quaint, reasonably priced inn that is bigger than a B&B but smaller than a Marriott? In the center of Edgartown, the Victorian Inn is a freshened-up version of those old-style hotels that used to exist in the center of every New England town. The inn has enough rooms that you don't feel like you are trespassing in someone's home, yet it retains a personal touch. With three floors of long, graceful corridors, the Victorian could serve as a stage set for a 1930s romance. Several rooms have canopy beds and a balcony with a harbor view. Each year innkeepers Stephen and Karen Caliri have improved and refined the inn, and they are always quick to dispense helpful advice with good humor.

24 S. Water St. (in the center of town), Edgartown, MA 02539. (C) 508/627-4784. www.thevic.com. 14 units (2 with tub/shower, 12 shower only). Summer $180–$385 double. Rates include full breakfast and afternoon tea. MC, V. Open year-round. Dogs welcome Nov–Mar. *In room:* A/C, TV, hair dryer, no phone.

MODERATE

The Arbor 🐾 *Value* This 1880 farm house is at the far edge of town, but still within walking distance from the center. The inside is stylish, with a lovely cathedral-ceilinged living room where you can seek comfort in an overstuffed chintz couch. The rooms range from tiny to spacious, but all are nicely appointed, largely with antiques. Most of the rooms have small televisions. In the morning, the fresh-baked breakfast is served on fine china in the dining room. The rates are very reasonable here compared to other Edgartown B&Bs.

222 Upper Main St., Edgartown, MA 02539. (C) 888/748-4383 or 508/627-8137. Fax 508/627-9104. www.arborinn.net. 10 units (2 with shared bathroom), 1 cottage. Summer $110–$120 room with shared bathroom; $145–$195 double; $1,000–$1,200 weekly cottage. Rates include continental breakfast. MC, V. Closed Nov–Apr. *In room:* A/C, no phone.

Edgartown Inn 🐾 *Value* This centrally located, historic inn offers perhaps the best value on the island. Nathaniel Hawthorne holed up here for nearly a year, and Daniel Webster also spent time here. It's a lovely 1798 Federal manse, a showplace even here on captain's row. Rooms are no-frills but pleasantly traditional; some have televisions. Breakfast, which is open to the public, is available in the dining room for an extra charge ranging from $5.50 to $8.50. Some rooms in the front of the house have harbor views, and two have private balconies. Modernists may prefer the two cathedral-ceilinged quarters in the annex out back, which offer lovely light and a sense of seclusion. Service is excellent here; be sure to say hello to Henry King, who has been on staff here for over 50 years.

56 N. Water St., Edgartown, MA 02539. © **508/627-4794.** Fax 508/627-9420. www.edgartowninn.com. 20 units, 4 with shared bathroom. Summer $115 double w/shared bathroom; $150–$250 double w/private bathroom. No credit cards. Closed Nov–Mar. No children under 8. *In room:* A/C, no phone.

OAK BLUFFS

Those looking for a basic motel with a central location will want to stay at **Surfside Motel** across from the ferry dock on Oak Bluffs Ave. in Oak Bluffs (© **800/537-3007** or 508/693-2500; www.mvsurf side.com). Summer rates are $195 to $220 double; $295 suites. Rooms have air-conditioning, televisions, minifridges, and telephones. Open year-round; well-behaved pets are allowed.

EXPENSIVE

The Dockside Inn ✿ Set close to the harbor, the Dockside is perfectly located for exploring the town of Oak Bluffs and is geared for families. The welcoming exterior, with its colonnaded porch and balconies, duplicates the inns of yesteryear. Once inside, the whimsical Victorian touches will transport you immediately into the spirit of this rollicking town. Most of the standard-size rooms have either a garden or harbor view; they're decorated cheerfully in pinks and greens. Suites have kitchenettes, and some have private decks. Location, charm, and flair mean this is a popular place, so book early. There are two accessible rooms for those with disabilities.

9 Circuit Ave. Extension (P.O. Box 1206), Oak Bluffs, MA 02557. © **800/245-5979** or 508/693-2966. Fax 508/696-7293. www.vineyardinns.com. 22 units. Summer $165–$210 double; $270–$360 suite. Rates include continental breakfast. AE, DISC, MC, V. Closed late Oct to early Apr. *In room:* A/C, TV, hair dryer, iron.

The Oak Bluffs Inn ✿ This homey, Victorian inn has a fun location at the top of Circuit Avenue, Oak Bluffs' main drag that is full of restaurants, ice cream parlors, clubs, and shops. The inn stands out with its whimsical, colorful Victorian paint scheme and its prominent cupola, from which guests can enjoy a 360-degree view of Oak Bluffs, including the beach and harbor a few blocks away. It's a 2-minute stroll from the inn to all the Oak Bluffs attractions, including the gingerbread cottages, the tabernacle, the Flying Horses Carousel, the waterfront park, the ferries, the harbor, and the beach.

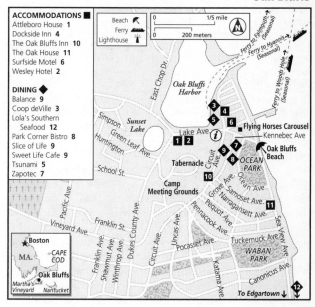

With its large veranda, the inn has a particularly welcoming appearance. As is typical in a house of this vintage, some of the rooms are a tad on the cozy side, but others are spacious and even have comfortable seating areas. All rooms have ceiling fans.

64 Circuit Ave. (at the corner of Pequot Ave.), Oak Bluffs, MA 02557. (C) **800/ 955-6235** or 508/693-7171. Fax 508/693-8787. www.oakbluffsinn.com. 9 units. $195–$255 double. Rates include continental breakfast. AE, MC, V. Closed Nov–Apr. *In room:* A/C, hair dryer, ceiling fan, no phone.

The Oak House (*Finds* An 1872 Queen Anne, bay-front beauty, this one-time home of former Massachusetts governor William Claflin has preserved all the luxury and leisure of the Victorian age. Innkeeper Betsi Convery-Luce trained at Johnson & Wales; her pastries (served at breakfast and tea) are sublime. The rooms toward the back are quieter, but those in front have Nantucket Sound views. The common rooms are furnished in an opulent Victorian mode, as are the 10 bedrooms (two are suites). This inn is very service-oriented, and requests for feather beds, down pillows, or non-allergenic pillows are accommodated. Anyone intent on decompressing is sure to benefit from this immersion into another era—the one that invented the leisure class.

75 Seaview Ave. (on the sound), Oak Bluffs, MA 02557. (𝄞 **800/245-5979** or 508/693-4187. Fax 508/696-7385. www.vineyardinns.com. 10 units (1 with tub/shower, 9 shower only). Summer $195–$230 double; $310–$315 suite. Rates include continental breakfast and afternoon tea. AE, DISC, MC, V. Closed late Oct to early May. *In room:* A/C, TV.

Wesley Hotel 🐾 *Value*   Formerly one of the grand hotels of Martha's Vineyard, this imposing 1879 property, right on the harbor, is now a solid entry in the good value category, especially with its low off-season rates. It occupies a terrific location in Oak Bluffs, across the street from the harbor, in the center of the action. Remnants remain from its years of grandeur—the rockers that line the spacious wraparound porch, and the lobby with its old photographs, dark-stained oak trim, old-fashioned registration desk, and Victorian reproductions. Most rooms are fairly compact and basic, though some are roomy with harbor views. The Wesley Arms, behind the main building, contains 33 air-conditioned rooms with private bathrooms, accessible by elevator. Eight suites and executive suites contain kitchenettes. There are five rooms equipped for those with disabilities. *Note:* Reserve early to specify harbor views, which do not cost more than regular rooms. This is one of the few Vineyard hotels that does not require a minimum stay in the off season.

70 Lake Ave. (on the harbor), Oak Bluffs, MA 02557. (𝄞 **800/638-9027** or 508/693-6611. Fax 508/693-5389. www.wesleyhotel.com. 95 units (all with shower only). Summer $195–$235 double; $290 suite. AE, DC, MC, V. Closed late Oct to Apr. *In room:* A/C, TV, no phone.

MODERATE

Attleboro House *Value*   As old-fashioned as the afghans that proprietor Estelle Reagan crochets for every bed, this harborside guesthouse—serving Camp Meeting visitors since 1874— epitomizes the simple, timeless joys of summer. None of the rooms is graced with a private bathroom, but the rates are so retro that you may not mind. What was good enough for 19th-century tourists more than suffices today.

42 Lake Ave. (on the harbor), Oak Bluffs, MA 02557. (𝄞 **508/693-4346.** 11 units, all with shared bathroom. Summer $125 double; $135–$220 suite. AE, DISC, MC, V. Closed Oct–May.

VINEYARD HAVEN (TISBURY)
VERY EXPENSIVE

The Mansion House 🐾🐾 *Finds*   After a fire burned down the 300-year-old Tisbury Inn several years ago, the owners decided to rebuild, making this one of the island's most full-service inns. The

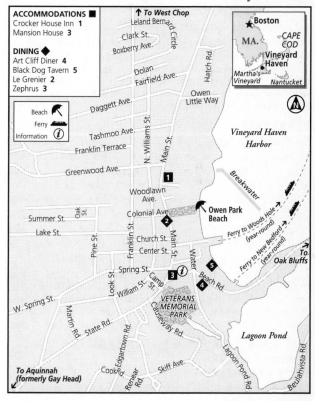

ACCOMMODATIONS ■
Crocker House Inn **1**
Mansion House **3**

DINING ◆
Art Cliff Diner **4**
Black Dog Tavern **5**
Le Grenier **2**
Zephrus **3**

Beach
Ferry
Information ⓘ

↑ To West Chop
Leland Bernard Circle
Clark St.
Boxberry Ave.
Dolan
Fairfield Ave.
Daggett Ave.
Hatch Rd.
Owen Little Way
Tashmoo Ave.
N. Williams St.
Franklin Terrace
Greenwood Ave.
Main St.

1

Woodlawn Ave.
Colonial Ave.
2
Summer St.
Oak St.
Lake St.
Franklin St.
Pine St.
Church St.
Center St.
Main St.
Water St.
Spring St.
3 ⓘ
5
Look St.
William St.
Camp
Beach Rd.
4
W. Spring St.
Martin Rd.
State Rd.
VETERANS MEMORIAL PARK
Causeway Rd.
Edgartown Rd.
Cook Rd.
Renear Rd.
Skiff Ave.
Lagoon Pond Rd.
Beulahvista Rd.

To Aquinnah (formerly Gay Head)

Vineyard Haven Harbor
Breakwater
↑ Owen Park Beach
Ferry to Woods Hole (year-round)
Ferry to New Bedford (year-round)
To Oak Bluffs
Lagoon Pond

★ Boston
MA.
CAPE COD
Vineyard Haven
Martha's Vineyard
Nantucket

building, occupying a prominent corner location in Vineyard Haven, a short walk from the ferry, is now a community hub, with a restaurant, health club, and shops. The three-story hotel is generous with comfortable amenities such as deluxe robes and bath products. The rooms range in size from cozy to spacious, and prices vary accordingly. Many have kitchenettes, plasma-screen televisions, and extra-large bathtubs. Some have harbor views and gas fireplaces. All rooms are equipped with high-speed Internet service at a cost of $9.99 per day. One unique feature of the inn is the 75-foot mineral spring (no chlorine) swimming pool in the inn's basement. There is still a lot of history here among the thoroughly modern amenities: For instance, an antique oak bar with elaborate carvings, saved from the old Island House, serves as the inn's bar. The roof deck offers wonderful panoramic views of Vineyard Haven and the harbor. A full gourmet breakfast is served buffet-style at Zephrus, the hotel's restaurant (see "Where to Dine," later in this chapter).

9 Main St., Vineyard Haven, MA 02568. © 800/332-4112 or 508/693-2200. Fax 508/693-4095. www.mvmansionhouse.com. 32 units. Summer $269–$449 double. Rates include full buffet breakfast. AE, MC, V. Open year-round. **Amenities:** Restaurant; indoor heated pool; health club; spa; room service to 8:30pm; shops. *In room:* A/C, TV, dataport, fridge, hair dryer, iron.

EXPENSIVE

Crocker House Inn ⊛   Jynell and Jeff Kristal have renovated this 1920s home near the harbor into a comfortable and casually elegant place to stay. Rooms are particularly light and airy here, all redone with new linens, beds, and furniture with a country flavor. The third-floor suite includes a deck, minifridge, and two-person Jacuzzi. Jynell has Marriott experience, and it shows in the room details and service-oriented hospitality. Jeff bakes the blueberry muffins in the morning, and guests rave about his chocolate chip cookies set out with iced tea and lemonade in the afternoon.

12 Crocker Ave. (P.O. Box 1658, off Main St.), Vineyard Haven, MA 02568. © 800/772-0206 or 508/693-1151. Fax 508/693-1123. www.crockerhouseinn.com. 8 units. Summer $225–$315 double; $395 suite. Rates include continental breakfast on weekdays, full breakfast on weekends. AE, MC, V. Open year-round. No children under 12. *In room:* A/C, TV, hair dryer, iron.

CHILMARK (INCLUDING MENEMSHA) & WEST TISBURY
VERY EXPENSIVE

Beach Plum Inn ⊛⊛ *Finds*   This family-owned country inn, recently renovated, is on 8 lush acres, with a lawn sloping graciously down to Vineyard Sound. It's a beautiful, secluded property tucked away in Menemsha, yet within walking distance of the harbor. On the grounds are a croquet course and Nova Grass tennis court, plus bikes to take exploring (extra charge). Rooms are in the main inn and in four cottages. The room decor is predominantly cottage-y, though some rooms lean toward elegance. Some of the rooms have canopied beds and are quite romantic. Linens are 275-count and above; towels are Egyptian cotton. Five of the rooms have a whirlpool bath. All but one room have decks or patios, some with views of Menemsha Harbor. One room is accessible for those with disabilities. Inn guests get beach passes to the private up-island beaches. The inn's restaurant is one of the best fine-dining spots on the island (see "Where to Dine," below).

Beach Plum Lane (off North Rd., ½ mile northeast of the harbor), Menemsha, MA 02552. © 877/645-7398 or 508/645-9454. Fax 508/645-2801. www.beachpluminn.com.

11 units (all with tub/shower). Summer $200–$400 double or cottage. Rates include full breakfast in season, continental off season. AE, DC, DISC, MC, V. Closed Jan–Apr. **Amenities:** Restaurant (fine dining); tennis court; croquet court; in-room massage; babysitting; laundry service for a charge; maid service twice daily; private beach passes. *In room:* A/C, TV, dataport, fridge, hair dryer, iron.

EXPENSIVE

The Inn at Blueberry Hill ✸ This bucolic property, formerly a farm dating from the late 1600s, is set on 56 acres in the up-island town of Chilmark. Book a room at this inn if you want a secluded vacation in the country, far away from the tourism crowds in Edgartown and Oak Bluffs. The comfortable rooms and suites are spread out in six traditional-style buildings. The overall feeling of the sunny rooms is serenity; they feature white cotton linens, ceiling fans, and hand-painted furniture. Many thoughtful extras are provided for guests, such as terrycloth robes, penlight flashlights (for evening strolls), and coolers for the beach. Exquisite Chilmark Chocolates are placed on pillows at night. Many have private balconies or porches. Though the property is ancient, the inn feels very up to date. The inn includes exercise and spa services, as well as a lap pool and a tennis court. Also on-site is Theo's, an attractive fine-dining restaurant specializing in fresh island cuisine. The restaurant is BYOB, as Chilmark is a dry town. The Inn at Blueberry Hill is surrounded by 2,000 acres of conservation land with a network of nature trails. Guests are given passes and offered shuttles to the private beaches, Lucy Vincent and Squibnocket, which are about 4 miles away. Children over 12 are welcome at the inn.

74 North Rd., Chilmark, MA 02535. ✆ **800/356-3322** or 508/645-3322. Fax 508/645-3799. www.blueberryinn.com. 25 units. $240–$285 double; $420–$1,035 suites and cottages. Rates include continental breakfast. AE, MC, V. Closed Dec–Apr. No children under 13. **Amenities:** Restaurant; 25-yd. lap pool; tennis court; exercise room (w/Cybex equipment, Stairmasters, and exercise bikes); Jacuzzi; facials and body treatments (extra charge); massage (extra charge). *In room:* A/C, TV (available upon request), hair dryer.

Lambert's Cove Country Inn ✸ A dedicated horticulturist created this haven in the 1920s, expanding on a 1790 farmstead. You can see the old adzed beams in some of the upstairs bedrooms. Among his more prized additions is the Greenhouse Room, a bedroom with its own conservatory. You'll find an all-weather tennis court on the grounds, and the namesake beach is a mile away. The inn's restaurant is known for skilled New American dinners. Set far off the main road and surrounded by apple trees and lilacs, this secluded estate suggests an age when time was measured in generations. There's no better place to relax.

Lambert's Cove Rd. (off State Rd., about 3 miles west of Vineyard Haven), West Tisbury, MA 02568. ✆ 508/693-2298. Fax 508/693-7890. www.lambertscoveinn. com. 15 units. Summer $195–$265 double. Rates include full breakfast. AE, MC, V. Closed Jan. **Amenities:** Restaurant; tennis court; private beach passes. *In room:* A/C, no phone.

Menemsha Inn and Cottages ✿✿   There's an almost Quaker-like plainness to this weathered waterside compound set in the pines near Menemsha Harbor, though many of the rooms are quite inviting. Mostly it's a place to revel in the outdoors (on 11 seaside acres) without distractions. The property is about a half-mile walk through a wooded path to the beach at Menemsha Harbor. The late *Life* photographer, Alfred Eisenstaedt, summered here for 4 decades, and the interior aesthetics would please any artist. There's no restaurant—just a restful breakfast room. Cottages have televisions, VCRs, dataports, outdoor showers, barbecue grills, kitchenettes, and hair dryers. The most luxurious suites are located in the Carriage House, which has a spacious common room with a fieldstone fireplace. The suites are equipped with minifridges, hair dryers, and ceiling fans. All rooms have private decks; most have water views. Guests have access to complimentary passes and shuttle bus service to the Lucy Vincent and Squibnocket private beaches.

Off North Rd. (about ½ mile northeast of the harbor), Menemsha, MA 02552. ✆ 508/645-2521. Fax 508/645-9500. www.menemshainn.com. 15 units, 12 cottages. Summer $240–$265 double; from $310 suite; $2,200–$3,100 weekly cottages. Rates include continental breakfast for rooms and suites. No credit cards. Closed Nov to mid-Apr. **Amenities:** Tennis court; fitness room (step machine, treadmill, exercise bike, and free weights); beach passes. *In room:* TV.

MODERATE

The Captain R. Flanders House ✿ *Finds*   Set amid 60 acres of rolling meadows crisscrossed by stone walls, this late-18th-century farmhouse, built by a whaling captain, has remained much the same for two centuries. The living room, with its broad-plank floors, is full of astonishing antiques, but there's none of that "for show" feel that's prevalent in more self-conscious B&Bs. This is a working farm, so there's no time for posing (even if it was featured in *Martha Stewart's Wedding Book*). Two new countrified cottages overlooking the pond have living rooms but not kitchenettes. After fortifying themselves with homemade muffins, island-made honey, and jam at breakfast, guests are free to fritter the day away. The owners will provide you with a coveted pass to

nearby Lucy Vincent Beach, or perhaps you'd prefer a long country walk.

North Rd. (about ½ mile northeast of Menemsha), Chilmark, MA 02535. ℭ **508/645-3123**. www.captainflanders.com. 5 units (3 with shared bathroom); 2 cottages. Summer $80 single with shared bathroom; $175 double with shared bathroom; $195 double with private bathroom; $275 cottage. Rates include continental breakfast. AE, MC, V. Closed Nov to early May. **Amenities:** Private beach; shuttle bus passes. *In room:* No phone.

INEXPENSIVE

Hostelling International Martha's Vineyard   The first "purpose-built" youth hostel in the United States, this homey, cedar-shake saltbox set at the edge of a vast state forest is still a front-runner. It hums with wholesome energy, from the huge group kitchen with recycling bins and two communal fridges, to the five sex-segregated dorms containing 74 beds. The hallways are plastered with notices of local attractions (some stores offer discounts to hostellers), and the check-in desk also serves as a tourist information booth. Outside, there's a volleyball court and a sheltered bike rack. By bike, the hostel is a little more than 7 miles from the Vineyard Haven ferry terminal; shuttle buses also make the rounds in summer. You'll have no trouble at all finding enjoyable ways to spend time during the "lockout," from 10am to 5pm; just don't forget the 11pm curfew.

525 Edgartown–West Tisbury Rd. (about 1 mile east of the town center), West Tisbury, MA 02575. ℭ **508/693-2665**. Fax 508/693-2699. www.hiusa.org. 74 beds. $22 for members, $24 for non-members. MC, V. Closed early Nov to Mar. *In room:* No phone.

3 Where to Dine

Restaurants tend to be rather expensive on the Vineyard, but the stiff competition has produced a bevy of places that offer excellent service, evocative settings, and creative cuisine. A note on spirits: Outside Oak Bluffs and Edgartown, all of Martha's Vineyard is "dry," including Vineyard Haven, so bring your own bottle; some restaurants charge a small fee for uncorking. **Great Harbour Gourmet & Spirits,** 40 Main St., Edgartown (ℭ **508/627-4390**), has a very good wine selection.

Refer to the accommodations maps earlier in this chapter for locations of many of the restaurants reviewed here.

EDGARTOWN
VERY EXPENSIVE

L'étoile ★★★ CONTEMPORARY FRENCH   Every signal (including the price) tells you that this is going to be one very special meal. Having passed through a pair of ormolu-laden sitting rooms, one comes upon a conservatory—a wonderfully summery room— sparkling with the light of antique brass sconces and fresh with the scent of potted citrus trees. Everything is perfection, from the table settings (gold-rimmed Villeroy & Boch) to a nouvelle-cuisine menu that varies seasonally but is always exquisite. Chef Michael Brisson, who came up through the kitchen of Boston's famed L'Espalier, is determined to dazzle, and he does, with an ever-evolving seven-course menu of delicacies flown in from the four corners of the earth. *Sevruga* caviar usually makes an appearance— perhaps as a garnish for chilled leek soup. An étouffée of lobster with cognac, and chervil sauce may come with littlenecks, bay scallops, and roasted corn fritters; or roasted pheasant breast in a cider, apple-brandy, and thyme sauce may be accompanied by apple, sun-dried cherry, and mascarpone-filled wild-rice crepes. A chef's tasting menu is offered for $120 per person.

At the Charlotte Inn, 27 S. Summer St. (off Main St.). ✆ **508/627-5187.** Reservations required. Jacket recommended for men. Fixed-price menu $75; chef's tasting menu $120. AE, MC, V. July–Aug daily 6:30–9:45pm; May–June and Sept–Oct Tues–Sun 6:30–9:45pm; mid-Feb to Apr and Nov–Dec Thurs–Sat 6:30–9:45pm. Closed Jan to mid-Feb.

EXPENSIVE

Alchemy 🐸🐸 FRENCH BISTRO   This spiffy bistro is a little slice of Paris on Edgartown's Main Street. Such esoteric choices as oyster brie soup and Burgundy Vintners salad share the bill with escargot and *chanterelle fricassee* and *lapin moutarde spatzle* (yes, that's rabbit). As befits a true bistro, there's also a large selection of cocktails, liqueurs, and wines. In addition to lunch and dinner, a bar menu is served from 2:30 to 11pm. This choice isn't for everyone, but sophisticated diners will enjoy the Continental flair here.

71 Main St. (in the center of town). ✆ **508/627-9999.** Reservations accepted for parties of 8 or more. Main courses $22–$33. AE, MC, V. Apr–Nov Mon-Sat noon–2:30pm and 5:30-10pm, Sun 5:30-10pm; call for off-season hours. Open year-round.

Atria 🐸🐸🐸 *Finds* NEW AMERICAN   This fine-dining restaurant set in an 18th-century sea captain's house on Upper Main Street in Edgartown gets rave reviews for its gourmet cuisine and high-caliber service. Pronounced with the emphasis on the second syllable (ah-*tree*-ah), the name refers to the brightest of three stars forming the Southern Triangle constellation. You can sit in the elegant dining room, the rose-covered wraparound porch, or the brick cellar bar downstairs for more casual dining. Chef/owner Christian Thornton's menu offers a variety of creative dishes with influences from around the country and around the world, with stops in the Mediterranean, Middle East, and Asia. It features organic island-grown produce, off-the-boat seafood, local shellfish, and aged prime meats. Popular starters include miso soup with steamed crab dumplings or seared foie gras with roasted quail. Unusual main courses include wok-fried Martha's Vineyard lobster or seared Georges Bank scallops with short-rib ragout and cauliflower puree. Half bottles of wine are available on the extensive wine list. Live entertainment, usually an acoustic guitar or a jazz trio, is on tap during weekends in the bar.

137 Main St. ✆ 508/627-5850. www.atriamv.com. Reservations recommended. Main courses $30–$48. AE, MC, V. June–Aug daily 5:30–10pm; call for off-season hours. Open year-round.

Chesca's 🍴🍴 *Finds* ITALIAN   This modern-decor restaurant at the Colonial Inn is a solid entry, with yummy food at reasonable prices, and you're sure to find favorites such as paella (with roasted lobster and other choice seafood), risotto (with roasted vegetables), and ravioli (with portobello mushrooms and asparagus). Smaller appetites can fill up on homemade soup and salad.

At the Colonial Inn, 38 N. Water St. ✆ 508/627-1234. Reservations not accepted. Main courses $22–$36. AE, MC, V. Late June to early Sept daily 6–10pm; call for off-season hours. Closed mid-Oct to mid-Apr.

The Coach House 🍴🍴 NEW AMERICAN   This is a terrific place to have a drink, or to dine with an exquisite view of Edgartown Harbor and the lighthouse. The long and elegant bar is particularly smashing. The menu is simple but stylish. To start, there's soft-shell crab with arugula and teardrop tomatoes. As a main course, try the caramelized sea scallops with a salad of Asian pear and apple. Service here is excellent; these are trained waiters, not your usual college surfer dudes. At the end of your meal, you may want to sit on the rockers on the Harbor View Hotel's wraparound porch and just watch the lights twinkling in the harbor.

At the Harbor View Hotel, 131 N. Water St. ✆ 508/627-7000. Reservations recommended. Main courses $24–$31. AE, MC, V. Daily 6am–10pm; call for off-season hours. Open year-round.

Lattanzi's 🍴🍴 NORTHERN ITALIAN   Some say Al Lattanzi cooks the best veal chops on Martha's Vineyard. Lattanzi's would be the ideal place to eat in the dead of winter, by the glow of the paneled living room's handsome fireplace. Service is exceptional, and the wine list has a wide range of well-priced bottles. Back to the veal chop. You have two choices: Piccolo Fiorentina, which is a hickory-grilled veal porterhouse chop with black peppercorns and lemon, or Lombatina di Vitello al Porcini, which serves the chop with porcini-mushroom cream. If it's July, get the striped-bass special; from local waters, it's luscious. Lattanzi also has a very good brick-oven pizzeria next door (② **508/627-9084**).

19 Church St. (Old Post Office Sq., off Main St. in the center of town). ② **508/627-8854**. Reservations recommended. Main courses $22–$38. AE, DC, DISC, MC, V. June–Sept daily 6–10pm; call for off-season hours. Open year-round.

Lure ★★ NEW AMERICAN   This elegant restaurant on the second floor of the new Winnetu Resort in Katama is quickly making a name for itself as a wonderful place for dinner. Those fortunate enough to get a window seat or a spot on the deck in good weather will enjoy a great sunset view over South Beach. Executive Chef Ed Gannon, formerly of the Four Seasons Hotel in Boston, wows diners with his stylish preparations. The menu is divided into two sections, with "simpler" items such as pan-roasted Chatham cod, as well as fancier fare such as lobster with coconut basmati rice. A special section of the restaurant, called Osprey, features a children's menu.

At the Winnetu Inn and Resort, Katama. ② **508/627-3663**. Reservations required. Main courses $24–$37. AE, MC, V. July–Aug daily 5:30–9:30pm; call for off-season hours. Closed Dec to mid-Apr.

MODERATE

Among the Flowers Cafe ★★ *Value* AMERICAN   Everything's fresh and appealing at this small outdoor cafe near the dock. Sit under the awning, and you'll just catch a glimpse of the harbor. The breakfasts are the best around, and all the crepes, waffles, and eggs are also available at lunch. The comfort-food dinners (chicken and black-pepper sauté over pasta, butter-and-crumb-crusted baked haddock with a sautéed lobster-and-shallot-butter cream) are among the most affordable options in this pricey town. There's almost always a wait, not just because it's so picturesque, but because the food is homey, hearty, and kind on the wallet.

17 Mayhew Lane ② **508/627-3233**. Reservations not accepted. Main courses $10–$18. AE, DC, DISC, MC, V. July–Aug daily 8am–10pm; May–June and Sept–Oct daily 8am–4pm. Closed Nov–Apr.

Seafood Shanty ★ SEAFOOD   This casual restaurant overlooking Edgartown Harbor features outdoor dining and cheerful service by college kids. This is a great place for lunch with a water view. Good lunch choices are the lobster roll or the cold poached salmon. For dinner, options include a classic bouillabaisse seafood stew or a prime rib plate. There is also a children's menu. The restaurant has a convenient walk-up counter in a shack on Dock Street in front of the restaurant where virtually the entire menu is available to go.

31 Dock St. ℂ **508/627-8622.** Reservations recommended. Main courses $9–$17 lunch, $17–$35 dinner. AE, MC, V. June–Aug daily 11am–10pm; call for off-season hours. Closed Nov–Apr.

INEXPENSIVE

Main Street Diner *Kids* AMERICAN   It's a little kitschy-cute, what with cartoon wallpaper decorated with vintage doodads, but tony Edgartown could use a place geared to folks not out to bust the budget. Kids and adults alike will enjoy this ersatz diner, where the food and trimmings hearken back to the 1950s. A one-egg breakfast with home fries and a buttermilk biscuit will set you back only $2; the burgers and sandwiches (including a classic open-face hot turkey with gravy, potatoes, and cranberry sauce) less than $6. Grab a grilled cheese or BLT, and wash it down with a cherry Coke.

Old Post Office Sq. (off Main St. in the center of town). ℂ **508/627-9337.** Reservations not accepted. Most items under $15. AE, MC, V. Daily 7am–8:30pm. Open year-round.

The Newes from America *Finds* PUB GRUB   This subterranean tavern is the place to come for pub food, including fish and chips and beer. Locals love the French onion soup here. Beers are a specialty: try a rack of five esoteric brews, or let your choice of food—from a wood-smoked oyster "Island Poor Boy" sandwich with linguica relish, to an 18-ounce porterhouse steak—dictate your draft; the menu comes handily annotated with recommendations. Don't miss their seasoned fries, accompanied by a savory Southwestern dipping sauce.

At The Kelley House, 23 Kelley St. ℂ **508/627-4397.** Reservations not accepted. Main courses $9–$11. AE, MC, V. Daily 11am–11pm. Open year-round.

OAK BLUFFS
EXPENSIVE

Balance NEW AMERICAN   Chef Benjamin deForest is the creative force behind this expansive restaurant, centrally located on Circuit Avenue in Oak Bluffs. The loftlike space features an open kitchen on one side and a 30-foot long bar on the other. The specialties here are seasonal island-grown produce and seafood that Mr. deForest claims to be the freshest served on the island. The menu changes frequently, but specialties include a delicate yellowfin tuna tartare and Pernod sundae, and a unique salad with artichoke hearts, frisée, and shaved beets with truffle vinaigrette. For main courses, big eaters will love the 16-ounce broiled salt-crusted New York strip steak with Roquefort Yukon potatoes. Fish lovers will find the grilled sake-marinated salmon with stir-fried baby bok choy to be a real treat. A six-course tasting menu costs $85 per person.

57 Circuit Ave. ℂ 508/696-3000. Reservations suggested. Main courses $28–$36. AE, MC, V. July–Aug daily 6–11pm (bar menu till midnight); call for off-season hours. Closed mid-Oct to mid-Apr.

Lola's Southern Seafood 🌟 SOUTHERN   This sultry New Orleans–style restaurant drips with atmosphere: Crystal chandeliers, intricate wrought-iron, arched doorways, and starched linens in an ocher palette. Specialties include the chicken-and-seafood jambalaya and the rib-eye steak spiced either "from heaven or hell." Meals are served family-style, with large helpings of side dishes. There's live entertainment nightly in season (Fri–Sat during off season), while Sunday brunch also features live music. A less-expensive pub menu is served in the bar with its mural of island personalities.

At the Island Inn, Beach Rd. ℂ **508/693-5007.** www.lolassouthernseafood.com. Reservations accepted only for 5 or more. Main courses $20–$36. DC, MC, V. Sun 10am–2pm; daily 5–11pm. Open year-round.

Park Corner Bistro 🌟🌟 NEW AMERICAN   The newest eatery in the center of Oak Bluffs is a quaint and cozy bistro that has a definite European aura. It's an intimate and romantic space for casual fine dining. Owner Josh Aronie and his partner, chef Jesse Martin, serve up creative offerings, and locals and visitors keep the place packed all summer. Favorite appetizers are the beet salad and the Parmesan gnocchi, which is sautéed with chanterelle and black trumpet mushrooms. The best main course choices are the Australian lamb loin with sweet-corn flan and champagne corn emulsion, and the Black Angus steak with arugula, Yukon Gold whipped potatoes, and Vidalia onion compote. For dessert, don't miss the warm fruit cobbler with vanilla ice cream.

20H Kennebec Ave. (across from the OB Post Office). ℂ **508/696-9922.** Reservations suggested. Main courses $26–$33. AE, MC, V. July–Aug daily 5:30–10pm (light menu till midnight); call for off-season hours. Open year-round.

Sweet Life Cafe 🌟🌟🌟 FRENCH/AMERICAN   Locals are crazy about this pearl of a restaurant, set in a restored Victorian house on upper Circuit Avenue and run by chef/owner Jackson Kenworth. In season, the most popular seating is outside in the gaily lit garden. Fresh island produce is featured, with seafood specials an enticing draw. The menu changes often and everything is terrific. Expect yummy soups such as vegetable white bean pistou and main

The Vineyard's Best Sweet Shops

Mad Martha's ℛ: Vineyarders are mad for this locally made ice cream, which comes in 2 dozen enticing flavors. You could opt for a restrained mango sorbet, which isn't to say you shouldn't go for a hot-fudge sundae. 10 Circuit Ave. (in the center of town). ℂ **508/693-9151**. Branches at 8 Union St., Vineyard Haven (ℂ **508/693-5883**), and 7 N. Water St., Edgartown (ℂ **508/627-8761**). Closed Oct–Apr.

Murdick's Fudge: Since 1887, the Murdick family has been serving up homemade fudge, brittle, clusters, and bark. Bring the kids and watch the candy-makers in progress. 5 Circuit Ave. and 21 N. Water St., Edgartown. ℂ **888/553-8343** or 508/627-8047. Summer Mon–Fri 10am–5pm, Sun–Sat 10am–8pm.

courses such as roast lamb loin with ratatouille. If the roasted lobster with potato-Parmesan risotto, roasted yellow beets, and smoked-salmon chive fondue is offered, order it.

63 Circuit Ave. ℂ **508/696-0200**. Reservations recommended. Main courses $23–$36. AE, DISC, MC, V. Mid-May to mid-Sept daily 5:30–10pm; Apr to mid-May and mid-Sept to Dec Thurs–Mon 5:30–9:30pm. Closed Jan–Apr.

MODERATE

Tsunami ℛ *(Finds* ASIAN/INTERNATIONAL   For something a little different in fine dining, look for the bright red, two-story cottage on Oak Bluffs Harbor. When you climb up the stairs and enter the second-floor dining room of this small restaurant, you'll feel like you've discovered something very special indeed. It's a picture-perfect view of Oak Bluffs Harbor in a spare room with Asian accents. But people also come to Tsunami for the food. While the restaurant specializes in seafood, there's also pheasant, duck, pork, and filet mignon, as well as wonderful pad Thai and tuna sashimi appetizers to start. The chef's specialty is the seared tuna with mango-mint mashed potatoes served with mixed vegetables and onion soy relish. The downstairs bar, with its cozy sitting area, has become quite a summer hangout in the evenings.

6 Circuit Ave. Extension. ℂ **508/696-8900**. Reservations accepted. Main courses $15–$29. AE, MC, V. June–Aug daily 11am–3pm and 5:30–10pm; call for off-season hours. Closed mid-Oct to mid-May.

Zapotec ⋇ *Value* MEXICAN/SOUTHWESTERN   Look for the chile-pepper lights entwining the porch of this clapboard cottage: They're a beacon leading to tasty regional Mexican cuisine, from mussels *Oaxaca* (with chipotle peppers, cilantro, lime, and cream) to crab cakes *Tulum* (mixed with grilled peppers and cilantro, served with dual salsas), plus the standard chicken and beef burritos. There are also tasty fish tacos, topped with a creamy yogurt dressing, and a small children's menu. A good mole is hard to find this far north; here you can accompany it with Mexico's unbeatable beers (including several rarely spotted north of the border), refreshing sangria, or perhaps a hand-picked, well-priced wine.

14 Kennebec Ave. (in the center of town). ℭ **508/693-6800**. www.zapotec restaurant.com. Reservations not accepted. Main courses $12–$20. AE, MC, V. May–Oct daily noon–3pm and 5–11pm. Closed Nov–Apr.

INEXPENSIVE

Coop deVille ⋇ SEAFOOD   Of the several open-air harborfront choices in Oak Bluffs, this one has the best service and food. This outdoor fried seafood shack serves up tasty beer-battered shrimp, grilled swordfish, lobster salad, and "world famous" chicken wings. Wing connoisseurs can choose from mild to suicide to 3-mile island, as well as Cajun, mango, and Maryland style, among others. It's a fun place to people-watch on sunny summer days, as boaters cruise around the harbor.

Dockside Market Place. ℭ **508/693-3420**. Reservations not accepted. Most items $9–$20. MC, V. June–Aug daily 11am–10pm; call for off-season hours. Closed mid-Oct to Apr.

Slice of Life *Finds* DELI   This deli at the upper end of Circuit Avenue is the place to head for gourmet sandwiches, salads, and soups. There are just a handful of tables inside and more tables out on the screened porch in front. The eclectic menu includes burgers and pizza. All of the food is very wholesome. There's also wine, beer, and specialty coffees.

50 Circuit Ave. ℭ **508/693-3838**. Reservations not accepted. Most items under $10. MC, V. June–Aug daily 8am–8pm; call for off-season hours. Open year-round.

VINEYARD HAVEN (TISBURY)
EXPENSIVE

Le Grenier ⋇⋇ FRENCH   If Paris is the heart of France, Lyons is its belly—and that's where chef/owner Jean Dupon grew up on his Mama's hearty cuisine (she now helps out here, cooking lunch). Dupon has the Continental moves down, as evidenced by such classics as steak au poivre; calf's brains Grenobloise with beurre noir and capers; and lobster Normande flambéed with calvados, apples, and cream. Despite the fact that Le Grenier means (and, in fact, is housed in) an attic, the restaurant is quite romantic, especially when aglow with hurricane lamps. *Remember:* You must BYOB here.

96 Main St. (in the center of town). ✆ 508/693-4906. Reservations suggested. Main courses $22–$32. AE, DC, DISC, MC, V. Daily 11am–2pm and 5:30–10pm. Open year-round.

Zephrus at the Mansion House ☞☞ INTERNATIONAL
This hip restaurant at the Mansion House in the center of Vineyard Haven is a great place to go for casual fine dining. Seating is at the sidewalk cafe on Main Street or inside by the hearth in view of the open kitchen. Menu items are creative at this high-energy venue, and portions are generous. For starters you may try the snow crab cakes or the spicy mussels. Main-course winners are pan-roasted pork tenderloin served with sweet 'tater tots; and shrimp and farfalle pasta. Though the menu is in constant flux, there is always a good vegetarian choice such as the delicious vegetable risotto with truffle vinaigrette. Since the restaurant is in BYOB Vineyard Haven, you'll want to bring your favorite wine to complement this winning cuisine. The corkage fee is $5 per table.

Main St. ✆ 508/693-3416. Reservations recommended. Main courses $18–$35. AE, DC, DISC, MC, V. July–Aug Mon-Sat 11:30am–3:30pm and 5:30–10pm, Sun 8am–2pm and 5:30–10pm; call for off-season hours. Open year-round.

MODERATE
Black Dog Tavern ☞ NEW AMERICAN How does a humble harbor shack come to be a national icon? Location helps. So do cool T-shirts. Soon after Shenandoah captain Robert Douglas decided, in 1971, that this hard-working port could use a good restaurant, influential vacationers, stuck waiting for the ferry, began to wander into this saltbox to tide themselves over with a bit of "blackout cake" or peanut-butter pie. The rest is history, as smart marketing moves extrapolated on word of mouth. The smartest of these moves was the invention of the signature "Martha's Vineyard Whitefoot," a black Lab whose stalwart profile now adorns everything from baby's overalls to doggy bandannas, golf balls, and needlepoint kits. Originally, the symbol signaled Vineyard ties to fellow insiders; now it merely bespeaks an acquaintance with mail-order catalogs.

Still, tourists love this rough-hewn tavern, and it's not just hype that keeps them happy. The food is still home-cooking good—heavy on the seafood, of course (including grilled swordfish with banana, basil, and lime; and bluefish with mustard soufflé sauce)—and the blackout cake has lost none of its appeal. Though the lines grow ever longer (there can be a wait to get on the waiting list!), nothing much has changed at this beloved spot. Eggs Galveston for breakfast at the Black Dog Tavern is still one of the ultimate Vineyard experiences—go early, when it first opens, and sit on the porch, where the views are perfect.

Beach St. Extension (on the harbor). © **508/693-9223.** Reservations not accepted. Main courses $14–$27. AE, MC, V. June to early Sept Mon–Sat 7–11am, 11:30am–2:30pm, and 5–10pm, Sun 7am–1pm and 5–10pm; call for off-season hours. Open year-round.

INEXPENSIVE

Art Cliff Diner ⭐ ECLECTIC DINER   Expect the best food you've ever had at a diner at this quirky establishment. It's a short walk from the center of Vineyard Haven. Be aware that the hours are a little unreliable and you should call to be sure it is open before making the trek. The food here is really scrumptious, whether you are having the fish of the day that has just been caught that morning served with herbs from the chef's garden, or a simple burger that is cooked just right. Desserts are homemade, of course.

39 Beach Rd. © **508/693-1224.** Reservations not accepted. Main courses all under $15. No credit cards. July–Aug daily 8am–8pm; call for off-season hours. Closed Nov–Apr.

TAKEOUT & PICNIC FARE

Black Dog Bakery ⭐   In need of a snack at 5am? That's when the doors to this fabled bakery open; from mid-morning on, it's elbow-room only. This selection of freshly baked breads, muffins, and desserts can't be beat. Don't forget some homemade doggie biscuits for your pooch.

Water St. (near the harbor). © **508/693-4786.** Summer daily 5:30am–7pm; winter daily 5:30am–5pm.

CHILMARK (INCLUDING MENEMSHA) & WEST TISBURY

VERY EXPENSIVE

The Beach Plum Inn & Restaurant ⭐⭐⭐ SEAFOOD   This jewel of a restaurant is located in an inn that sits on a bluff overlooking the fishing village of Menemsha. Extensive renovations and attention to quality have made this one of the island's top dining venues. Guests can dine inside in the spare, but elegant, dining room, or outside on the new tiled patio. Either way, diners enjoy sunset views of the harbor. Chef James McDonough's most popular dishes include hazelnut-encrusted halibut with Marsala wine beurre blanc sauce; and Alaskan king salmon, grilled over Peruvian blue

mashed potatoes with a morel mushroom sauce and crabmeat timbale. The most winning appetizer is the blackened lobster tips, served
with mango cream sauce and house-cured gravlax with homemade
wild rice and corn pancakes. For dessert, you'll flip for the chocolate
quadruple-layer cake made with white and dark chocolate mouse and
Chambord. In the spring and fall, there is usually an ethereal soufflé
on the menu, either Grand Marnier or chocolate.

At the Beach Plum Inn. 50 Beach Plum Lane (off North Rd.), Menemsha. ℂ 508/
645-9454. www.beachpluminn.com. Reservations required. Main courses
$32–$40; 4-course fixed-price menu $68. Off season only 3-course fixed-price menu
$50. Mid-June to early Sept daily seatings 5:30–6:45pm and 8–9:30pm; call for off-
season hours. Closed Dec–Apr.

Home Port 🐾🐾 *Kids* SEAFOOD   When the basics—a lobster
and a sunset—are what you crave, head to this classic Vineyard
establishment, a favorite of locals and visitors alike. At first glance,
prices for the lobster dinners may seem a bit high, but note that they
include an appetizer of your choice (go with the stuffed quahog),
salad, amazing fresh-baked breads, a non-alcoholic beverage
(remember, it's BYOB in these parts), and dessert. The decor is on
the simple side, but who really cares? It's the riveting harbor views
that have drawn fans to this family-friendly place for over 60 years.
Locals not keen on summer crowds prefer to order their lobster dinners for pickup (less than half-price) at the restaurant door, then
head down to Menemsha Beach for a private sunset supper.

North Rd., Menemsha. ℂ 508/645-2679. Reservations required. Fixed-price dinners $25–$45. MC, V. Mid-June to Labor Day daily 5–10pm; call for off-season
hours. Closed early Oct to mid-May.

EXPENSIVE

At The Cornerway 🐾🐾 NEW AMERICAN/CARIBBEAN
This elegant fine-dining restaurant in Chilmark was opened by
Jamaican chef Deon Thomas. It's a good dining option if you are
staying at one of the up-island inns in Chilmark or West Tisbury.
Chef Thomas, who cooks with Caribbean flair, specializes in com-
bining the freshest ingredients with wonderful spices. The menu is
changed daily, but be on the lookout for tasty starters such as the
spicy cilantro-laced gazpacho, smoked mako bites, and Dutch-pot
jerk venison. As a main course, consider the unusual fish dish, the
rosemary-roasted whole pompano; the celebratory oven-crisped
Oriental spice duck; or, of course, Jamaican jerk chicken. Remember this restaurant is in a "dry" town, so you must BYOB. Corkage
fee is $4 per table.

13 State Rd., Chilmark. ✆ **508/645-9300.** Reservations recommended. Main courses $24–$38. MC, V. July–Aug 5–10pm; call for off-season hours. Closed Nov–Apr.

Bittersweet ✿✿ NEW AMERICAN   It's a bit of an adventure to take the long drive down winding country roads into the heart of the Vineyard to this very fine restaurant. This pricey but popular up-island restaurant is earning raves for the high quality of the food and service. It's also a hip venue, the place where island-insiders who wouldn't be caught dead in the down-island towns go to see and be seen. From the outside, it looks like a modest roadhouse, but the inside is stylishly decorated with fine dining in mind. The menu changes often, as the chef combines unusual ingredients with island produce, meats, and locally caught fish. The restaurant is located in West Tisbury, a dry town, so you must BYOB here. Also, no credit cards are accepted, so bring plenty of cash.

688 State Rd., West Tisbury. ✆ **508/696-3966.** Main courses $25–$36. No credit cards. July–Aug daily 6–10pm; call for off-season hours. Closed Jan–Apr.

Lambert's Cove Country Inn Restaurant ✿✿ NEW AMERI-CAN   One of the Vineyard's favorite chefs, Joe Silva, is now cooking at this romantic country inn and drawing enthusiastic reviews. If you are staying in one of the down-island towns, such as Edgartown or Oak Bluffs, driving through the wooded countryside to this secluded inn feels like an expedition to an earlier time. The interior of the inn's fine-dining restaurant is charming, with crisp white tablecloths and antique furniture. In good weather, you can dine al fresco on a deck surrounded by flowering trees and shrubs. Many people believe that Lambert's Cove is the perfect place for a special occasion, say an anniversary dinner or a Mother's Day brunch. The menu features fresh island seafood, veal, beef, poultry, and vegetables from local gardens and farms. You may begin your meal with a crab and asparagus Napoleon, or simply with a luscious cream of mushroom soup. Special dinner entrees include grilled marinated duck breast with orange sauce and green apple chutney, or sea scallop and leek casserole baked in a sherry lobster cream sauce. Desserts are homemade delicacies. Don't forget: The town of West Tisbury is "dry," so you must bring your own alcoholic beverage. Corkage fee is $4.

Lambert's Cove Rd. (off State Rd., about 3 miles west of Vineyard Haven), West Tisbury. ✆ **508/693-2298.** www.lambertscoveinn.com. Reservations suggested. Main courses $24–$32. AE, MC, V. July–Aug daily 6–9pm; call for off-season hours. Open year-round.

MODERATE

The Bite *ᏒᏒ* *(Finds)* SEAFOOD   It's usually places like "The Bite" that we crave when we think of New England. This is your quintessential "chowdah" and clam shack, flanked by picnic tables. Run by two sisters using their grandmother's recipes, this place makes superlative chowder, potato salad, fried fish, and so forth. The food comes in graduated containers, with a jumbo portion of shrimp topping out at around $26.

Basin Rd. (off North Rd., about ¼ mile northeast of the harbor), Menemsha. ℂ **508/ 645-9239.** Main courses $18–$30. No credit cards. July–Aug daily 11am–3pm and 5–7pm; call for off-season hours. Closed late Sept to Apr.

TAKEOUT & PICNIC FARE

Alley's General Store *(Finds)*   That endangered rarity, a true New England general store, Alley's—in business since 1858—nearly foundered in the profit-mad 1980s. Luckily, the Martha's Vineyard Preservation Trust interceded to give it a new lease on life, along with a much-needed structural overhaul. The stock is still the same, though: basically, everything you could possibly need, from scrub brushes to fresh-made salsa. Best of all, the no-longer-sagging front porch still supports a popular bank of benches, along with a blizzard of bulletin board notices. For a local's-eye view of noteworthy activities and events, this is the first place to check.

State Rd. (in the center of town), West Tisbury. ℂ **508/693-0088.** Summer Mon–Sat 7am–7pm, Sun 8am–6pm; winter Mon–Sat 7am–6pm, Sun 8am–5pm. Open year-round.

West Tisbury Farmer's Market *(Finds)*   This seasonal outdoor market, open Wednesday from 2:30 to 5:30pm and Saturday from 9am to noon, is among the biggest and best in New England, and certainly the most rarefied, with local celebrities loading up on prize produce and snacking on pesto bread and other international goodies. The fun starts in June and runs for 18 Saturdays and 10 Wednesdays.

Old Agricultural Hall, West Tisbury. ℂ **508/693-3638.**

6

Exploring Martha's Vineyard

Martha's Vineyard offers many activities and diversions to occupy your time. Whether you want to shop, fish, sail, golf, run, sightsee, or just relax, this chapter tells you where to find the best of everything.

1 Beaches & Recreational Pursuits

BEACHES Most down-island beaches in Vineyard Haven, Oak Bluffs, and Edgartown are open to the public and just a walk or short bike ride from town. In season, shuttle buses make stops at **State Beach** between Oak Bluffs and Edgartown. Most of the Vineyard's magnificent up-island shoreline, alas, is privately owned or restricted to residents, and thus off-limits to transient visitors. Renters in up-island communities, however, can obtain a beach sticker (around $35–$50 for a season sticker) for those private beaches by applying with a lease at the relevant **town hall: West Tisbury, *©* 508/696-0147; Chilmark, *©* 508/645-2113** or 508/ 645-2100; or **Aquinnah, *©* 508/645-2300.** Also, many up-island inns offer the perk of temporary passes to a hot spot such as Lucy Vincent Beach (see below). In addition to the public beaches listed below, you may also track down a few hidden coves by requesting a map of conservation properties from the **Martha's Vineyard Land Bank** (*©* 508/627-7141). Below is a list of visitor-friendly beaches:

- **Aquinnah Beach** ✴✴✴ (Moshup Beach), off Moshup Trail: Parking costs $15 a day (in season) at this peaceful ½-mile beach just east (Atlantic side) of the colorful cliffs. Go early, since the lot is small and a bit of a hike from the beach. I suggest that all but one person get off at the wooden boardwalk along the road with towels, toys, lunches, and so on, while the remaining one heads back up to park. In season, you can also take the shuttle buses from down-island to the parking lot at the Aquinnah cliffs and walk to the beach. Although it is against the law, nudists tend to gravitate toward this beach.

Remember that climbing the cliffs or stealing clay for a souvenir here is against the law for environmental reasons: The cliffs are suffering from rapid erosion. Restrooms are near the parking lot.

- **East Beach** *&&*, Wasque (pronounced *Way*-squee) Reservation, Chappaquiddick: Relatively few people go to the bother of biking or hiking (or four-wheel-driving) this far, so this beach remains one of the Vineyard's best-kept secrets (and an ideal spot for bird-watching). You should be able to find all the privacy you crave. If you're staying in Edgartown, the Chappy ferry is probably minutes by bike from your inn. Biking on Chappaquiddick is one of the great Vineyard experiences, but the roads can be quite sandy, and you may have to dismount during the 5-mile ride to Wasque. Because of its exposure on the east shore of the island, the surf here is rough. Pack a picnic, and make this an afternoon adventure. Sorry, no facilities.

- **Joseph A. Sylvia State Beach** *&&&*, midway between Oak Bluffs and Edgartown: Stretching a mile and flanked by a paved bike path, this placid beach has views of Cape Cod and Nantucket Sound and is prized for its gentle and (relatively) warm waves, which make it perfect for swimming. The wooden drawbridge is a local landmark, and visitors and islanders alike have been jumping off it and into the water for years. Be aware that State Beach is one of the Vineyard's most popular; come midsummer, it's packed. The shuttle bus stops here, and roadside parking is also available—but it fills up fast, so stake your claim early. Located on the eastern shore of the island, this is a Nantucket Sound beach, so waters are shallow and rarely rough. There are no restrooms, and only the Edgartown end of the beach, known as Bend-in-the-Road Beach, has lifeguards.

- **Lake Tashmoo Town Beach** *&*, off Herring Creek Road, Vineyard Haven: The only spot on the island where lake meets the ocean, this tiny strip of sand is good for swimming and surf casting but is somewhat marred by limited parking and often brackish waters. Nonetheless, this is a popular spot, as beachgoers enjoy a choice between the Vineyard Sound beach with mild surf or the placid lake beach. Bikers will have no problem reaching this beach from Vineyard Haven; otherwise, you have to have access to a car to get to this beach.

- **Lighthouse Beach** *&*, off North Water Street, Edgartown: Even though tiny, unattended, lacking parking, and often seaweed-strewn, it's terribly scenic and a perfect place to watch

Exploring Martha's Vineyard

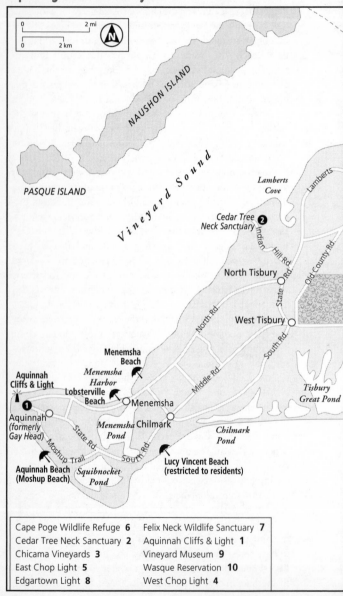

Cape Poge Wildlife Refuge **6**	Felix Neck Wildlife Sanctuary **7**
Cedar Tree Neck Sanctuary **2**	Aquinnah Cliffs & Light **1**
Chicama Vineyards **3**	Vineyard Museum **9**
East Chop Light **5**	Wasque Reservation **10**
Edgartown Light **8**	West Chop Light **4**

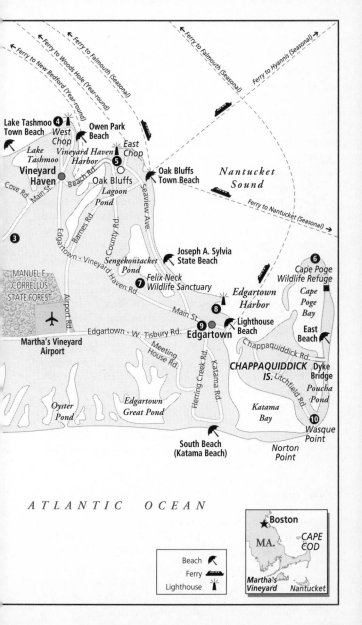

Lake Tashmoo **4** Owen Park
Town Beach **West** Beach
Lake **Chop** *East*
Tashmoo *Vineyard Haven* **Chop**
Vineyard *Harbor* **5**
Haven *Beach Rd.* Oak Bluffs
Cove Rd. **Oak Bluffs** Town Beach
Main St. *Lagoon*
Pond *Nantucket*
Sound

Ferry to Falmouth (Seasonal)
Ferry to Woods Hole (Year-round)
Ferry to New Bedford (Year-round)
Ferry to Falmouth (Seasonal)
Ferry to Hyannis (Seasonal)
Ferry to Nantucket (Seasonal)

3

MANUEL F.
CORRELLUS
STATE FOREST

Sengekontacket
Pond
Joseph A. Sylvia
State Beach
Felix Neck
Wildlife Sanctuary
7

6
Cape Poge
Wildlife Refuge
Cape
Poge
Bay

Edgartown
Harbor

Main St **8**
9 Lighthouse
Edgartown Beach
East
Beach
Chappaquiddick Rd.

Martha's Vineyard
Airport

Edgartown - W. Tisbury Rd.
Meeting
House Rd.

CHAPPAQUIDDICK
IS. *Litchfield Rd.* Dyke
Bridge
Poucha
Pond

Airport Rd.

Edgartown - Vineyard Haven Rd.
Barnes Rd.
County Rd.
Seaview Ave.

Herring Creek Rd.
Katama Rd.

Katama
Bay
10
Wasque
Point

Oyster
Pond

Edgartown
Great Pond

South Beach
(Katama Beach)
Norton
Point

A T L A N T I C   O C E A N

Beach
Ferry
Lighthouse

★ Boston
MA. CAPE
COD
Martha's
Vineyard Nantucket

the boats drift in and out of the harbor. Fuller Beach, nearby, is popular with a college crowd. No lifeguards or restrooms. Both beaches are within walking distance of the center of Edgartown.

- **Lobsterville Beach** ⭐⭐, at the end of Lobsterville Road in Aquinnah (restricted to residents): This 2-mile beauty on Menemsha Pond boasts calm, shallow waters that are ideal for children. It's also a prime spot for birding—just past the dunes are nesting areas for terns and gulls. Surf casters tend to gravitate here, too. The only drawback is that parking is for residents only. This is a great beach for bikers to hit on their way back from Aquinnah before taking the bike ferry over to Menemsha.

- **Lucy Vincent Beach** ⭐⭐⭐ (restricted to residents), off South Road, Chilmark: It's a shame that the island's most secluded and breathtaking beach is restricted to Chilmark town residents and guests only (don't forget that many up-island inns offer guest passes). Lined with red and brown clay cliffs, this wide stretch of sand and pounding surf is a virtual oasis. If you want to let it all hang out, head left down the beach.

- **Menemsha Beach** ⭐⭐, next to Dutchers Dock in Menemsha Harbor: Despite its rough surface, this small but well-trafficked strand, with lifeguards and restrooms, is popular with families. In season, it's virtually wall-to-wall colorful umbrellas and beach toys. Nearby food vendors in Menemsha sell everything from ice cream and hot dogs to steamers and shrimp cocktail—also a plus here. *Tip:* This beach is the ideal place for a sunset. I suggest you get a lobster dinner to go at the famous **Home Port restaurant** next to the beach in Menemsha (see listing in chapter 5), grab a blanket and a bottle of wine, and picnic here for a spectacular evening. If you are staying at an up-island inn, Menemsha is a fun bike ride downhill. Energetic bikers can make it from down-island towns; plan to make it part of an entire day of scenic biking. Otherwise, you'll need a car to get here.

- **Oak Bluffs Town Beach,** Seaview Avenue: This sandy strip extends from both sides of the ferry wharf, which makes it a convenient place to linger while waiting for the next boat. This is an in-town beach, within walking distance for visitors staying in Oak Bluffs. The surf is consistently calm and the sand smooth, so it's also ideal for families with small children. Public restrooms are available at the ferry dock, but there are no lifeguards.

- **Owen Park Beach,** off Main Street in Vineyard Haven: A tiny strip of harborside beach adjoining a town green with swings and a bandstand will suffice for young children, who, by the way, get lifeguard supervision. There are no restrooms, but this in-town beach is probably a quick walk from your Vineyard Haven inn.

- **South Beach** ⚓⚓⚓ (Katama Beach), about 4 miles south of Edgartown on Katama Road: If you have time for only one trip to the beach and you can't get up-island, I'd go with this popular, 3-mile barrier strand that boasts heavy wave action (check with lifeguards for swimming conditions), sweeping dunes, and, most important, relatively ample parking space. It's also accessible by bike path or shuttle. Lifeguards patrol some sections of the beach, and there are sparsely scattered toilet facilities. The rough surf here is popular with surfers. *Tip:* Families tend to head to the left, college kids to the right.

- **Wasque Beach** ⚓⚓, Wasque Reservation, Chappaquiddick: Surprisingly easy to get to (via the On-Time ferry and a bike or car), this ½-mile-long beach has all the amenities—lifeguards, parking, restrooms—without the crowds. Wasque Beach is a Trustees of Reservations property, and if you are not a member of this land-preservation organization, you must pay at the gatehouse (© **508/627-7260;** $3 per car and $3 per person) for access in season.

BICYCLING What's unique about biking on Martha's Vineyard is that you'll find not only the smooth, well-maintained paths indigenous to the Cape, but also long stretches of virtually untrafficked roads that, while rough in spots, traverse breathtaking country landscapes with sweeping ocean views. Serious cyclists will want to do a 1-day **circle-the-island tour** through the up-island towns and out to Aquinnah, stopping in Menemsha before heading back down-island. You'll pass through all six Vineyard towns and some unique off-the-beaten-track businesses.

For much of the trek, you'll be traveling country roads, so beware of sandy shoulders and blind curves. You'll avoid tour buses by taking routes outlined below, such as the Moshup Trail to Aquinnah or the triangle of paved bike paths between the down-island towns. These bike paths, roughly 8 miles to a side, link the down-island towns of Oak Bluffs, Edgartown, and Vineyard Haven (the Sound portion along Beach Road, flanked by water on both sides, is especially scenic). From Edgartown, you can also follow the bike path to South Beach (also known as Katama Beach). The bike paths are accessible off Edgartown–West Tisbury Road in Oak Bluffs, West Tisbury, and Edgartown.

The up-island roads leading to West Tisbury, Chilmark, Menemsha, and Aquinnah are a cyclist's paradise, with sprawling, unspoiled pastureland, old farmhouses, and brilliant sea views reminiscent of Ireland's countryside. But keep in mind that the terrain is often hilly, and the roads are narrow and a little rough around the edges. Try **South Road** from the town of West Tisbury to Chilmark Center (about 5 miles). En route, you'll pass stone walls rolling over moors, clumps of pine and wildflowers, verdant marshes and tidal pools, and, every once in awhile, an old Vineyard farmhouse. About halfway, the road becomes hillier as you approach a summit, **Abel's Hill,** home to the **Chilmark Cemetery,** where comedian John Belushi is buried. A mile farther, don't miss the view of **Allen Farm,** an operating sheep farm amongst picturesque pastureland. **Middle Road** is another lovely ride with a country feel and will also get you from West Tisbury to Chilmark (it's usually less trafficked, too).

My favorite up-island route is the 6-mile stretch from Chilmark Center out to Aquinnah via **State Road** and **Moshup Trail** ⟨⟩. The ocean views on this route are spectacular. Don't miss the **Quitsa Pond Lookout,** about 2 miles down **State Road,** which provides a panoramic vista of Nashaquitsa and Menemsha ponds, beyond which you can see Menemsha, the Vineyard Sound, and the Elizabeth Islands—it's an amazing place to watch the sunset on a clear evening. A bit farther, just over the Aquinnah town line, is the Aquinnah spring, a roadside iron pipe where you can refill your water bottle with the freshest and coldest water on the island. At the fork after the spring, turn left on Moshup Trail—in fact, a regular road—and follow the coast, with its gorgeous views of the water and the sweeping sand dunes. You'll soon wind up in Aquinnah, where you can explore the red-clay cliffs and pristine beaches. On the return trip, you can take the handy bike ferry ($7 round-trip) from Aquinnah to Menemsha. It runs daily in the summer and on weekends in May.

A word about Aquinnah: Almost every visitor to the Vineyard finds his or her way to the cliffs, and with all the tour buses lined up in the huge parking lot and the rows of tacky concession stands and gift shops, this can seem like a rather outrageous tourist trap. You're right; it's not the Grand Canyon. But the observation deck, with its view of the colorful cliffs, the adorable brick lighthouse, and the Elizabeth Islands beyond, will make you glad you bothered. Instead of rushing away, stop for a cool drink and a clam roll at the snack bar with the deck overlooking the ocean.

The adventurous **mountain biker** will want to head to the trails in the **Manuel F. Correllus State Forest** (© 508/693-2540), a vast spread of scrub oak and pine smack-dab in the middle of the island that boasts paved paths and hiking and horseback-riding trails. If you seek an escape from the multitudes, the trails are so extensive that even during peak summer season you may not see another soul for hours. On most of the conservation land on the Vineyard, however, mountain biking is prohibited for environmental reasons.

Bike-rental operations are ubiquitous near the ferry landings in Vineyard Haven and Oak Bluffs, and there are also a few outfits in Edgartown. For information on bike-rental shops, see "Getting Around," in chapter 5.

A very good outfit out of Boston, called **Bike Riders** (© 800/473-7040; www.bikeriderstours.com), runs 6-day island-hopping tours of Martha's Vineyard and Nantucket. The cost is $2,180 per person, plus $60 if you need to borrow one of their bikes. It's a perfect way to experience both islands.

The Chamber of Commerce has a great bike map available at its office on Beach Road in Vineyard Haven (see "Visitor Information," in chapter 5).

BIRD-WATCHING **Felix Neck Wildlife Sanctuary,** Edgartown–Vineyard Haven Road, Edgartown (© 508/627-4850), is an easy 2-mile bike ride from Edgartown. A Massachusetts Audubon Property, its visitor center is staffed by naturalists who lead bird-watching walks, among other activities. You'll see osprey nests on your right on the way to the center. Pick up a trail map at the center before heading out. Several of the trails pass Sengekontacket Pond, and the orange trail leads to Waterfowl Pond, which has an observation blind with bird-sighting information. While managed by the conservation group Sheriff's Meadow Foundation, the 300-acre **Cedar Tree Neck Sanctuary** 🐦🐦🐦 (State Rd., follow to Indian Hill Rd. to Obed Daggett Rd. and follow signs), Tisbury (see "Nature Trails," below), was acquired with the assistance of Massachusetts Audubon. The area has several trails, but you'll eventually arrive out on a picturesque bluff overlooking Vineyard Sound and the Elizabeth Islands. Check out the map posted at the parking lot for an overview of the property. The range of terrain here—ponds, fields, woods, and bogs—provides diverse opportunities for sightings. **Wasque Reservation** ★★★ on Chappaquiddick, Martha's Vineyard (see "Nature Trails," below), a sanctuary owned by the Trustees of Reservations and located on the easternmost reaches of the island, is accessible by bike or four-wheel-drive (see "Getting Around," in chapter 5). The hundreds of untouched acres here draw flocks of nesting shorebirds, including egrets, herons, terns, and plovers.

FISHING For shellfishing, you'll need to get information and a permit from the appropriate town hall (for the telephone numbers, see "Beaches," above). Popular spots for surf casting include **Wasque Point** on Chappaquiddick (see "Nature Trails," below). The party boat *Skipper* (© **508/693-1238;** www.mvskipper.com) offers half-day trips out of Oak Bluffs harbor in season. The cost is $40 for adults and $25 for children 12 and under. Bring your own poles and bait. You can arrange deep-sea excursions aboard **Big Eye Charters** (© **508/627-3649;** www.bigeyecharters.com) out of Edgartown and **Summer's Lease** (© **508/693-2880**) out of Oak Bluffs. Up-island, there is **North Shore Charters** (© **508/645-2993;** www.bassnblue. com) and **Flashy Lady Charters** (© **508/645-2462;** www.flashy ladycharters.com) both out of Menemsha, locus of the island's com-mercial fishing fleet (you may recognize this weathered port from *Jaws*). Charter costs are about $400 for a half-day for five people and $750 for a full day.

IGFA world-record holder Capt. Leslie Smith operates **Backlash Charters** (© **508/627-0148;** www.backlashcharters.com), special-izing in light tackle and fly-fishing, out of Edgartown. Cooper Gilkes III, proprietor of **Coop's Bait & Tackle** at 147 W. Tisbury Rd. in Edgartown (© **508/627-3909**), which offers rentals as well as supplies, is another acknowledged authority. He's available as an instructor or charter guide, and even amenable to sharing hard-won pointers on local hot spots.

FITNESS Gym addicts can get their workout fix at the **Health Club at the Tisbury Inn** on Main Street in Vineyard Haven (© **508/693-7400**), which accepts visitors for a $10 fee.

GOLF The 9-hole **Mink Meadows Golf Course** off Franklin Street in Vineyard Haven (© **508/693-0600**), which, despite occu-pying a top-dollar chunk of real estate, is open to the general pub-lic. There is also the semiprivate, championship-level 18-hole **Farm Neck Golf Club** off Farm Neck Road in Oak Bluffs (© **508/693-3057**). The Cafe at Farm Neck serves a wonderful lunch overlooking their manicured greens. In season, greens fees at Mink Meadows are $42 for 9 holes and $63 for 18 holes. In season greens fees at Farm Neck are $50 for 9 holes and $90 for 18 holes.

ICE-SKATING   The **Martha's Vineyard Ice Arena** on Edgartown–Vineyard Haven Road, Oak Bluffs (© **508/693-4438**), offers public skating from mid-July to mid-April; call for details.

IN-LINE SKATING   In-line skaters are everywhere on the island's paved paths. You'll find rentals at **Sports Haven,** 5 Beach St., Vineyard Haven (© **508/696-0456**). Rates are about $15 to $30 per day, including pads.

NATURE TRAILS   About a fifth of the Vineyard's land mass has been set aside for conservation, and it's all accessible to energetic bikers and hikers. The **West Chop Woods,** off Franklin Street in Vineyard Haven, comprise 85 acres with marked walking trails. Midway between Vineyard Haven and Edgartown, the **Felix Neck Wildlife Sanctuary** (see "Bird-Watching," above) includes a 6-mile network of trails over varying terrain, from woodland to beach. Accessible by ferry from Edgartown, quiet Chappaquiddick is home to two sizable preserves: The **Cape Pogue Wildlife Refuge** 🐾🐾🐾 and **Wasque Reservation** 🐾🐾🐾 (© **508/627-7260,** gatehouse), covering much of the island's eastern barrier beach, have 709 acres that draw flocks of nesting or resting shorebirds. Also on the island, 3 miles east on Dyke Road, is another Trustees of Reservations property, the distinctly poetic and alluring **Mytoi,** a 14-acre Japanese garden that is an oasis of textures and flora and fauna.

The 633-acre **Long Point Wildlife Refuge** 🐾🐾🐾 off Waldron's Bottom Road in West Tisbury (© **508/693-7392,** gatehouse) offers heath and dunes, freshwater ponds, a popular family-oriented beach, and interpretive nature walks for children. In season, the Trustees of Reservations charges a $7 parking fee, plus $3 per adult over age 16. The 4,000-acre **Manuel F. Correllus Vineyard State Forest** occupies a sizable, if not especially scenic, chunk mid-island; it's riddled with mountain-bike paths and horseback-riding trails. This sanctuary was created in 1908 to try to save the endangered heath hen, a species now extinct. In season, there are free interpretive and birding walks.

Up-island, along the Sound, the **Menemsha Hills Reservation** off North Road in Chilmark (© **508/693-7662**) encompasses 210 acres of rocks and bluffs, with steep paths, lovely views, and even a public beach. **The Cedar Tree Neck Sanctuary,** off Indian Hill

Road southwest of Vineyard Haven (© **508/693-5207**), offers some 300 forested acres that end in a stony beach (alas, swimming and sunbathing are prohibited). It's still a refreshing retreat.

Some remarkable botanical surprises can be found at the 20-acre **Polly Hill Arboretum,** 809 State Rd., West Tisbury (© **508/693-9426**). Legendary horticulturist Polly Hill has developed this property over the past 40 years and allows the public to wander the grounds Thursday through Tuesday from 7am until 7pm. This place is particularly magical from mid-June to July when the Dogwood Allee is in bloom. Wanderers pass old stone walls on the way to The Tunnel of Love, an arbor of pleached hornbeam. There are also witch hazels, camellias, magnolias, and rhododendrons. To get there from Vineyard Haven, go south on State Road, bearing left at the junction of North Road. The entrance is just under a half-mile on the right. A donation of $5 for adults and $3 for children under 12 is requested.

TENNIS Public courts typically charge a small fee, and you can reserve one in person a day in advance. You'll find clay courts on **Church Street** in Vineyard Haven; non-clay in Oak Bluffs' **Niantic Park,** West Tisbury's **grammar school** on Old County Road, and the **Chilmark Community Center** on South Road. Three public courts—plus a basketball court, roller-hockey rink, softball field, and children's playground—are located at the **Edgartown Recreation Area** on Robinson Road. You can also book a court (1 day in advance only) at two semiprivate clubs in Oak Bluffs: the **Farm Neck Tennis Club** (© **508/693-9728**) and **the Island Country Club** on Beach Road (© **508/693-6574**). In season, expect to pay around $18 to $24 per hour for court time at these clubs.

WATERSPORTS **Wind's Up,** 199 Beach Rd., Vineyard Haven (© **508/693-4252**), rents canoes, kayaks, and various sailing craft, including windsurfers, and offers instruction on-site on a placid pond; it also rents surfboards and boogie boards. Canoes and kayaks rent for $18 to $20 per hour. Rank beginners may enjoy towing privileges at **M. V. Parasail** at pier 44 off Beach Road in Vineyard Haven (© **508/693-2838**), where you'll be airborne by parachute.

2 A Stroll Around Edgartown

A good way to get acclimated to the pace and flavor of the Vineyard is to walk the streets of Edgartown. This walk starts at the Dr. Daniel

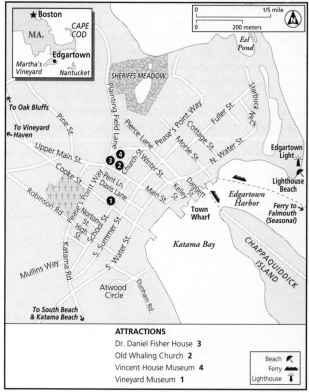

ATTRACTIONS

Dr. Daniel Fisher House **3**

Old Whaling Church **2**

Vincent House Museum **4**

Vineyard Museum **1**

Beach 🏖
Ferry ⛴
Lighthouse 🗼

Fisher House and meanders along for about a mile; depending on how long you linger at each stop, it should take about 2 to 3 hours.

If you're driving, park at the free lots at the edge of town (you'll see signs on the roads from Vineyard Haven and West Tisbury) and bike or take the shuttle bus (it only costs 50¢) to the Edgartown Visitor Center on Church Street. Around the corner are three local landmarks: the Dr. Daniel Fisher House, Vincent House Museum, and Old Whaling Church.

The **Dr. Daniel Fisher House,** 99 Main St. (© **508/627-8017**), is a prime example of Edgartown's trademark Greek revival opulence. A key player in the 19th-century whaling trade, Dr. Fisher amassed a fortune sufficient to found the Martha's Vineyard National Bank. Built in 1840, his prosperous and proud mansion boasts such classical elements as colonnaded porticos, as well as a delicate roof walk. The only way to view the interior (now head-quarters for the Martha's Vineyard Preservation Trust) is with a guided **Vineyard History Tour** (© **508/627-8619;** see "Organized Tours," later in this chapter). This tour originates next door at the **Vincent House Museum,** off Main Street between Planting Field Way and Church Street. The transplanted 1672 full Cape is considered the oldest surviving dwelling on the island. Plexiglas-covered cutaways permit a view of traditional building techniques, and three rooms have been refurbished to encapsulate the decorative styles of 3 centuries, from bare-bones Colonial to elegant Federal. The tour also takes in the neighboring **Old Whaling Church,** 89 Main St., a magnificent 1843 Greek revival edifice designed by local architect Frederick Baylies, Jr., and built as a whaling boat would have been, out of massive pine beams. With its 27-foot windows and 92-foot tower (a landmark easily spotted from the sea), the building, which is maintained by the Preservation Trust and still supports a Methodist parish, is now primarily used as a performance site.

Continuing down Main Street and turning right onto School Street, you'll pass another Baylies monument, the 1839 **Baptist Church,** which, having lost its spire, was converted into a private home with a rather grand, column-fronted facade. Two blocks farther, on your left, is the **Vineyard Museum,** 59 School St. (© **508/627-4441**), a fascinating complex assembled by the Dukes County Historical Society. An absorbing display of island history, these buildings hold exhibits of early Native American crafts; an entire 1765 house; an extraordinary array of maritime art, from whalers' logs to WPA-era studies by Thomas Hart Benton; a carriage house to catch odds and ends; and the Aquinnah Lighthouse's decommissioned Fresnel lens.

Give yourself enough time to explore the museum's curiosities before heading south 1 block on Cooke Street. Cater-cornered across South Summer Street, you'll spot the first of Baylies's impressive endeavors, the 1828 **Federated Church.** One block left are the offices of the *Vineyard Gazette,* 34 S. Summer St. (© **508/627-4311**). Operating out of a 1760 house, this exemplary small-town newspaper has been going strong since 1846; its 14,000 subscribers span the globe. If you are wandering by on a Thursday afternoon, you may catch a press run in progress.

Now, head down Main Street toward the water, stopping in at any inviting shops along the way. Veer left on Dock Street to reach the **Old Sculpin Gallery,** 58 Dock St. (© **508/627-4881;** open late June to early Sept). The output of the Martha's Vineyard Art Association displayed here tends to be amateurish, but you might happen upon a find. The real draw is the stark old building itself, which started out as a granary (part of Dr. Fisher's vast holdings) and spent the better part of the 20th century as a boat-building shop. Keep an eye out for vintage beauties when you cross the street to survey the harbor from the deck at Town Wharf. It's from here that the tiny On-Time ferry makes its 5-minute crossing to **Chappaquiddick Island,** hauling three cars at a time and a great many more sightseers—not that there's much to see on the other side. Just so you don't waste time tracking it down, the infamous **Dyke Bridge,** scene of the Kennedy/Kopechne debacle, has been dismantled and, at long last, replaced. However, the island does offer great stretches of conservation land that will reward the hearty hiker or mountain biker.

Mere strollers may want to remain in town to admire the many formidable captains' homes lining **North Water Street,** some of which have been converted into inns. Each has a tale to tell. The 1750 **Daggett House** (no. 59), expanded upon a 1660 tavern, and the original beehive oven is flanked by a "secret" passageway. Nathaniel Hawthorne holed up at the **Edgartown Inn** (no. 56) for nearly a year in 1789 while writing *Twice Told Tales*—and, it is rumored, romancing a local maiden who inspired *The Scarlet Letter.* On your way back to Main Street, you'll pass the **Gardner–Colby Gallery** (no. 27), filled with beautiful island-inspired paintings.

WINDING DOWN For a refreshment after all that walking, **The Newes from America,** at The Kelley House, 23 Kelley St. (just off N. Water St.; ✆ **508/627-4397**), is a classic old-world tavern with specialty beers and the best French onion soup on the island.

3 Museums & Historic Landmarks

Cottage Museum ✿ Oak Bluffs' famous "Camp Ground," a 34-acre circle with more than 300 multicolored, elaborately trimmed Carpenter's Gothic cottages, looks very much the way it might have more than a hundred years ago. These adorable little houses, loosely modeled on the revivalists' canvas tents that inspired them, have been handed down through the generations. Unless you happen to know a lucky camper, your best chance of getting inside one is to visit this homey little museum, which embodies the late-19th-century *Zeitgeist* and displays representative artifacts: bulky black bathing costumes and a melodeon used for informal hymnal singalongs.

The compact architecture is at once practical and symbolic. The Gothic-arched French doors off the peak-roofed second-story bedroom, for instance, lead to a tiny balcony used for keeping tabs on community doings. The daily schedule was, in fact, rather hectic. In 1867, when this cottage was built, campers typically attended three lengthy prayer services daily. Today's denizens tend to blend in with the visiting tourists, though opportunities for worship remain: at the 1878 Trinity Methodist Church within the park, or just outside, on Samoset Avenue, at the non-sectarian 1870 Union Chapel, a magnificent octagonal structure with superb acoustics (posted signs give the lineup of guest preachers and musicians).

At the very center of the Camp Grounds is the striking **Trinity Park Tabernacle** 𝒜𝒜. Built in 1879, the open-sided chapel is the largest wrought-iron structure in the country. Thousands can be accommodated on its long wooden benches, which are usually filled to capacity for the Sunday-morning services in summer, as well as for community sings (Wed in July–Aug) and occasional concerts (see "Martha's Vineyard After Dark," later in this chapter). Give yourself plenty of time to wander this peaceful enclave, where spirituality is tempered with a taste for harmless frivolity.

1 Trinity Park (within the Camp Meeting Grounds), Oak Bluffs. ℂ 508/693-7784. Admission $1.50 (donation). Mid-June to Sept Mon–Sat 10am–4pm. Closed Oct to mid-June.

Flying Horses Carousel 𝒜𝒜 *Kids*   You don't have to be a kid to enjoy the colorful mounts adorning what is considered to be the oldest working carousel in the country. Built in 1876 at Coney Island, this National Historic Landmark maintained by the Martha's Vineyard Preservation Trust predates the era of horses that "gallop." Lacking the necessary gears, these merely glide smoothly in place to the joyful strains of a calliope. The challenge lies in going for the brass ring that entitles the lucky winner to a free ride. Some regulars, adults included, have grown rather adept—you'll see them scoop up several in a single pass. In between rides, take a moment to admire the intricate hand-carving and real horsehair manes, and gaze into the horses' glass eyes for a surprise: tiny animal charms glinting within.

33 Circuit Ave. (at Lake Ave.), Oak Bluffs. ℂ 508/693-9481. Tickets $1 per ride, or $8 for 10. Late May to early Sept daily 9:30am–10pm; call for off-season hours. Closed mid-Oct to mid-Apr.

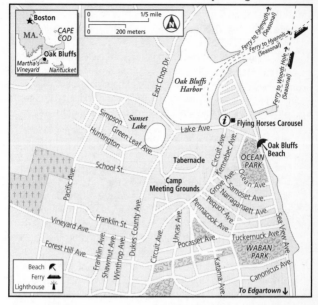

The Martha's Vineyard Historical Society ✿ All of Martha's Vineyard's colorful history is captured here, in a compound of historic buildings. To acclimate yourself chronologically, start with the pre-Colonial artifacts—from arrowheads to colorful Gay Head clay pottery—displayed in the 1845 **Captain Francis Pease House;** there's also an oral history exhibit, a gift shop, and a gallery to showcase local students' work.

The **Gale Huntington Reference Library** houses rare documentation of the island's history, from genealogical records to whale-ship logs. The recorded history of Martha's Vineyard (the name has been attributed, variously, to a Dutch seaman named Martin Wyngaard, and to the daughter and/or mother-in-law of early explorer Bartholomew Gosnold) begins in 1642 with the arrival of missionary Thomas Mayhew, Jr., whose father bought the whole chain of islands, from Nantucket through the Elizabeths, for £40, as a speculative venture. Mayhew, Jr., had loftier goals in mind, and it is a tribute to his methodology that long after he was lost at sea in 1657, the Wampanoags whom he had converted to Christianity continued to mourn him (a stone monument to his

Menemsha: A New England Fishing Village

For an authentic slice of the Vineyard, leave the hordes down-island and take the winding roads up-island to picturesque Menemsha, one of the few remaining fishing villages in New England. Shuttle buses make the trip a few times daily, or you can take the bike ferry from Aquinnah—a spectacularly scenic but exhausting bike ride. It seems appropriate to approach Menemsha from its colorful harbor, alongside the commercial fishing fleet, the sportfishing vessels, and the pleasure boats. You can spend the afternoon strolling the wharves at leisure and watching the fishermen unloading their catches—lobsters, tuna, and swordfish. Or simply wander over to the town beach, a colorful mélange of umbrellas, plastic buckets, and splashing youngsters. The water here can be quite cold, but after all that biking, you'll appreciate it.

For charter fishing trips operating out of Menemsha, contact **North Shore Charters** (② **508/645-2993;** www.bassnblue.com) and **Flashy Lady Charters** (② **508/645-2462;** www.flashyladycharters.com).

For a wonderful boat ride around Menemsha Harbor, take Hugh Taylor's catamaran *Arabella* (② **508/645-3511;**

memory survives by the roadside opposite the airport). In his brief sojourn on-island, Mayhew helped to found what would become Edgartown (named for the British heir apparent). The library's holdings on this epoch are extensive, and some extraordinary memorabilia, including scrimshaw and portraiture, are on view in the adjoining **Francis Foster Maritime Gallery.** Outside, a reproduction "tryworks" shows the means by which whale blubber was reduced to precious oil.

To get a sense of daily life during the era when the waters of the East Coast were the equivalent of a modern highway, visit the **Thomas Cooke House,** a shipwright-built Colonial, built in 1765, where the Customs collector lived and worked. A few of the house's 10 rooms are decorated as they might have been at the height of the maritime trade; others are devoted to special exhibits on other

www.outermostinn.com). A sunset cruise before dinner at the Home Port (see below) will be a most perfect evening.

There are several charming clothing, craft, and antiques shops in the village, as well as a fried-fish shack—**The Bite** *((508/645-9239)—which some have dubbed the best restaurant on Martha's Vineyard. Or if you prefer, have a celebrity-monikered sandwich (I like the Art Buchwald) at the **Menemsha Deli** ((508/645-9902). Two family-owned fish markets within yards of each other enjoy a healthy competition. **Larsen's** ((508/645-2680) has picnic tables for on-site eating; **Poole's Fish Market** ((508/645-2282) is strictly takeout.

At dinnertime, you may prefer to eat at the casual **Home Port** *((508/645-2679), perhaps the most famous restaurant on the Vineyard; it has perfect sunset views. Places to stay in Menemsha with ocean views include the **Menemsha Inn and Cottages** *((508/645-2521), a serene compound; and the **Beach Plum Inn** *((508/645-9454), an antique farmhouse with a full-service restaurant. See chapter 5 for details on both inns.

fascinating aspects of island history, such as the revivalist fever that enveloped Oak Bluffs. Further curiosities are stored in the nearby Carriage Shed. Among the vintage 19th-century vehicles are a painted peddler's cart, a whaleboat, a hearse, and a fire engine, and the odds and ends include some touching mementos of early tourism.

The Fresnel lens on display outside the museum was lifted from the Aquinnah Lighthouse in 1952, after nearly a century of service. Though it no longer serves to warn ships of dangerous shoals (that light is automated now), it still lights up the night every evening in summer, just for show.

59 School St. (corner of Cooke St., 2 blocks southwest of Main St.), Edgartown. (508/627-4441. www.marthasvineyardhistory.org. Admission in season $7 adults, $4 children 6–15. Mid-June to mid-Oct Tues–Sat 10am–5pm; mid-Oct to late

Dec and mid-Mar to mid-June Wed–Fri 1–4pm, Sat 10am–4pm; early Jan to mid-Mar Wed–Fri by appointment, Sat 10am–4pm.

4 Organized Tours

Arabella 𝒢   Hugh Taylor (James's brother) alternates with a couple of other captains in taking the helm of his swift 50-foot catamaran for daily trips to Cuttyhunk Island, and sunset cruises around the Aquinnah cliffs; you can book the whole boat, if you like, for a private charter. Zipping along at 15 knots, it's a great way to see lovely coves and vistas otherwise denied the ordinary tourist.

Menemsha Harbor (at North Rd.), Menemsha. © **508/645-3511.** www.outermost inn.com. Evening sail $50 adults; day sail $60 adults, $30 children under 12. Departures mid-June to mid-Sept daily 10:30am, 6pm (or 2 hr. before sunset). Reservations required. Closed mid-Sept to mid-June.

Ghosts, Gossip, and Downright Scandal Walking Tours 𝒢𝒢
Laced with local lore and often led by the entertaining local historian Liz Villard, this 75-minute walking tour of Edgartown by the organization Vineyard History Tours gives a fun look at town history. Other tours provide access to the interiors of the 1672 Vincent House (the island's oldest surviving dwelling), the 1840 Dr. Daniel Fisher House (an elegant Greek revival mansion), and the splendid Old Whaling Church, a town showpiece built in 1843. There are also a variety of other van and walking tours including "A-Whaling We Will Go," in Edgartown, and "Cottages, Campgrounds, and Flying Horses" in Oak Bluffs (which includes admission to the Cottage Museum and a ride on the Flying Horses).

From the Vincent House Museum, behind 99 Main St., Edgartown. © **508/627-8619.** Also, from the Cottage Museum, 1 Trinity Park, Oak Bluffs, and at the Steamship Authority kiosk in Vineyard Haven. $7–$10 adults, free for children 12 and under. June–Sept Mon–Sat noon–3pm; call for off-season hours. Closed Nov–Apr.

Trustees of Reservations Natural History Tours 𝒢𝒢𝒢   The Trustees, a statewide land conservation group, offers several fascinating 2½-hour tours by safari vehicle or kayak around this idyllic nature preserve. The kayak tour, which takes place at 9am and 2pm, on Poucha Pond and Cape Poge Bay is designed for all levels. It costs $30 for adults and $18 for children. There's also a tour of the Cape Poge lighthouse at 10am and 1pm. The cost is $15 for adults and $10 for children.

Cape Poge, Chappaquiddick Island. © **508/627-3599.** www.thetrustees.org. $30 adults, $15 children 15 and under. In season, Mon–Fri 8:30am, 3pm. Call for reservations. Meet at Mytoi on Chappaquiddick. Closed mid-Oct to May.

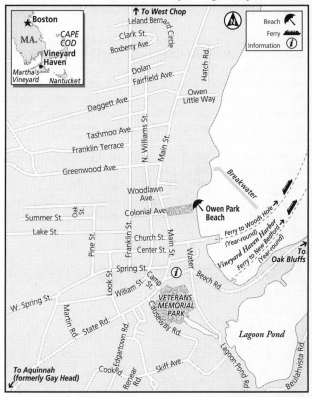

5 Kid Stuff

A must for tots to preteens is the unique **Flying Horses Carousel** in the center of Oak Bluffs (see above). Directly across the street, the **Dreamland Fun Center** (© **508/693-5163**) features dozens of video games, air hockey, skee-ball, and even a small bumper-car arena. For an atmospheric minigolf course, visit **Island Cove Mini Golf,** on State Road outside Vineyard Haven (© **508/693-2611**), a family-friendly setup with a snack bar serving Mad Martha's ice cream, an Island favorite. Island Cove is closed October through March. On weekends, from 10am to 3pm, children may enjoy the **World of Reptiles** off Edgartown–Vineyard Haven Road on Bachelder Avenue, Edgartown (© **508/627-5634**), where they'll meet various snakes, including a 21-foot python; turtles; and even an alligator. There's also a new bird park. Admission is $4. Call for hours. World of Reptiles is closed October through March. Nearby, the **Felix Neck Wildlife Sanctuary** (© 508/627-4850) on Edgartown–Vineyard Haven Road, is a popular destination with its exhibit room and self-guided trails (see "Beaches & Recreational Pursuits," earlier in this chapter). On Sundays in season, there are natural history talks and activities geared to children. Pony-cart rides ($1.50) are offered summer afternoons at the **Nip 'n' Tuck Farm** on State Road in West Tisbury (© 508/693-1449). Many families plan their vacations around the **Agricultural Society Annual Livestock Show and Fair** (© 508/693-9549) in West Tisbury in mid-August. It's an old-fashioned country fair with animals, food, and entertainment. An island event to remember is **Illumination Night** in Oak Bluffs, when all the cottages in the campground are lit up with Japanese lanterns. The exact day is a secret, but it's usually on a Wednesday evening at 7:30pm in mid-August.

6 Shopping

ANTIQUES/COLLECTIBLES For the most exquisite Asian furniture, lamps, porcelains, and jewelry, visit **All Things Oriental** at 123 Beach Rd. in Vineyard Haven (© 508/693-8375). The treasures here are handpicked in China by owner Shirley Seaton.

You don't have to be a bona fide collector to marvel at museum-quality marine antiques at **C. W. Morgan Marine Antiques,** Beach Road, just east of the town center, Vineyard Haven (© 508/693-3622). The collection encompasses paintings and prints, intricate ship models, nautical instruments, sea chests, and scrimshaw.

ARTS & CRAFTS Stop by **C. B. Stark Jewelers,** 53A Main St., Vineyard Haven (© 508/693-2284), and 27 N. Water St., Edgartown (© 508/627-1260), where proprietor Cheryl Stark started fashioning island-motif charms back in 1966.

No visit to Edgartown would be complete without a peek at the wares of scrimshander Thomas J. DeMont, Jr., at the **Edgartown Scrimshaw Gallery** at 43 Main St. (© 508/627-9439). In addition to DeMont's work, the shop carries the work of a number of the country's top scrimshaw artists. All the scrimshaw in the gallery is hand-carved using ancient mammoth ivory or antique fossil ivory.

In the center of Edgartown, stop in at **Gardner Colby Gallery** on 27 N. Water St. (© 888/969-9500 or 508/627-6002), a soothing and sophisticated art showroom filled with Vineyard-inspired paintings by such popular artists as Robert Cardinal, whose landscapes often feature haunting purple skies; and Ovid Osborn Ward, who paints graphically realistic portrayals of Vineyard motifs.

The **Chilmark Pottery,** off State Road (about 4 miles southwest of Vineyard Haven), West Tisbury (℃ **508/693-6476**), features tableware fashioned to suit its setting. Geoffrey Borr takes his palette from the sea and sky and produces highly serviceable stoneware with clean lines and a long life span. Summer pottery classes are also available.

The Field Gallery, State Road (in the center of town), West Tisbury (℃ **508/693-5595**), set in a rural pasture, is where Marc Chagall meets Henry Moore and where Tom Maley's playful figures have enchanted locals and passersby for decades. You'll also find paintings by Albert Alcalay and drawings and cartoons by Jules Feiffer. The Sunday-evening openings are high points of the summer social season. Closed mid-October to mid-May.

Don't miss the **Granary Gallery at the Red Barn,** Old County Road (off Edgartown–West Tisbury Rd., about ¼ mile north of the intersection), West Tisbury (℃ **800/472-6279** or 508/693-0455), which displays astounding prints by the late longtime summerer Alfred Eisenstaedt, dazzling color photos by local luminary Alison Shaw, and a changing roster of fine artists—some just emerging, some long since discovered. A fine selection of country and provincial antiques are also sold here. Open April to December, and by appointment only January through March.

At **Martha's Vineyard Glass Works,** State Road, North Tisbury (℃ **508/693-6026**), world-renowned master glassblowers sometimes lend a hand at this handsome rural studio/shop for the fun of it. The three resident artists—Andrew Magdanz, Susan Shapiro, and Mark Weiner—are no slouches themselves, having shown nationwide to considerable acclaim. Their output is decidedly avant-garde and may not suit all tastes, but it's an eye-opening array and all the more fascinating once you've witnessed a work in progress.

Etherington Fine Art (℃ **508/693-9696**), South Road in Chilmark, features estimable work such as Vineyard- and Venice-inspired paintings by Rez Williams, nature collages by Lucy Mitchell, pastels and oils by Wolf Kahn, and the colorful, iconographic sculptures by Sam Milstein that grace the front yard. Gallery owner Mary Etherington's selection is a giant step up from the usual seascapes and lighthouses offered by other Vineyard galleries. Big-name museum people such as Thomas Hoving and Agnes Gund all stop here when on the island.

BOOKS   Edgartown Book Store, Main Street (in the center of town), Edgartown (© **508/627-8463**), has a lively presentation of timely titles highlighting local endeavors; inquire about readings and signings. Closed January to March.

Bunch of Grapes, 44 Main St. (in the center of town), Vineyard Haven (© **800/693-0221** or 508/693-2291), offering the island's broadest selection (some 40,000 tomes), is a year-round institution and a browser's haven.

FASHION   The Great Put On, Dock Street (in the center of town), Edgartown (© **508/627-5495**), dates back to 1969, but always keeps up with the latest styles, including lines by Vivienne Tam, Moschino, and BCBG.

Treading a comfortable middle ground between functional and fashionable, the women's and men's labels at **LeRoux,** 89 Main St. (in the center of town), Vineyard Haven (© **508/693-6463**), include some nationally known names, such as Patagonia, Columbia Sportswear, and Tommy Bahama. It also carries Woodland Waders, an island-made line of sturdy woolen outerwear—everyday clothes for both sexes that are neither staid nor trendy.

GIFTS/HOME DECOR   Bramhall & Dunn, 23 Main St., Vineyard Haven (© **508/693-6437**), contains the kind of chunky, eclectic extras that lend character to country homes. Expect to find the requisite rag rugs, rustic pottery, a smattering of English country antiques, bed linens, and a large selection of sweaters.

My favorite place for gifts in Oak Bluffs, **Craftworks,** 149 Circuit Ave. (© **508/693-7463**), is filled to the rafters with whimsical, colorful contemporary American crafts, some by local artisans.

Carly Simon owns a shop called **Midnight Farm,** 18 Water-Cromwell Lane, Vineyard Haven (© **508/693-1997**), named after her popular children's book. This home store offers a world of high-end, carefully selected, and imaginative gift items starting with soaps and candles and including children's clothes and toys, rugs, furniture, books, clothes, and glassware.

A handsome shop on upper Circuit Avenue (no. 73), **Argonauta** (© **508/696-0097**) carries hand-painted vintage furniture, country pine, wicker, topiary, and artwork. **Third World Trading Co.,** 52 Circuit Ave., Oak Bluffs (© **508/693-5550**), features well-priced clothing, accessories, and home accents from around the globe.

SEAFOOD   **Feel like whipping up your own lobster feast? For the freshest and biggest crustaceans on the island, head to **The Net

Result, 79 Beach Rd., Vineyard Haven (✆ **800/394-6071** or 508/693-6071). Run by the Larsen family, you'll find everything from shrimp, scallops, and swordfish to bluefish and tuna. Their spreadable seafood salad makes a perfect hors d'oeuvre, and if you're feeling sorry for your friends back home, they'll ship fresh lobsters, quahogs, and other aquatic delicacies anywhere in the United States overnight. If you're up-island, stop by **Poole's Fish Market** or **Larsen's Fish Market,** both on the docks at Menemsha Harbor.

WINE   With a name like Martha's Vineyard, you probably expected to find wild grapes, which in fact have always grown on the island. But who knew whether fussy French vinifera would take? California transplants George and Catherine Mathiesen had high hopes when they started cultivating 3 backwoods-acres in 1971, and their faith has been borne out in **Chicama Vineyards,** Stoney Hill Road (off State Rd., about 3 miles southwest of Vineyard Haven), West Tisbury (✆ **508/693-0309;** www.chicamavineyards.com), a highly successful winery yielding some 100,000 bottles a year. The dozen-plus varieties not only are palatable drinking wines, but also lend themselves beautifully to such gourmet uses as jellies, jams, and flavored oils and vinegars, all prepared and sold on the premises. Visitors are always welcome for a tasting, and in high season, they're treated to an entertaining 20-minute tour of the production line.

7 Martha's Vineyard After Dark

The Vineyard has an active summer social life. TV journalism and pop-culture firmament types such as Diane Sawyer, Mike Wallace, Walter Cronkite, Carly Simon, and Art Buchwald may be busy attending private dinner parties, but they are apt to join the rest of us later at a nightspot. While the number one club on the island is the Hot Tin Roof at the airport, there are plenty of other places within walking distance in the down-island towns. Hit Oak Bluffs for the rowdiest bar scene and best nighttime street life. In Edgartown, you may have to hop around before you find the evening's most happening spot; for instance, you could happen upon an impromptu performance by Vineyard Sound, a grooving all-male *a cappella* group. In addition, there are interesting cultural offerings almost every night in summer, so check local papers for details.

PUBS, BARS, DANCE CLUBS & LIVE MUSIC

Atlantic Connection   Disco lives! As do karaoke and comedy, on occasion. Locals such as Spike Lee and Ted Danson seem to love the hodgepodge, and the unofficial house band, Entrain, has begun to attract a wide following (both on the island and on the mainland) with their funky, reggae-laced rock. There's entertainment nightly in season. June to early September, 9pm to 1am. Call for off-season hours. 124 Circuit Ave. (in the center of town), Oak Bluffs. © 508/693-7129. Cover ranges from free to $12.

David Ryans People have been known to dance on the tables at this boisterous bar. The bartender decides the canned tunes, from Sinatra to the Smashing Pumpkins. There's also a martini bar upstairs. Open June to September, daily 11:30am to 1am; call for off-season hours. 11 N. Water St., Edgartown. © 508/627-4100.

The Lampost/Rare Duck Young and loud are the watchwords at this pair of clubs; the larger features live bands and a dance floor, the smaller (in the basement), acoustic acts. This is where the young folk go, so entertainment includes such prospects as "'80s night" and "male hot-body contest." Closed November to March. 111 Circuit Ave. (in the center of town), Oak Bluffs. © 508/696-9352. Cover varies $1–$5.

Lola's With a large dance floor for the over-30 crowd, Lola's always has a hip and fun-loving crowd. There's live music 7 nights a week from June to Labor Day. In the off season, bands play on Thursday, Friday, and Saturday nights. Open year-round. At the Island Inn, Beach Rd., Oak Bluffs. © 508/693-5007.

Offshore Ale Company *Finds* In 1602, the first barley in the New World was grown on Martha's Vineyard. A few years ago, the Vineyard's first and only brewpub opened, featuring eight locally made beers on tap ($2.75–$5). It's an attractively rustic place, with high ceilings, oak booths lining the walls, and peanut shells strewn on the floor. There's a raw bar, and late-night munchies are served till 10pm, featuring pizza and hamburgers, among other offerings. Local acoustic performers entertain 6 nights a week in season. Open June to September, daily noon to midnight; call for off-season hours. 30 Kennebec Ave., Oak Bluffs. © 508/693-2626. Cover $2.

The Ritz Cafe Locals and visitors alike flock to this down-and-dirty hole-in-the-wall that features live music every night in season and on weekends year-round. The crowd, a boozing, brawling lot, enjoy the pool tables in the back. 1 Circuit Ave. (in the center of town), Oak Bluffs. © 508/693-9851. Cover $2–$3.

LOW-KEY EVENINGS

Old Whaling Church This magnificent 1843 Greek revival church functions primarily as a 500-seat performing-arts center offering lectures, symposia, films, plays, and concerts. Such Vineyard luminaries as actress Patricia Neal have taken their place at the pulpit, not to mention Livingston Taylor and Andre Previn, whose annual gigs always sell out. It's also the Edgartown United Methodist Church with a 9am service Sundays. 89 Main St. (in the center of town), Edgartown. © 508/627-4442. Ticket prices vary.

THEATER & DANCE

The Vineyard Playhouse   In an intimate (112-seat) black-box theater, carved out of an 1833 church-turned-Masonic-lodge, Equity professionals put on a rich season of favorites and challenging new work, followed, on summer weekends, by musical or comedic cabaret in the gallery/lounge. Children's theater selections are performed on Saturdays at 10am. Townspeople often get involved in the outdoor Shakespeare production, a 3-week run starting in mid-July at the Tashmoo Overlook Amphitheatre about a mile west of town, where tickets for the 5pm performances Tuesday to Sunday run $5 to $10. Open June to September, Tuesday through Saturday at 8pm, Sunday at 7pm; call for off-season hours. 24 Church St. (in the center of town), Vineyard Haven. © 508/696-6300 or 508/693-6450. www.vineyardplayhouse.org. Tickets $15–$30. MC, V.

The Yard   For over 25 years, The Yard has been presenting modern dance performances on Martha's Vineyard. The choreographer residency program here is nationally recognized, and there are classes open to the public. Open late May to late September. Performances are at 8:30pm. A Colony for the Performing Arts (off Middle Rd. near Beetlebung Corner), Chilmark. © 508/645-9662. www.dancetheyard.org. Tickets $12 adults, $9 students.

MOVIES

The **Entertainment Cinemas** at 65 Main St. (© 508/627-8008) in Edgartown has two screens. The Vineyard has three vintage Art Deco movie theaters: **Capawok** (© 508/626-9200), Main Street, Vineyard Haven; **Island Theater** (© 508/626-8300), at the bottom of Circuit Avenue, Oak Bluffs; and **The Strand** (© 508/626-8300), Oak Bluffs Avenue Extension, Oak Bluffs.

ONLY ON THE VINEYARD

Aquinnah Lighthouse   Though generally closed to the public, this 1856 lighthouse opens its doors on summer-weekend evenings to afford an awe-inspiring view of the sunset over the Devil's Bridge shoals. The light has been automated since 1952 (the original lens lights up the night sky in Edgartown), but the experience continues to be romantic. Tour times begin 90 minutes before sunset and end a half-hour past sunset. Open late June to late September, Friday through Sunday, 7 to 9pm. Off State Rd., Aquinnah. ✆ 508/645-2211. Admission $2 adults, free for children under 12.

Trinity Park Tabernacle   Designed by architect J. W. Hoyt of Springfield, Massachusetts, and built in 1879 for just over $7,000, this open-air church, now on the National Register of Historic Places, is the largest wrought-iron-and-wood structure in America. Its conical crown is ringed with a geometric pattern of amber, carmine, and midnight-blue stained glass. Old-fashioned community sings take place Wednesday at 8pm, and concerts are scheduled irregularly on weekends. James Taylor and Bonnie Raitt have regaled the faithful here, but usually the acts are more homespun. Open July to August. Trinity Park (within the Camp Meeting Grounds), Oak Bluffs. ✆ 508/693-0525. Admission varies: free to $20.

Where to Stay & Dine in Hyannis or Woods Hole

It's a good idea to have a backup plan just in case you miss the last ferry, or in the event that the ferry and airplanes are canceled or delayed due to inclement weather. This chapter contains information on where to stay and dine if you find yourself spending more time in Hyannis or Woods Hole than you had planned.

1 Hyannis (a Village in the Town of Barnstable)

As the commercial center and transportation hub of the Cape, hyperdeveloped Hyannis—a mere "village"—can be a hectic place in the summer. It's no wonder many visitors experience "post-Camelot letdown" the first time they venture to Hyannis. The downtown area, sapped by the strip development that proliferated at the edges of town after the Cape Cod Mall was built in 1970, is making a valiant comeback, with attractive banners and a pretty public park flanking the wharf where frequent ferries depart for the Islands. If you were to confine your visit to this one town, however, you'd get a warped view of the Cape. Along routes 132 and 28, you could be visiting Anywhere, USA: They're lined by the standard chain stores, restaurants, and hotels, and mired with maddening traffic.

VISITOR INFORMATION The **Hyannis Area Chamber of Commerce,** 1481 Rte. 132, Hyannis, MA 02601 (© 877/492-6647 or 508/362-5230; fax 508/362-9499; www.hyannis.com); and the **Cape Cod Chamber of Commerce,** Routes 6 and 132, Hyannis, MA 02601 (© 888/332-2732 or 508/362-3225; fax 508/362-2156; www.capecodchamber.org), are open year-round, mid-April to mid-November daily from 9am to 5pm, mid-November to mid-April Monday through Saturday, from 10am to 4pm.

WHERE TO STAY

There are a variety of large, generic, but convenient hotels and motels in Hyannis.

Heritage House Hotel, 259 Main St. (in the center of town), Hyannis (© **800/352-7189** or 508/775-7000; www.heritagehouse hotel.com) is ideally located, within walking distance from restaurants, shops, and the ferries to Nantucket and Martha's Vineyard. The hotel has an indoor and an outdoor pool, hot tub and saunas, and a restaurant/lounge on-site. The 143 rooms are priced at $169 to $189 double and $209 for a family suite.

Also centrally located on Main Street within strolling distance of restaurants, shopping, and the ferries is the **Hyannis Inn Motel,** 473 Main St., Hyannis (© **800/922-8993** or 508/775-0255; www. hyannisinn.com). Summer rates are $132 to $155 double—a real value. During the Kennedy administration, this motel served as the press headquarters. It has an indoor pool, a breakfast restaurant (not included with room rates), and a cocktail lounge. Closed late October to mid-March.

If you prefer more amenities, the **Four Points by Sheraton Hyannis Resort** is at the West End Circle just off Main Street (© **800/598-4559** or 508/775-7775; www.sheraton.com). Summer rates are $199 to $309 double. Out the back door is an 18-hole, par-3 executive golf course. The Sheraton also has four tennis courts, an indoor and an outdoor pool, four restaurants, and a fitness center.

A great choice for families is the **Cape Codder Resort and Spa,** 1225 Iyanough Rd. (Rte. 132), Hyannis (at the intersection of Bearse's Way (© **888/297-2200** or 508/771-3000; www.capecodder resort.com). It features two restaurants (VJ's Grille Room and, for families, the Hearth 'n Kettle) plus a wine bar and a spa (massage and other body treatments). Kids love the indoor wave pool with water slides. Summer rates in the 261 rooms are $159 to $189 double, $479 suite. Rooms have all the usual amenities, plus high-speed Internet access and Nintendo.

EXPENSIVE

Simmons Homestead Inn *Kids* *Finds*   The first thing passersby notice is all the classic red sports cars: 55 at last count. A former ad exec and race-car driver, innkeeper Bill Putman likes to collect them. He's made his sports car collection into a small museum open to the public (admission: $8 adults, $4 children) called Toad Hall, after *The Wind in the Willows*. Inside the inn is his animal collection. The stuffed toys, sculptures, needlepoint, and wallpaper differentiate the rather traditional rooms in this rambling 1820s captain's manse. This is an inn where you'll find everyone mulling around the

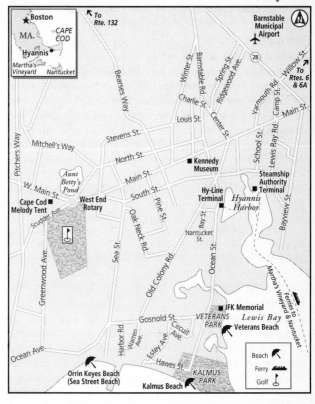

hearth, sipping complimentary wine (served at "6-ish") while they compare notes and nail down dinner plans. To help his guests plan their days and evenings, Putman has typed up extensive notes on day trips (including the Islands), bike routes (he supplies the bikes), and his own personal, quirky restaurant reviews. Guests who prefer privacy may book the spiffily updated "servants' quarters," a spacious, airy wing with its own private deck. Rooms vary in size, but all are decorated with comfort and a sense of humor in mind. Four hammocks swing from trees in the shady backyard of this home-y establishment.

288 Scudder Ave. (about ¼ mile west of the West End rotary), Hyannisport, MA 02647. ✆ **800/637-1649** or 508/778-4999. Fax 508/790-1342. www.simmons homesteadinn.com. 14 units. Summer $220–$260 double; $350 2-bedroom suite.

Rates include full breakfast. AE, DISC, MC, V. Dogs welcome. **Amenities:** 6-person hot tub; loaner bikes; billiards parlor. *In room:* Hair dryer, iron, no phone.

MODERATE

Trade Winds Inn ⦿ *Finds*   Many rooms in this attractive motel have patios and balconies with wonderful views of Craigville Beach, one of the Cape's most popular strips of sand. However, since it's hard to see the sand once the summer crowds hit, this property also has its own immaculate 500-foot private stretch of beach. Beach chairs and beach towels are provided. On cloudy days, guests may enjoy strolling up to the Craigville Campground next door, a compound of 19th-century gingerbread-style cottages that still serves as a Methodist meeting camp preserve. The motel, which is on 6 acres, also abuts tiny Lake Elizabeth, where young Jack and Ted Kennedy learned to sail.

780 Craigville Beach Rd. (across the street from Craigville Beach), Centerville, MA 02632. ⦿ **877/444-7966** or 508/775-0365. www.twicapecod.com. 46 units. Summer $129–$199 double; $199–$239 suite. Rates include continental breakfast in season. AE, MC, V. Closed Nov–Apr. **Amenities:** Small bar; putting green. *In room:* A/C, TV.

WHERE TO DINE
EXPENSIVE

Alberto's Ristorante ⦿⦿ ITALIAN   Alberto's explores the full range of Italian cuisine, with a classicist's attention to components and composition. Owner/chef Felisberto Barreiro's most popular dishes are his treatments of lobster, rack of lamb, and beef tenderloin. Hand-cut pasta is also a specialty, including the ultra-rich seafood ravioli cloaked in saffron-cream sauce. Though the atmosphere is elegant, with sconces shedding a warm glow over well-spaced, linen-draped tables, it is not one of hushed reverence: People clearly come to have a good time, and the friendly service and fabulous food ensure that they do. Locals know to come between 3 and 6pm, when a full dinner, with soup, salad, and dessert, costs as little as $10 to $15. There's live jazz or piano music daily year-round.

360 Main St., Hyannis. ⦿ **508/778-1770.** Reservations recommended. Main courses $11–$27. AE, DC, DISC, MC, V. Daily 11:30am–10pm. Open year-round.

The Black Cat ⦿ NEW AMERICAN   Located on Hyannis Harbor less than a block from the Hy-Line ferries, this is a fine place to catch a quick bite or full meal while you wait for your boat to come in. The menu is basic—steak, pasta, and, of course, fish—but attention is paid to the details; the onion rings, for instance, are made fresh. The dining room, with a gleaming mahogany and brass bar, will appeal to chilled travelers on a blustery day; in fine weather, you may prefer the porch. There's live jazz on the weekends in season.

165 Ocean St. (opposite the Ocean St. Dock), Hyannis. ℂ **508/778-1233.** Reservations not accepted. Main courses $15–$29. AE, DC, DISC, MC, V. Apr–Oct daily 11:30am–10pm; call for off-season hours. Closed Jan to mid-Feb.

The Naked Oyster Bistro and Raw Bar 𝒢𝒢 NEW AMERICAN

Overlook the fact that this fun bistro restaurant is located in an office complex and just enjoy the experience. The specialty here is fresh local seafood, and oyster fans will be fascinated by the selection of "dressed oysters" from the traditional Rockefeller to a more exotic baked oishi with wasabi and soy. The main courses feature spicy options such as sautéed Thai shrimp and blackened Cajun swordfish, as well as hearty dishes such as grilled filet mignon with garlic mashed potatoes. Portions are large and service is professional and cheerful. In the evenings, local young professionals make this a bar scene.

20 Independence Drive (just off Rte. 132 at Park Place), Hyannis. ℂ **508/778-6500.** Reservations accepted. Main courses $14–$24. AE, MC, V. Mon–Fri 11:30am–3pm; daily 4–10pm. Open year-round.

The Paddock 𝒢𝒢 CONTINENTAL

In the almost 30 years that the Zartarian family has run this large, traditional restaurant, they have maintained a solid reputation in the community with consistently good food and service. The decor might be a little dated, but grandma will love the Victorian motifs; better yet, you can dine on the plant-and-wicker-filled summer porch. The menu combines creative options with traditional choices (you can still order extra béarnaise sauce on the side). For appetizers, you'll find chicken-liver pâté right alongside polenta crab cakes with chipotle chile cream and sweet mango salsa. Among the main courses, you can choose filet mignon or sesame-encrusted yellowfin tuna served rare with Asian greens. The 300-bottle wine list has received awards from *Wine Spectator* for 16 years. There is free valet parking, and a pianist entertains nightly in the pub area. Because the Cape Cod Melody Tent is right next door, you'll need to go after 9pm to avoid the crowds if there is an act playing.

West End Rotary (at the intersection of W. Main St. and Main St.), Hyannis. ℂ **508/775-7677.** www.paddockcapecod.com. Reservations recommended. Main courses lunch $7–$13, dinner $17–$28. AE, DC, DISC, MC, V. Apr to mid-Nov Mon–Sat 11:30am–2:30pm and 5–10pm, Sun noon to 10pm. Closed mid-Nov to Mar.

Ristorante Barolo ✹✹ NORTHERN ITALIAN   This is the best Italian restaurant in town. Part of a smart-looking brick office complex, this thoroughly up-to-date establishment does everything right, from offering extra-virgin olive oil in which to dunk its crusty bread to getting those pastas perfectly al dente. Appetizers perfect for sharing are *Polpette Gartinate alla Romana* (homemade meatballs in a tomato-and-basil sauce) and *Gamberi al Martini* (shrimp sautéed with fresh scallions and martini-wine sauce). Entrees include a number of tempting veal choices, like *Vitello alla Sorrentina* (Provimi-brand veal, mozzarella, and basil with plum-tomato sauce), as well as such favorites as *Linguine al Frutti di Mare,* with littlenecks, mussels, shrimp, and calamari. The desserts are brought in daily from Boston's famed North End.

1 Financial Place (297 North St., just off the West End rotary), Hyannis. ✆ 508/ 778-2878. Reservations recommended. Main courses $10–$27. AE, DC, MC, V. June–Sept Sun–Thurs 4:30–10pm, Fri–Sat 4:30–11pm; call for off-season hours.

Roadhouse Café ✹✹ AMERICAN/NORTHERN ITALIAN This is neither a roadhouse nor a cafe, but it is a solid entry in the Hyannis dining scene. The extensive menu is pretty much split between American standards such as steak (not to mention oysters Rockefeller or casino) and real Italian cooking, unstinting on the garlic. There's also a less expensive lighter-fare menu, including what some have called "the best burger in the world," served in the snazzy bistro in back. Among the appetizers are such delicacies as beef capriccio with fresh-shaved Parmesan, and vine-ripened tomatoes and buffalo mozzarella drizzled with balsamic vinaigrette. The latter also makes a tasty marinade for native swordfish headed for the grill. The signature dessert, a distinctly non-Italian cheesecake infused with Baileys Irish Cream, is a must-try. Music-lovers know to come on Monday nights for the live jazz in the bistro.

488 South St. (off Main St., near the West End rotary), Hyannis. ✆ 508/775-2386. Reservations recommended. Main courses $15–$26. AE, DC, DISC, MC, V. Daily 4pm–midnight.

Roobar ✹ BISTRO   This stylish bistro is one of the few truly hip spots in Hyannis. You may want to sit at the bar and have a few appetizers, such as the chicken pot sticker (pan-seared wonton wrappers filled with an Asian chicken and vegetable stuffing with an orange marmalade dipping sauce) or a simple plate of oysters on the half shell. The most popular entree may be the seafood Provençale (jumbo shrimp and sea scallops sautéed with fresh tomatoes and basil in a white-wine garlic sauce and served over fresh angel-hair pasta), but there are a number of other lobster, fish, and steak dishes, as well as a selection of delicious gourmet pizzas.

586 Main St., Hyannis. ℂ **508/778-6515**. Reservations recommended. Main courses $9–$25. AE, DC, MC, V. Daily 5–10pm.

MODERATE

Harry's ℛ CAJUN   Seemingly transported from the French Quarter, this small restaurant/bar—park benches serve as booths—has added some Italian and French options to its menu, but it's the authentic Cajun cooking that keeps customers coming back: ribs, jambalaya, hoppin' John, red beans, and rice. On the weekends, get set for a heaping serving of R&B. The blues bar here hops until 1am.

700 Main St. (near the West End rotary), Hyannis. ℂ **508/778-4188**. Reservations not accepted. Main courses $10–$19. MC, V. Daily 5–9:30pm.

Tugboats ℛ AMERICAN   This harborside perch is especially appealing for munching and ogling. Two spacious outdoor decks are angled just right to catch the sunset, with cocktail/frappes to match, or perhaps a bottle of Moët et Chandon. Forget fancy dining and chow down on blackened-swordfish bites (topping a Caesar salad, perhaps); lobster fritters; or the double-duty Steak Neptune, topped with scallops and shrimp. Among the "decadent desserts" is a Key lime pie purportedly lifted straight from Papa's of Key West.

21 Arlington St. (at the Hyannis Marina, off Willow St.), Hyannis. ℂ **508/775-6433**. Reservations not accepted. Main courses $11–$18. AE, DC, DISC, MC, V. Late May to Oct daily 11:30am–10:30pm; mid-Apr to late May Tues–Sun 11:30am–10:30pm. Closed Nov to mid-Apr.

INEXPENSIVE

Baxter's Boat House ℛ *Value* *Kids* SEAFOOD   A shingled shack on a jetty jutting out into the harbor, Baxter's has catered to the boating crowd since the mid-1950s with Cape classics such as fried clams and fish virtually any way you like it, from baked to blackened, served on paper plates at picnic tables. This is a good place to bring a brood of kids. If you sit out on the deck, be wary of swooping seagulls looking to spirit away your lunch.

177 Pleasant St. (near the Steamship Authority ferry), Hyannis. ℂ **508/775-7040**. Reservations not accepted. Main courses $8–$14. AE, MC, V. Late May to early Sept Mon–Sat 11:30am–10pm, Sun 11:30am–9pm; hours may vary at the beginning and end of the season. Closed mid-Oct to Mar.

Collucci Brothers Diner DINER   In the tradition of great diners, this one has a tin ceiling, comfy booths, and a shiny counter. It also has sassy waitresses who pour really good coffee. Selections from the children's menu are under $4. Wash down a tuna melt with a root beer float or splurge on the roast turkey dinner. It's a block from Main Street and about a half-mile from the Hy-Line ferry terminal with boats to Nantucket.

50 Sea St. (at the corner of South St.). (*C*) **508/771-6896**. Reservations not accepted. All items under $10. AE, MC, V. Late May to Sept Mon–Sat 7am–3pm, Sun 7am–1pm; call for off-season hours.

TAKEOUT

Left Bank Cafe, 349 Main St., in the center of town ((*C*) **508/771-4445**), serves scrumptious croissants, breads, and pastries, all baked on-site. For lunch, there are homemade soups, quiches, and crepes, as well as sandwiches and salads. Open Monday to Saturday 7am to 10pm. Closed January to mid-March.

A branch of the popular **Box Lunch** ((*C*) **508/790-5855**), serving pita "rollwiches," is right on Main Street (no. 357) in Hyannis. These are the best—and fastest—sandwiches in town.

2 Woods Hole (a Village in the Town of Falmouth)

Falmouth is a classic New England town, complete with 19th-century churches beside the village green and a walkable and bustling Main Street. Those rushing to catch the ferry to the Vineyard tend to bypass Falmouth's Main Street and head straight down to the Steamship Authority ferry terminal in the village of Woods Hole. Two other ferries to the Vineyard, *The Island Queen* to Oak Bluffs and the *Pied Piper* to Edgartown, leave from Falmouth Inner Harbor.

Officially a village within Falmouth (one of eight), tiny **Woods Hole** ꧁꧁꧁ has been a world-renowned oceanic research center since 1871, when the U.S. Commission of Fish and Fisheries set up a primitive seasonal collection station. Today, the various scientific institutes crowded around the harbor—principally, the National Marine Fisheries Service, the Marine Biological Laboratory (founded in 1888), and the Woods Hole Oceanographic Institute (a newcomer as of 1930)—have research budgets in the tens of millions of dollars and employ thousands of scientists.

The Woods Hole community is one of the hipper communities on the Cape. There are good shops, galleries, restaurants, inns, and bars, most with water views. Be forewarned that it is very difficult to find a parking space on Water Street in the summer, and the dreaded meter maid is notoriously vigilant.

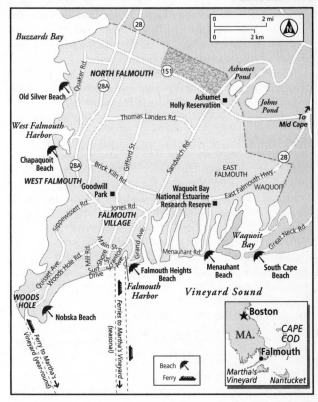

VISITOR INFORMATION Contact the **Falmouth Chamber of Commerce,** 20 Academy Lane, Falmouth, MA 02541 (© **800/ 526-8532** or 508/548-8500; fax 508/548-8521; www.falmouth-capecod.com); or the **Cape Cod Chamber of Commerce,** Routes 6 and 132, Hyannis, MA 02601 (© **888/332-2732** or 508/362-3225; fax 508/362-2156; www.capecodchamber.org); open year-round, mid-April to mid-November daily from 9am to 5pm, mid-November to mid-April Monday through Saturday from 10am to 4pm.

WHERE TO STAY

For a basic motel with a great location, try the **Tides Motel** ⊛ (© **508/548-3126**) at the west end of Grand Avenue in Falmouth

Heights. The 1950s-style no-frills (no air-conditioning, no phone) motel sits on the beach at the head of Falmouth Harbor facing Vineyard Sound. Rates in season are $150 for double occupancy, and $195 for a suite. Closed late October to April.

The **Red Horse Inn** ✦ (© **800/628-3811** or 508/548-0053; www.redhorseinn.com) is a family-friendly option just a short walk from Falmouth Harbor in Falmouth Heights. The 22 rooms are priced from $150 to $250, and kids will love the large outdoor pool.

EXPENSIVE

Inn on the Sound ✦✦ *Finds*   The ambience here is as breezy as the setting, high on a bluff beside Falmouth's premier sunning beach, with a sweeping view of Nantucket Sound from the large front deck. Innkeeper Renee Ross is an interior decorator, and it shows: There's none of the usual frilly/cutesy stuff in these well-appointed guest rooms, most of which have ocean views, several with their own private decks. Many of the bathrooms have been renovated with large, luxurious tiled showers. The focal point of the living room is a handsome boulder hearth (nice for those nippy nights). Breakfast is delivered to your room in a bountiful basket of home-baked goodies.

313 Grand Ave., Falmouth Heights, MA 02540. © **800/564-9668** or 508/457-9666. Fax 508/457-9631. www.innonthesound.com. 10 units (5 with tub/shower, 5 shower only). Summer $150–$295 double. Rates include continental breakfast. AE, DISC, MC, V. No children under 16. *In room:* TV, no phone.

Scallop Shell Inn ✦✦✦ *Finds*   Some call this new deluxe inn, located just steps from Falmouth Heights Beach, Falmouth's best. Several rooms have wonderful views of Vineyard Sound and Martha's Vineyard. Guests are apt to lounge on the wide front porch during the day. Falmouth Heights Beach is one of the area's most picturesque, and the neighborhood is an old summer community with narrow streets, lots of pedestrian traffic, and beautiful Victorian cottages. The inn is also a short walk from a fun bar/restaurant, the British Beer Company. Several rooms have gas fireplaces and two- or three-person whirlpool tubs. In addition to air-conditioning and those brisk ocean breezes, the rooms have ceiling fans. All rooms are thoughtfully appointed with extras such as robes and high-quality toiletries. Two rooms have mahogany balconies, and several have private entrances. In the billiard and sitting room, guests can enjoy a drink from the wet bar and sit by the fireplace. Guests also have free rein in a 24-hour guest kitchenette that is stocked with hot and cold beverages and homemade treats. The

four-course gourmet breakfast, with a different entree every day, may include crème brûlée French toast or lobster, asparagus, and Gruyère cheese omelets.

16 Massachusetts Ave., Falmouth Heights, MA 02540. ℂ 800/249-4587 or 508/495-4900. Fax 508/495-4600. www.scallopshellinn.com. 7 units. Summer $295–$360 double. Rates include full breakfast. AE, DISC, MC, V. **Amenities:** Laundry room. *In room:* A/C, TV/VCR, safe, 1 room for those w/limited mobility.

MODERATE

Coonamessett Inn 🐾🐾   A gracious inn built around the core of a 1796 homestead, the Coonamessett Inn is Falmouth's most traditional lodging choice. The original inn was a few miles away and flanked the namesake river. Set on 7 lushly landscaped acres overlooking a pond, it has the feel of a country club where all comers are welcome. Some of the rooms, decorated in reproduction antiques, can be a bit somber, so try to get one with good light. Most have a separate sitting room attached. On-site is a restaurant featuring a very comfortable tavern room as well as a more formal dining room. The extensive Sunday buffet brunch brings out people from all over town.

Jones Rd. and Gifford St. (about ½ mile north of Main St.), Falmouth, MA 02540. ℂ 508/548-2300. Fax 508/540-9831. www.capecodrestaurants.org/coonamessett. 27 units, 1 cottage. Summer $150–$180 double; $175–$230 2-bedroom suite; $200–$260 cottage. Rates include continental breakfast. AE, MC, V. **Amenities:** 2 restaurants (1 fancy, 1 tavern w/entertainment). *In room:* A/C, TV, coffeemaker, hair dryer.

Mostly Hall 🐾   Set conveniently on the Village Green, a short stroll from Main Street, this charming B&B has long been a popular choice. The plantation-style house itself is unusual. It was built by a sea captain to please his New Orleans–born bride. The six stately, high-ceilinged corner bedrooms each boast a canopied four-poster bed. The mature gardens are particularly lovely in spring when the dogwoods, azaleas, and cherry trees are in bloom. The garden gazebo makes a pleasant retreat. Loaner bikes are provided for exploring the nearby Shining Sea Bicycle Path to Woods Hole.

27 W. Main St. (west of the Village Green), Falmouth, MA 02540. ℂ 800/682-0565 or 508/548-3786. Fax 508/548-5778. www.mostlyhall.com. 6 units (with shower only). Summer $150–$249 double. Rates include full breakfast. AE, DC, DISC, MC, V. Closed mid-Dec to mid-Mar. No children under 18. **Amenities:** Loaner bikes. *In room:* A/C, no phone.

Nautilus Motor Inn 🐾   The Nautilus is a crescent-shaped motel poised above Woods Hole's picturesque Little Harbor. The two tiers of rooms are standard motel-ish, but each room comes with a private balcony for taking in the view and/or sunning. An unusual restaurant used for private parties, The Dome, is right on the premises. An architectural landmark, this very sturdy geodesic dome was R. Buckminster Fuller's first, and must have seemed grandly futuristic in 1953. The Martha's Vineyard ferry is a very short stroll away. Not so much a destination in and of itself, the Nautilus makes an ideal launching pad for a day trip to the Vineyard or an exploration of Woods Hole.

539 Woods Hole Rd., Woods Hole, MA 02543. © **800/654-2333** or 508/548-1525. Fax 508/457-9674. www.nautilusinn.com. 54 units (all with tub/shower). Summer $102–$170 double. AE, DC, DISC, MC, V. Closed mid-Oct to mid-Apr. Pets allowed. **Amenities:** Good-size outdoor pool w/large deck; 2 tennis courts. *In room:* A/C, TV, dataport.

Sands of Time Motor Inn & Harbor House 🌟🌟

This property, which is across the street from the Woods Hole ferry terminal, consists of two buildings: a two-story motel in front of a shingled 1879 Victorian mansion. The motel rooms feature crisp, above-average decor, plus private porches overlooking the harbor. The rooms in the Harbor House are more lavish and romantic—some with four-poster beds, working fireplaces, wicker furnishings, and harbor views. There is a small heated pool on the grounds, and guests can use the tennis court at the motel property next door. All rooms are equipped with computer jacks.

549 Woods Hole Rd., Woods Hole, MA 02543. © **800/841-0114** or 508/548-6300. Fax 508/457-0160. www.sandsoftime.com. 36 units, 2 with shared bathroom. Summer $130–$190 double. Rates include continental breakfast. AE, DC, DISC, MC, V. Closed Nov–Mar. **Amenities:** Small heated pool; 2 tennis courts. *In room:* A/C, TV, dataport.

INEXPENSIVE

Inn at One Main Though a centenarian (built in 1892), this shingled house with Queen Anne flourishes has a crisp, youthful air. The bedrooms embody barefoot romance, rather than the Victorian brand. Lace, chintz, and wicker have been laid on lightly, leaving plenty of room to kick about. The Turret Room, with its big brass bed, is perhaps the most irresistible. Breakfasts would instantly convert a "Just coffee, please" morning grouch: gingerbread pancakes, orange-pecan French toast, homemade scones—it's a good thing the Shining Sea Bicycle Path is right at hand.

1 Main St. (1 block northwest of the Village Green), Falmouth, MA 02540. © **888/281-6246** or 508/540-7469. www.innatonemain.com. 6 units. Summer $110–$150 double. Rates include full breakfast. AE, DISC, MC, V. *In room:* A/C, hair dryer, no phone.

WHERE TO DINE
EXPENSIVE

The Boat House Restaurant and Lounge ⚓ NEW AMERICAN/SEAFOOD

Set harborside, the large plate-glass windows of this casual restaurant overlook mainly power boats stacked high in a marina on Falmouth Inner Harbor. Service is very friendly, and the atmosphere, especially from the large bar area, tends to be quite jovial. The food, though pricey, is very good. Standouts are bouillabaisse and garlic-oil-rubbed sirloin. A number of pasta and fried fish choices are also on the menu. This place turns into a rowdy club with live music on summer evenings. It's particularly appealing at lunchtime when prices are lower and the bar scene is quieter.

88 Scranton Ave. (on Falmouth Inner Harbor), Falmouth. © 508/548-7800. Reservations recommended. Main courses $18–$26. AE, MC, V. Mid-June to mid-Sept daily 11:30am–10pm; call for off-season hours. Closed mid-Oct to mid-May.

Fishmonger's Cafe ⚓⚓ NATURAL

A cherished carry-over from the early 1970s, this sunny, casual cafe attracts local young people and scientists, as well as Bermuda-shorted tourists, with an ever-changing array of imaginatively prepared dishes. Prices have risen substantially over the past couple of years, making dinner in this casual setting feel like a splurge. Chefs Anne Hunt and Harold Broadstock change the eclectic dinner menu every few days and have added some Thai entrees. Regulars sit at the counter to enjoy a bowl of the fisherman's stew while schmoozing with staff bustling about the open kitchen. Newcomers usually go for the tables by the window, where you can watch boats come and go from Eel Pond. The menu ranges widely (lunch could be a tempeh burger made with fermented soybeans, or ordinary beef), and longtime customers look to the blackboard for the latest innovations, which invariably include delectable desserts like pumpkin-pecan pie.

56 Water St. (at the Eel Pond drawbridge), Woods Hole. © 508/540-5376. Reservations not accepted. Main courses $15–$25. AE, MC, V. Mid-June to Oct Mon–Fri 7–11am, 11:30am–4pm, and 5–10pm, Sat–Sun 7–11:30am, noon–4:30pm, and 5:30–10:30pm; call for off-season hours. Closed mid-Dec to mid-Feb.

La Cucina Sul Mare ⚓⚓ Finds ITALIAN

Locals and tourists alike line up outside this popular Main Street restaurant, craving its hearty Italian fare. The interior features cheerful murals and a tin ceiling, and large picture windows overlook Main Street. Chef/owner Mark Ciflone's signature dishes include classic Italian specialties such as lasagna, braised lamb shanks, *osso buco,* lobster *fra diavolo* over linguine, zuppa de pesce, rigotoni a la vodka, chicken

Parmesan, and veal piccata, among others. The desserts here are homemade and truly delicious.

237 Main St., Falmouth. © 508/548-5600. Reservations not accepted. Main courses $15–$25. AE, MC, V. Daily 11:30am–2pm and 5–10pm; call for off-season hours. Open year-round.

Phusion Grille 🐟🐟 NEW AMERICAN   This restaurant has a terrific location on Eel Pond in Woods Hole. The interior is all blond wood and Asian screens, but nothing blocks the views of the wraparound floor-to-ceiling windows. The food can be inconsistent here, though it is frequently very good. Favorites are filet mignon on a wild mushroom risotto cake, and diver scallops with fresh herbed pasta. Waitstaff are well-skilled. The dessert menu features a very special fresh-fruit strudel.

71 Water St., Woods Hole. © 508/457-3100. Reservations not accepted. Main courses $21–$27. AE, MC, V. Daily 11:30am–2:30pm and 5–10pm. Closed mid-Oct to mid-May.

Roobar 🐟🐟 NEW AMERICAN   Opened in August 2001, Roo-bar is the best thing that has happened restaurant-wise in Falmouth in decades. Owner Dana Heilman, who also owns Roobar in Hyan-nis, has created an exciting bistro with handblown glass lamps over the bar and metal sconce sculptures on the walls; it's an arty and hip setting. An eclectic crowd fills the bar area, which has picture win-dows overlooking Falmouth's Main Street. The food is exceptionally yummy if pricey. Creative appetizers include red curry coconut shrimp and crisp, fried polenta. Good main course choices include the fire-roasted half chicken rubbed with toasted fennel and cumin, and seafood Provençal with shrimp, scallops, and mussels. Look to the daily specials for meals with a distinctly Asian spin. Pizzas from the wood-burning oven come with unusual toppings like scallop and prosciutto and beef satay. For dessert, skip the heavy Key lime pie and go for the crème brûlée. The professional and charming service is a welcome surprise here, and unusual on Cape Cod.

285 Main St. (at Cahoon Ct.). © 508/548-8600. Reservations not accepted. Main courses $15–$25. AE, MC, V. May–Oct daily noon–2pm and 4–10pm; call for off-season hours.

The Waterfront 🐟🐟 NEW AMERICAN   This upscale restau-rant on pretty Eel Pond is in the same building as the down-and-dirty Cap'n Kidd (see below) and is serviced by the same kitchen. Unlike the Kidd, The Waterfront is open only for a few months in the summer. It offers expensive dinners served by fresh-faced and professional staff. Sitting on the back deck overlooking Eel Pond is a very pleasant way to spend a summer evening. The cavernous room inside is also comfortable, with romantic lighting. The food is fairly standard for these parts: fresh fish, steaks, and chicken prepared with an attempt at a flourish. Good choices are turbans of sole stuffed with crab and topped with a rich lobster sauce. A lighter choice is Mediterranean shrimp and scallops sautéed with olive oil, garlic tomatoes, olives, asparagus, mushrooms, and capers over angel-hair pasta. It's perhaps a tad pricey for what it is, but the atmosphere is top-notch.

77 Water St. (next to the Cap'n Kidd), Woods Hole. © **508/548-8563.** Reservations accepted after 4pm. Main courses $19–$30. AE, MC, V. Mid-June to early Sept daily 5:30–10pm. Closed early Sept to mid-June.

MODERATE

The Flying Bridge ⓡ *(Kids* AMERICAN/CONTINENTAL Seafood, appropriately enough, predominates at this shipshape harborside mega-restaurant (capacity: nearly 600). With three bars tossed into the mix and live music upstairs on weekends, things can get a bit crazy; you'll find comparative peace and quiet—as well as tip-top nautical views—out on the deck. In addition to basic bar food (Buffalo chicken wings and the like), you'll find hefty hunks of protein and fish in many guises, from fish and chips—with optional malt vinegar—to appealing blackboard specials. Kids will enjoy wandering onto the attached dock to watch the ducks in the harbor.

220 Scranton Ave. (about ½ mile south of Main St.). © **508/548-2700.** Reservations not accepted. Main courses $8–$20. AE, MC, V. Apr–Dec daily 11:30am–10pm; call for off-season hours.

Landfall ⓡⓡ *(Kids* SEAFOOD A terrific harbor setting, Cape Cod-y cuisine, and good service make this Woods Hole seafood restaurant stand out. This is the type of place where you'll see the owner bussing tables on busy nights. Besides the usual fish and pasta dishes, there's "lite fare" such as burgers and fish and chips for under $15. This is a great place to bring the kids; a children's menu comes with games and crayons. Or come for a drink at the half-dory bar to enjoy this massive wooden building constructed of salvage, both marine and terrestrial. The "ship's knees" on the ceiling are the ribs of an old schooner which broke up on the shores of Cuttyhunk Island; the big stained-glass window came from a mansion on nearby Penzance Point. A large bank of windows looks out onto the harbor, and the Martha's Vineyard ferry, when docking, appears to be making a beeline straight for your table.

Luscombe Ave. (½ block south of Water St.), Woods Hole. ℂ 508/548-1758. Reservations recommended. Main courses $7–$26. AE, MC, V. Mid-May to Sept daily 11:30am–9:30pm; call for off-season hours. Closed late Nov to mid-Apr.

INEXPENSIVE

Betsy's Diner 𝕉 𝘍𝘪𝘯𝘥𝘴 𝘒𝘪𝘥𝘴 DINER   I once had the best piece of baked scrod ever at this vintage 1950s diner. It was breaded with corn flakes. This is hearty food like your mother used to make, if your mother was a variation of June Cleaver. The menu features turkey dinner, breakfast all day, and homemade soups. Some say the fried clams here are the best in town. Many people come for the large selection of scrumptious homemade pies, which may be the best on Cape Cod. Each red vinyl booth is equipped with its own jukebox with retro hits.

457 Main St. (in the center of town). ℂ 508/540-0060. Reservations not accepted. All items under $11. AE, MC, V. May–Oct Mon–Sat 6am–8pm, Sun 6am–2pm; call for off-season hours.

The British Beer Company 𝕉 PUB FARE/PIZZA   The view is great at this faux British pub across the street from Falmouth Heights Beach. The food quality, though, is inconsistent. Stick with the fish and chips or the lobster bisque, which has won local awards, and you'll be fine. Of course, there is beer, 23 drafts available, including Guinness and John Courage, as well as bottled selections.

263 Grand Ave. (across from the beach), Falmouth Heights. ℂ 508/540-9600. All items under $15. AE, DC, DISC, MC, V. Daily 11am–10pm.

Cap'n Kidd 𝕉𝕉 𝘍𝘪𝘯𝘥𝘴 PUB GRUB/SEAFOOD   The semi-official heart of Woods Hole, this well-worn pub comes into its own once the tourist hordes subside. It's then that the year-round scientists and fishing crews huddle around the fireplace, congregate on the glassed porch overlooking Eel Pond and order reasonably priced seafood, or belly up to the hand-carved mahogany bar (thought to date from the early 1800s) and drink to their heart's content. The notorious 17th-century pirate is rumored to have debarked in Woods Hole on his way back to England to be hanged, and he'd probably get a warm reception here today. Although the Kidd shares a kitchen with a fancier restaurant called The Waterfront (see above), the fare here is pub grub and some seafood, with individual pizzas, burgers, and sandwiches the mainstays. Homemade clam chowder is thick as paste, with large chunks of potato and clam; stuffed quahogs are piled high; and french fries are the real deal, thickly sliced.

77 Water St. (west of the Eel Pond drawbridge), Woods Hole. (℃ **508/548-9206.** Reservations not accepted. Main courses $12–$18. AE, MC, V. Daily 11:30am–3pm and 5–9pm.

Carolina BBQ Barn 🐾 (Value) AMERICAN/BARBECUE   A couple from North Carolina have introduced authentic barbecue in heaping portions at very reasonable prices. Customers choose from a smokehouse barbecue half chicken or mouth-whoppin' baby back ribs, Carolina-style pulled pork, or fried catfish, among other items. Then choose two sides. My favorites are corn on the cob and green beans, but other choices include homemade mashed potatoes, baked beans, and collards. Dessert is free with the meal; try the yummy banana pudding or homemade peach pie topped with vanilla ice cream. Service is cheerful and efficient. The owners will likely greet you on the way in and out.

100 Davis Straits (near the center of town), Falmouth. (℃ **508/540-1915.** Reservations accepted. Main courses $6–$18. MC, V. Daily 11am–9pm. Open year-round.

The Clam Shack 🐾 (Kids) SEAFOOD   This classic clam shack sits at the head of Falmouth harbor and offers steaming plates of fried seafood that you carry to a picnic table inside, outside, or up on the roof deck with the best view in town. The food is basic clam-shack fare, but the fish is fresh and you can't beat the view.

227 Clinton Ave. (off Scranton Ave., about 1 mile south of Main St.). (℃ **508/540-7758.** Reservations not accepted. Main courses $5–$15. No credit cards. Daily 11:30am–7:45pm. Closed mid-Sept to late May.

McMenamy's Seafood Restaurant (Kids) (Value) SEAFOOD   The McMenamy family has been serving heaping plates of fried, broiled, and baked seafood at this location for 25 years. Deliveries of fresh fish are brought in daily and make their way onto the specials board. The lobster roll is superb, as is the fish sandwich. The chowders, both fish and quahog, are made from scratch. Fish sandwiches here are the best in town. Onion rings are made fresh on-site. On a clear night, you may want to sit out on the screened porch. Acoustic entertainment is offered on weekends in season.

70 Davis Straits (Rte. 28; 1 mile east of the town center). (℃ **508/540-2115.** Reservations not accepted. Main courses $8–$16. AE, DISC, MC, V. Mid-May to mid-Oct 11:30am–10pm; mid-Oct to mid-May 11:30am–9pm.

Peking Palace 🐾🐾 CHINESE/JAPANESE/THAI   This popular Chinese restaurant recently underwent a major renovation from the ground up, also expanding its menu to offer Japanese and Thai food. Three regional Chinese cuisines (Cantonese, Mandarin, and

Szechuan) are served, as well as Polynesian. Sip a fanciful drink while you take in the menu, and be sure to solicit your server's opinion: That's how I learned of some heavenly spicy chilled squid.

452 Main St. (in the center of town). ℂ 508/540-8204. Main courses $5–$15. AE, MC, V. Daily 11:30am–midnight. Open year-round.

TAKEOUT

Cape Cod Bagel Co., 419 Palmer Ave. (ℂ 508/548-8485), carries the usual bagel sandwiches, soups, coffee, and other beverages, but the bagels, made on the premises, are definitely the best in town. **Box Lunch,** 781 Main St. (ℂ 508/457-7657), serves pita "rollwiches." These are the best—and fastest—sandwiches in town. **Laureen's,** at 170 Main St. in the center of town (ℂ 508/540-9104), is a sophisticated coffee bar/deli, ideal for a quick bite or sip. It specializes in vegetarian and Middle Eastern fare. Try one of the feta pizzas. Everything is available to go or in-house. Kitchen gear and gifts, including some great stuff for kids, round out the stock.

SWEETS

Locals know to get to **Pie in the Sky Dessert Café and Bake Shop,** 10 Water St., Woods Hole (ℂ 508/540-5475), by 9am for sticky buns, the best anywhere. Those bound for Martha's Vineyard stop at this small cafe for treats before hopping on the ferry.

Ben & Bill's Chocolate Emporium ✎, at 209 Main St., in the center of town (ℂ 508/548-7878), draws crowds even in winter, late into the evening. They come for the homemade ice cream, not to mention the hand-dipped candies showcased in a wraparound display—a chocoholic's nightmare or dream come true, depending. Those who can trust themselves not to go hog-wild might enjoy watching the ice cream being made.

Index

See also Accommodations and Restaurant indexes below.

ACCOMMODATIONS

RESTAURANTS

FROMMER'S® COMPLETE TRAVEL GUIDES

Alaska
Alaska Cruises & Ports of Call
American Southwest
Amsterdam
Argentina & Chile
Arizona
Atlanta
Australia
Austria
Bahamas
Barcelona, Madrid & Seville
Beijing
Belgium, Holland & Luxembourg
Bermuda
Boston
Brazil
British Columbia & the Canadian Rockies
Brussels & Bruges
Budapest & the Best of Hungary
Calgary
California
Canada
Cancún, Cozumel & the Yucatán
Cape Cod, Nantucket & Martha's Vineyard
Caribbean
Caribbean Ports of Call
Carolinas & Georgia
Chicago
China
Colorado
Costa Rica
Cruises & Ports of Call
Cuba
Denmark
Denver, Boulder & Colorado Springs
England
Europe
Europe by Rail
European Cruises & Ports of Call

Florence, Tuscany & Umbria
Florida
France
Germany
Great Britain
Greece
Greek Islands
Halifax
Hawaii
Hong Kong
Honolulu, Waikiki & Oahu
India
Ireland
Italy
Jamaica
Japan
Kauai
Las Vegas
London
Los Angeles
Maryland & Delaware
Maui
Mexico
Montana & Wyoming
Montréal & Québec City
Munich & the Bavarian Alps
Nashville & Memphis
New England
Newfoundland & Labrador
New Mexico
New Orleans
New York City
New York State
New Zealand
Northern Italy
Norway
Nova Scotia, New Brunswick & Prince Edward Island
Oregon
Ottawa
Paris
Peru

Philadelphia & the Amish Country
Portugal
Prague & the Best of the Czech Republic
Provence & the Riviera
Puerto Rico
Rome
San Antonio & Austin
San Diego
San Francisco
Santa Fe, Taos & Albuquerque
Scandinavia
Scotland
Seattle
Shanghai
Sicily
Singapore & Malaysia
South Africa
South America
South Florida
South Pacific
Southeast Asia
Spain
Sweden
Switzerland
Texas
Thailand
Tokyo
Toronto
Turkey
USA
Utah
Vancouver & Victoria
Vermont, New Hampshire & Maine
Vienna & the Danube Valley
Virgin Islands
Virginia
Walt Disney World® & Orlando
Washington, D.C.
Washington State

FROMMER'S® DOLLAR-A-DAY GUIDES

Australia from $50 a Day
California from $70 a Day
England from $75 a Day
Europe from $85 a Day
Florida from $70 a Day
Hawaii from $80 a Day

Ireland from $80 a Day
Italy from $70 a Day
London from $90 a Day
New York City from $90 a Day
Paris from $90 a Day
San Francisco from $70 a Day

Washington, D.C. from $80 a Day
Portable London from $90 a Day
Portable New York City from $90 a Day
Portable Paris from $90 a Day

FROMMER'S® PORTABLE GUIDES

Acapulco, Ixtapa & Zihuatanejo
Amsterdam
Aruba
Australia's Great Barrier Reef
Bahamas
Berlin
Big Island of Hawaii
Boston
California Wine Country
Cancún
Cayman Islands
Charleston
Chicago
Disneyland®
Dominican Republic
Dublin

Florence
Frankfurt
Hong Kong
Las Vegas
Las Vegas for Non-Gamblers
London
Los Angeles
Los Cabos & Baja
Maine Coast
Maui
Miami
Nantucket & Martha's Vineyard
New Orleans
New York City
Paris

Phoenix & Scottsdale
Portland
Puerto Rico
Puerto Vallarta, Manzanillo & Guadalajara
Rio de Janeiro
San Diego
San Francisco
Savannah
Vancouver
Vancouver Island
Venice
Virgin Islands
Washington, D.C.
Whistler

FROMMER'S® NATIONAL PARK GUIDES

Algonquin Provincial Park
Banff & Jasper
Family Vacations in the National
  Parks

Grand Canyon
National Parks of the American
  West
Rocky Mountain

Yellowstone & Grand Teton
Yosemite & Sequoia/Kings
  Canyon
Zion & Bryce Canyon

FROMMER'S® MEMORABLE WALKS

Chicago
London

New York
Paris

San Francisco

FROMMER'S® WITH KIDS GUIDES

Chicago
Las Vegas
New York City

Ottawa
San Francisco
Toronto

Vancouver
Walt Disney World® & Orlando
Washington, D.C.

SUZY GERSHMAN'S BORN TO SHOP GUIDES

Born to Shop: France
Born to Shop: Hong Kong,
  Shanghai & Beijing

Born to Shop: Italy
Born to Shop: London

Born to Shop: New York
Born to Shop: Paris

FROMMER'S® IRREVERENT GUIDES

Amsterdam
Boston
Chicago
Las Vegas
London

Los Angeles
Manhattan
New Orleans
Paris
Rome

San Francisco
Seattle & Portland
Vancouver
Walt Disney World®
Washington, D.C.

FROMMER'S® BEST-LOVED DRIVING TOURS

Austria
Britain
California
France

Germany
Ireland
Italy
New England

Northern Italy
Scotland
Spain
Tuscany & Umbria

THE UNOFFICIAL GUIDES®

Beyond Disney
California with Kids
Central Italy
Chicago
Cruises
Disneyland®
England
Florida
Florida with Kids
Inside Disney

Hawaii
Las Vegas
London
Maui
Mexico's Best Beach Resorts
Mini Las Vegas
Mini Mickey
New Orleans
New York City
Paris

San Francisco
Skiing & Snowboarding in the
  West
South Florida including Miami &
  the Keys
Walt Disney World®
Walt Disney World® for
  Grown-ups
Walt Disney World® with Kids
Washington, D.C.

SPECIAL-INTEREST TITLES

Athens Past & Present
Cities Ranked & Rated
Frommer's Best Day Trips from London
Frommer's Best RV & Tent Campgrounds
  in the U.S.A.
Frommer's Caribbean Hideaways
Frommer's China: The 50 Most Memorable Trips
Frommer's Exploring America by RV
Frommer's Gay & Lesbian Europe
Frommer's NYC Free & Dirt Cheap

Frommer's Road Atlas Europe
Frommer's Road Atlas France
Frommer's Road Atlas Ireland
Frommer's Wonderful Weekends from
  New York City
The New York Times' Guide to Unforgettable
  Weekends
Retirement Places Rated
Rome Past & Present

Travel Tip: Make sure there's customer service
for any change of plans — involving
friendly natives, for example.

One can plan and plan, but if you don't book with the
right people you can't seize le moment and canoodle
with the poodle named Pansy. I, for one, am all for
fraternizing with the locals. Better yet, if I need to
extend my stay and my gnome nappers are willing, it
can all be arranged through the 800 number at, oh look,
how convenient, the lovely company coat of arms.

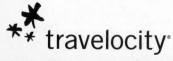

travelocity®